EARLY DEVELOPMENT AND ITS DISTURBANCES

EARLY DEVELOPMENT AND ITS DISTURBANCES

Clinical, Conceptual, and Empirical Research on ADHD and other Psychopathologies and its Epistemological Reflections

Edited by

Marianne Leuzinger-Bohleber, Jorge Canestri and Mary Target

Routledge
Taylor & Francis Group
LONDON AND NEW YORK

First published 2010 by Karnac Books Ltd

Published 2018 by Routledge
2 Park Square, Milton Park, Abingdon, Oxon OX14 4RN
711 Third Avenue, New York, NY 10017, USA

Routledge is an imprint of the Taylor & Francis Group, an informa business

British Library Cataloguing in Publication Data

A C.I.P. for this book is available from the British Library

ISBN-13: 978-1-85575-745-5 (pbk)

Typeset by Vikatan Publishing Solutions (P) Ltd., Chennai, India

CONTENTS

PREFACE ix

ACKNOWLEDGEMENTS xv

ABOUT THE EDITORS AND CONTRIBUTORS xvii

PART I: INTRODUCTION 1

CHAPTER ONE
Controversies on different approaches in psychoanalytic research on early development and ADHD 3
Marianne Leuzinger-Bohleber, Jorge Canestri and Mary Target

PART II: EARLY DEVELOPMENT AND ITS DISTURBANCES 51

CHAPTER TWO
Attachment, trauma, and psychoanalysis: Where psychoanalysis meets neuroscience 53
Peter Fonagy

DISCUSSION OF PETER FONAGY'S PAPER
Developmental risks and their sequelae: Effects on attachment and mentalization 77
Gerd Lehmkuhl

DISCUSSION OF PETER FONAGY'S PAPER
Attachment, trauma, and psychoanalysis: Where psychoanalysis meets neuroscience 87
Björn Salomonsson

CHAPTER THREE
Coping with children's temperament 97
William B. Carey, M.D.

DISCUSSION OF WILLIAM B. CAREY'S PAPER
Coping with children's temperament: Early development and its disturbances 113
Jorge Canestri

CHAPTER FOUR
Motion and meaning: Psychoanalytic inquiry of so-called ADHD children 123
Heidi Staufenberg

DISCUSSION OF HEIDI STAUFENBERG'S PAPER
ADHD from the empirical and clinical perspectives 143
Annette Streeck-Fischer

CHAPTER FIVE
Further comments on Sophia's mimetic autism, with special reference to Bion's theory of thinking 153
Jorge L. Ahumada and Luisa C. Busch de Ahumada

DISCUSSION OF JORGE L. AHUMADA AND LUISA C. BUSCH DE AHUMADA'S PAPER 175
Angela Joyce

CHAPTER SIX
Early affect regulations and its disturbances: Approaching ADHD in a psychoanalysis with a child and an adult 185
Marianne Leuzinger-Bohleber

PART III: PSYCHOANALYTIC RESEARCH: HOPES, VIEWS, CONTROVERSIAL DISCUSSION 207

CHAPTER SEVEN
Logic, meaning, and truth in psychoanalytic research 209
Charles Hanly

CHAPTER EIGHT
Trauma or drive—drive and trauma: Revisited 219
Ilse Grubrich-Simitis

CHAPTER NINE
Pluralism in theory and in research—and what now? A plea for connectionism 239
Anna Ursula Dreher

CHAPTER TEN
New orleans congress panel: What does conceptual research have to offer? 267
Jorge L. Ahumada and Roberto Doria-Medina

INDEX 281

PREFACE

We are very pleased to present here one of the first psychoanalytic books devoted to Attention Deficit Hyperactivity Disorder (ADHD) and other disturbances of early development. Some of the papers of this volume were presented at the ninth Joseph Sandler Research Conference which took place in Frankfurt for the first time. It was organized by both Research Subcommittees of the International Psychoanalytical Association (IPA): the Research Subcommittee for Empirical Research (Chair: Peter Fonagy) and the Research Subcommittee for Clinical, Conceptual, Historical and Epistemological Research (Chair: Marianne Leuzinger-Bohleber).

The research conference carries the name of Joseph Sandler as he is known as one of the most productive psychoanalytic researchers of the last few decades. It is not so well-known that it was Joseph Sandler who created the so-called "Conceptual Resarch" in Psychoanalysis, and who organized a 'concept group' and developed the famous 'Hampstead Index', which was taught in the unique psychoanalytic training courses at the Hampstead Clinic (now the Anna Freud Centre) in London. Since 1980 Joseph Sandler has also worked with a 'concept group' at the Sigmund-Freud-Institut in Frankfurt, although he has also been Freud Memorial Professor at the University College London and since 1989 president of the International Psychoanalytical Association. We three editors share his conviction that the validity and usefulness of psychoanalytic concepts must show themselves in clinical practice. They are in constant change and thus have to be further developed and researched again and again. Joseph Sandler is indeed the father of conceptual research in psychoanalysis.

Institutionally it took more than 40 years until the former president of the IPA, Daniel Widlöcher, appointed a second Subcommittee for Clinical, Conceptual, Historical and Epistemological Research which should supplement the very successful Research Committee for Empirical Research by supporting conceptual, clinical, epistemological and historical resarch in contemporary psychoanalysis. The commitee members were Rachel Blass (Jerusalem and Essex), Jorge Canestri (Rom), Anna Ursula Dreher (Frankfurt), Paulo Duarte (Sao Paulo), Norbert Freedman (New York), Ilse Grubrich-Simitis (Frankfurt), Mark Solms (Cape Town/London), Mary Target (London), Susana Vinocur de Fischbein (Buenos Aires), Sverre Varvin (Oslos), and Samuel Zysman (Buenos Aires). The three editors of this volume were all members of this sub-committee.

To come back to Joseph Sandler: he is admired for his unique and innovative openness to all kinds of different forms of research in psychoanalysis as well as for his engagement in building bridges and creating dialogue between psychoanalysts working in their private offices, psychoanalytic researchers in universities and other institutions, and non-psychoanalytic researchers and intellectuals. This attitude cannot be taken for granted: the dialogue among psychoanalysts with diffferent convictions in the field of psychoanalyic research cannot always be described as open, friendly, and productive. And often a withdrawal into an exclusively psychoanalytic exchange within the psychoanalytic societies is like a form of seduction for all of us. Reading this volume you will recognize that a withdrawal into the psychoanalytical ivory tower often might be more convenient than to confront ourselves with intensive controversial discourses in the non-psychoanalytical scientific community. We will touch on the conflictual discussions on ADHD in this respect, which often are connected with intensive affects, devaluations, and even paranoid suspicion. To mention just one example: some psychoanalysts are deeply concerned about the dramatic increase of medication in the case of children with ADHD. (From 1993 to 2006, there was a 3,591% increase in medication in this area, from 34 kg to 1,221 kg of medication per year.) Some authors talk about the danger of a 'medicalization of social problems'. Others, particularly the representatives of the pharmacological industry, still postulate, conversely, that we have an under-supply of medication. Not offering medication to an ADHD child would be, according to this opinion, unethical, and could be compared to refusing to offer insulin to a child suffering from diabetes. In this volume we will argue the importance of psychoanalysts engaging in this debate. It will be shown that psychoanalysis—due to the richness of clinical experiences and conceptualizations on early developments and its disturbances—have something unique to offer for a deepening of the understanding of children suffering from so-called ADHD and other developmental disturbances.

With this volume we would like to contribute to a more intensive engagement of psychoanalysts in this field. We are very sad that one outstanding psychoanalyst and researcher, who has been a model for such an engagement for us, Stuart Hauser, unfortunately died suddenly in 2008. He was the Chair of the Sub-committee for Empirical Research and should have opened the ninth Joseph Sandler Research Committee. His death is a great loss for all of us and for the psychoanalytic community in general. We are dedicating this volume to him, especially as many of his most important empirical and clinical studies focused on early development and its disturbances. His last book, co-authored with Allen and Golden (2006), was devoted to one of the most central research questions of this volume. The question as to why some of the children who have gone through severe infantile traumatizations develop more or less 'normally', while others become seriously ill. It is the question which nowadays is discussed in the so-called 'resiliency research'

Hauser *et al.* report on their follow-up studes of late adolescents who had been hospitalized in a psychiatric clinic because of drug abuse, violence and/or suicidality. In the *High Valley Resilience Study* Stuart Hauser and his co-workers had interviewed 150 teenagers each year between 1978 and 1983. Half of them had been hospitalized in the Children's Center of High Valley Hospital, a psychiatric institution. Around 24 children and adolescents from different milieus and different parts of the US had been treated there. Their stay was expensive but mostly payed for by public institutions. Some of the young people suffered from a psychosis or an autistic disease, many of them from severe depression. Some had neurological symptoms (for example, the so-called Tourette syndrome). But all of them shared one commonality: they had an uncontrollable anger and rage inside of them and were highly violent.

According to the authors this was one reason why clear rules and 'punishments' were indispensible in this institution. The most important rule was that everyone should talk about emotions. The children were not allowed to withdraw from the social group; they were forced to remain in contact with the others. 'There was no escape from unit society, because unit society—for the kids who could learn to stand it—was the basic instrument of the Center's healing works.'

For Stuart Hauser and his co-workers the most surprising result of their follow-up interviews was that some of these children, in spite of the pessimistic prognoses, developed into 'normal adults'. In order to understand these findings, 16 of the late adolescents were investigated in great detail. This revealed that none of them had actually 'recovered' from their severe crises during adolescence. The researchers summarize their findings in four extensive and very impressive case studies.

For years professionals explained similar positive developments by postulating the particularly strong personalities of such children who, it was argued, due to a surprising genetic potentiality, had the strength to adapt to reality in spite of severe traumatizations. Hauser, Allen and Golden characterize this position as an idealization. They prefer a different definition of resiliency:

> For children of adversity *are* wounded, often severely. To imply otherwise is to deny the acuteness of suffering in children, who don't *come* resilient but *become* resilient—*after* they have been hurt. There is no shield that keeps them safe from all harms, no intrinsic toughness such as the older terms imply. It is not the illusory invulnerability of resilient children that should command attention and respect, but their powers of self-healing. And these are powers that vary with circumstance: people's styles of adaptation change and evolve over their lifetimes.

> In order to speak of 'resiliency', two conditions have to be fullfilled: i) a person must develop more or less normally and ii) this person must have been exposed to high risk, severe unhappiness and/or suffering and was able to overcome this situation by their own efforts.

In the *High Valley Resilience Study* 13% of the late adolescents had been diagnosed as 'resilient' according to objective test results. The interviews with these 'resilient adolescents' showed narratives more complex, vivid and clearer than the ones of the non-resilient adolescents. They also contained sequences in which the adolescent reflected in a different way about their own part and responsibilities for the former severe crises. Stuart Hauser and his co-authors interprete these findings as an indicator that these resilient adolesents had memories and representations of at least one good inner object due to at least one positive object relationship during childhood. This good relationship had enabled them to believe in 'something good in this world' in spite of all the traumatic cruelty which they had gone through. They had helped them to believe in the '*Prinzip Hoffnung*' (Ernst Bloch), the principle of hope, and to not resign completely or give up a basic wish for a better life. Therefore resiliency, accoring to Stuart Hauser, cannot develop by the child's inner world alone: it is dependent on some supporting object relations in their outside reality.

For the following discussion in this volume these findings are extremely important. It is also impressive that one of the most convincing case studies is also connected to the so called ADHD. Pete, one of the extremely violent children in the book, had also been diagnosed as 'hyperactive'. The interviews with him—up to the age of 25—illustrate how important it had been for him that, in spite of the most severe and violent crises, both of his parents did not withdraw from him completely but, within their limits, tried to keep a basic positive relationship with their difficult and aggressive child. This partially good object relationship enabled Pete to finally 'forgive' them their failures during his upbringing and to see his own part in his crises. He sees that he was 'an extremely difficult child' and now, in his late adolescence, is able to take responsibility for his own behaviour.

> Taking responsibility was always one of Pete's strong suits and it still is. [...] The adult Pete knows that relationships are the psychological work that remains to him. And he looks forward to it. He knows what relationships can give him, if he will let it: I look for the best in a person and I try to learn something from them. This is exciting to him: Those people turn me on. And then his battle cry, and the battle cry of resilient kids all over: Because, Jesus, that's the way it should be ...
>
> (Hauser *et al.* 2006)

Medications would not have allowed Pete to become resilient: it was only human relationships (in his family and later to the staff in the clinic) that helped him to develop the coping possibilities with his life that he did in spite of all his sufferings, vulnerabilities, and traumatizations.

This is one of the main messages in all the contributions of this volume. In this sense we feel very grateful to the enormous engagement and outstanding and courageous findings of Stuart Hauser. We will try to take up his engagement with traumatized children and adolescents, and his attempts to understand their sufferings and struggles to overcome them, as a sensitive psychoanalyst and gifted researcher.

ACKNOWLEDGEMENTS

We would like to thank all the authors of this volume for their most interesting contributions and the good cooperation. We are grateful to the International Psychoanalytical Association and to the Sigmund-Freud-Institute for giving us the chance to organize the Joseph Sandler Research Conference on the topic of this volume. We also thank Jannine Kuhlewey, Renate Stebahne and Ute Ochtendung for helping us organizing this conference as well as for preparing this publication. Finally special thanks to all the different translators who—in spite of the time pressure—offered us their professionalism in order to produce a „real English book". Many thanks to all of them!

ABOUT THE EDITORS AND CONTRIBUTORS

Jorge L. Ahumada, Supervising and Training Analyst, Argentine Psychoanalytic Association. Distinguished Fellow, British Psychoanalytical Society. Mary S. Sigourney Awardee, 1996. Editor for Latin America, *The International Journal of Psychoanalysis*, 1993–1998. Author of *The Logics of the Mind: A Clinical View* (Karnac 2001) and over forty papers published in eight languages.

Luisa C. Busch de Ahumada is a full member of the Buenos Aires Psychoanalytic Association and an International Psychoanalytical Association (IPA)-certified child psychoanalyst. Her clinical papers on child dynamics have been published in English, Spanish, French, German, and Italian.

Jorge Canestri is a training and supervising analyst for the Italian Psychoanalytical Association and for the Argentine Psychoanalytic Association. He is also Professor of Psychology of Health at the Roma 3 University, co-author of *The Babel of the Unconscious: Mother Tongue and Foreign Languages in the Psychoanalytic Dimension* and co-editor (with Marianne Leuzinger-Bohleber and Anna Ursula Dreher) of *Pluralism and Unity? Methods of Research in Psychoanalysis and of Psychoanalysis: From Practice to Theory.*

William B. Carey, M.D., is a paediatrician educated at the Harvard Medical School and the Children's Hospital of Philadelphia. He spent 31 years in primary care. For the last 20 years he has been Clinical Professor of Pediatrics back at CHOP. He received the Aldrich Award in Child Development from the American Academy of Pediatrics and was elected to the Institute of Medicine of the National Academy of Sciences.

Roberto Doria-Medina, Prof. Dr., Chair, Dept. Mental Health, University Hospital. Full Professor, School of Medicine, University of Buenos Aires. Co-Chair, Latin America, Programme Committee, International Psychoanalytic Congress 2011. Past Editor of *Revista de Psicoanálisis, Libro Anual de Psicoanálisis*, and *Revista Latinoamericana de Psicoanálisis.* Past Member of the Editorial Board L A, *The International Journal of Psychoanalysis.* Past Chair, Department History of Psychoanalysis. Training Analyst, Argentine Psychoanalytical Association.

Anna Ursula Dreher is a psychoanalyst and supervisor in private practice in Frankfurt am Main, trained in the German Psychoanalytic Association. Member of the Research Committee of the IPA (sub-committee: conceptual research). Author of publications on the foundations of research in psychoanalysis, conceptual research, and basic psychoanalytic concepts.

Peter Fonagy, PhD FBA is Freud Memorial Professor of Psychoanalysis and Head of the Research Department of Clinical, Educational and Health Psychology at University Collage London. He is Chief Executive at the Anna Freud Centre, London. He is a clinical psychologist and a training and supervising analyst in the British Psycho-Analytical in child and adult analysis. His clinical interests centre around issues of borderline psychopathology, violence, and early attachment relationships. His work attempts to integrate empirical research with psychoanalytic theory. He holds a number of important positions, which include chairing the Postgraduate Centre of the International Psychoanalytic Association and Fellowship of the British Academy.

Ilse Grubrich-Simitis is a training analyst of the German Psychoanalytical Association and is working in private practice in Frankfurt a.M. She is a member of the IPA Research Subcommittee for Conceptual Research and of the IPA Committee of History of Psychoanalysis. She was a member of the IPA Research Advisory Board

1997–2007. She is an editor of Sigmund Freud's works and letters in German. Her main research fields are Freud research; the history of psychoanalysis; and clinical and theoretical work on trauma and severe traumatization, especially the second generation of holocaust survivors.

Charles Hanly is in full-time psychoanalytic practice; a training and supervising analyst in the Canadian Institute of Psychoanalysis (Toronto Branch); and a Professor Emeritus (philosophy) University of Toronto. He has published a number of books including *Psychoanalysis and Philosophy, Existentialism and Psychoanalysis,* and *Method in Applied Psychoanalysis*, along with numerous articles in major international journals, and chapters in books on clinical psychoanalysis, psychoanalytic theory, and applied psychoanalysis. He is President-elect of the International Psychoanalytical Association.

Angela Joyce, Training Analyst and Fellow of the Institute of Psychoanalysis, London; Child Psychoanalyst; at the Anna Freud Centre in London she is a Consultant Parent Infant Psychotherapist in the pioneering Parent Infant Project; and Project Lead (training) in the child psychotherapy service. She has co-edited the forthcoming *Reading Winnicott* with Lesley Caldwell, which will be published by Routledge in the Teaching Series of the New Library of Pyschoanalysis.

Gerd Lehmkuhl, full professor for child and adolescent psychiatry at the University of Cologne, specialist for neurology, child- and adolescent psychiatry, psychotherapy and psychoanalysis. Since October 1988 director of the clinic and outdoor clinic for psychiatry and psychotherapy for children and adolescents of the University of Cologne. Psychoanalytical training at the Alfred Adler Institute Cologne/Aachen, training analyst (DGIP, DGPPT, DAGG), respnsible editor of the Zeitschrift für Individualpsychologie, co-editor of the Zeitschrift für Kinder- und Jugendpsychiatrie und Psychotherapie.

Marianne Leuzinger-Bohleber is a training analyst in the German Psychoanalytical Association, former Chair of the Research Subcommittees for Conceptual Research, and a member of the Swiss Psychoanalytical Society. Vice Chair of the Research Board of the IPA, Full Professor for Psychoanalytic Psychology at the University of Kassel and head Director of the Sigmund-Freud-Institut, Frankfurt/Main. Her main research fields include epistemology and methods of clinical and empirical research in psychoanalysis, interdisciplinary discouse with embodied cognitive science, educational sciences, and modern German literature.

Björn Salomonsson is a training and child psychoanalyst at the Swedish Psychoanalytical Society, Stockholm. He runs a research project at the Child and Adolescent Psychiatric Unit, Karolinska Institute, investigating the results of psychoanalytic mother–infant treatments. Björn has published papers on containment, the analysis of children with ADHD, infant–mother psychoanalysis, the aesthetic experience and, together with Johan Norman, on analytic case presentation according to the weaving thoughts method. From 2001 to 2006, he was chair of the Child Forum of the European Psychoanalytic Federation. He is a member of the Societé Européenne pour la Psychanalyse de l'Enfant et de l'Adolescent, Paris.

Adelheid Staufenberg Study of the German language and literature, sociology, science of the politics, state exam, and internship. Freelance active in the pedagogic area and adult's education. Education in the institute for analytic child- and youth psychotherapy in Frankfurt am Main, practising and working in her practice since 1996, lecturer in the education and continuing education. Cooperation, amongst others, in the 'prevention and intervention study in order to prevent psychosocial integration disturbances (in particular from ADHD)' in the Sigmund-Freud-Institut.

Annette Streeck-Fischer is director of the department 'Clinical psychotherapy of children and adolescents' at Asklepios Fachklinikum Tiefenbrunn/Güettingen. She is Professor of Clinical Psychology and Psychoanalysis at International Psychoanalytic University (IPU) in Berlin. She is training and supervising analyst at Lou-Andreas-Salomé-Institut Goettingen and member of DPG. She is editor of the journal *Praxis der Kinderpsychologie und Kinderpsychiatrie*. Since 2007 she is president elect of the International Society of Adolescent Psychiatry and Psychotherapy (ISAPP). Her interests centre on adolescence, violence, trauma, and maltreatment.

Mary Target PhD is Professor of Psychoanalysis at University College London, and Professional Director of the Anna Freud Centre, London. She is a Clinical Associate Professor in the Yale University School of Medicine. She is a Fellow of the Institute of Psycho-Analysis in London, and maintains a half-time adult psychoanalytic practice.

PART I

INTRODUCTION

CHAPTER ONE

Controversies on different approaches in psychoanalytic research on early development and ADHD

Marianne Leuzinger-Bohleber, Jorge Canestri and Mary Target

1 *Introductory remarks*

Surprisingly, psychoanalysts have only during the past few years actively engaged in the on-going and very important controversial discussions on attention deficit hyperactivity disorder (ADHD) (for example, the casebook on learning disabilities by Rothstein and Glenn, 1999; the special volume of Psychoanalytic Inquiry, 2002; and the panel on ADHD and trauma at the IPA Congress in Rio 2005 reported by Sugarman, 2006 and at the IPA Congress in Chicago, 2009, summarized by Sugarman, 2010).[1] Carney (2002: 301) writes in his prologue to this volume: 'Not so long ago, some practitioners both inside and outside psychoanalysis discouraged the use of psychodynamic treatment for patients with AD/HD.' Salomonsson (2004: 132) agrees, writing: 'Psychoanalysis is an often-neglected treatment method for children with neuropsychiatric disorders.'

There may be many reasons for the increasing interest in this topic over the past few years. We wish to mention just four possible ones, which for us were essential in the decision to become involved in this topic:

i. The dialogue between psychoanalysis and contemporary neurobiology/brain research opens a fascinating window on an old problem in European culture: the mind–body problem. This exchange also promises to enlarge the understanding of psychic problems probably connected with some neurobiologically founded pathologies, as postulated for ADHD.
ii. Twin studies postulate a strong genetic component in ADHD (see, for example, Faraone *et al.*, 2005, Romanos *et al.*, 2008). Only during the last years could epigenetic researchers empirically demonstrate that early traumatization might strongly influence the 'triggering' of gene disposition (see, for example, Caspi *et al.*, 2003; Schulte-Körne and Allgaier, 2008; Goldberg, 2009; Risch *et al.*, 2009; Rutter, 2009; Soumi, 2010). Therefore psychoanalysts feel more reassured to treat children with ADHD psychoanalytically: They are experts in understanding and treating children with early trauma, independent of their genetic disposition.
iii. New developments in psychoanalytic theory, taking up findings from empirical infant, attachment, and memory research, offer alternative conceptualizations and techniques for treating early disturbances in affect regulation, and in the development of symbolization and mentalization—all of which are central dysfunctions in ADHD.
iv. The growing 'competition' with other therapeutic approaches (for example, medication with Ritalin®, cognitive behavioural programmes, and so forth) and the political realities of a modern zeitgeist in the Western world probably motivate many self-critical psychoanalysts to engage intensely in relevant public and professional debates. One of these is about ADHD, which is considered to be one of the most heated controversies that child psychiatry has ever gone through (see Riedesser, 2006).

These heated debates on the medical treatment of even very young children were one of the main reasons that the Sigmund-Freud-Institut in Frankfurt conceptualized the so-called *Frankfurt Prevention Study* (*FPS*) in cooperation with the Institute for Psychoanalytic

Treatments of Children and Adolescents in Frankfurt. The representative, cluster randomized *Frankfurt Prevention Study*[2] was carried out from September 2003 to September 2006. In order to be able to draw a representative sample of roughly n = 500 children in the prevention/intervention group and a control-comparison group of another n = 500 children, we had to perform a basic assessment in all public kindergartens in Frankfurt (114 kindergartens with around 4,500 children). The main hypothesis of the study was that a two-year psychoanalytic (and non-psychopharmacological) prevention and intervention programme would result in a statistically significant decrease in the number of children suffering from psychosocial disturbances (particularly aggressive conflicts, frequently the main problem of ADHD children in social situations) in their first year of school (compared with the control group). The psychoanalytic prevention and intervention programme consisted of several components based on the psychoanalytic understanding of ADHD: psychoanalytic supervision of the kindergarten teams, a weekly offering of a psychoanalytically oriented educational programme for individual children or the children's group, including a violence prevention programme called FAUSTLOS ('NO FISTS'; a modification of the US American programme SECOND STEPS) developed by Cierpka and his group (see Cierpka and Schick, 2006); psychoanalytic therapies (always including the parents) offered to children with severe psychopathologies (including ADHD) mostly in the Kindergartens themselves; consultations and educational courses for parents; and finally intensive collaboration with medical doctors, child psychiatrists, mental health and welfare institutions and potential schools, if necessary.

In the meantime, we have obtained statistical results which support our main hypothesis: the level of aggression and anxiety of the children in the prevention group has decreased significantly compared with the control group (interestingly, there is a statistically significant decrease of hyperactivity only in girls). We have published these results in detail in other papers (see Leuzinger-Bohleber *et al.*, 2007, 2008). In this introduction we only want to mention one aspect that is important for the topic of this volume. Seen from a psychoanalytical perspective, we found several different psychodynamic backgrounds with a final common pathway to ADHD syndrome according to DSM–IV: a) known brain damage (due to organic traumata during birth, an accident, encephalitis, and so on); b) early emotional neglect; c) personal and family trauma (for example, in refugees' families); d) chronic under-stimulation of highly talented children in kindergarten; e) a mismatch of the temperament of the child with their primary caregiver, or object; f) a mismatch of family culture with the cultural 'rules' of the host country (for example, a Moroccan family living in Germany); and g) growing up with a chronically depressed mother (or 'dead mother', according to André Green[3]).

To summarize: in this large empirical and clinical study it was shown that in all of the children investigated, early disturbances of affect regulation had—in different and idiosyncratic combinations—led to behaviour then assigned an ADHD diagnosis. This is one of the major reasons that we argue for psychoanalysis to get involved in the public discussion of diagnosis and treatment for this group of children. Causation does not necessarily mean that treatment is required in the same domain, but we need to take seriously a developmental model which can make sense of such diverse aetiological pathways.

To this end, we decided to devote the ninth Joseph Sandler Research Conference 2008 to this topic: *Early development and its disturbances: clinical, conceptual and empirical research on AD/HD and other psychopathologies.* In this volume we are publishing some of the main papers given at this conference, in combination with some papers dealing with epistemological and methodological problems connected to research in this field.

We will begin our introduction with some remarks on the ongoing public and professional debates (2). In the following section we would like to summarize briefly some of the consequences of different theoretical positions towards the preferred therapy of ADHD children (3). First the so-called 'multimodal treatment of ADHD' (cognitive-behavioural treatment in combination with medication) and the implications for diagnosis and therapy will be shortly summarized (3.1) in order to contrast this view with psychoanalytical concepts (3.2). We think that the richness of psychoanalytic concepts, encompassing possible idiosyncratic biographical and psychodynamic as well as genetic and biological roots of ADHD, seems to be in impressive concordance with contemporary neurobiological memory research (4). In the penultimate section we will illustrate this thesis with some short case examples (5). In the last section we will summarize the various approaches of the different authors of this book toward investigating early development and its disturbances (6).

2 The dramatic increase in treating ADHD[4] by medication (for example, Ritalin®)—a warning sign of medicalizing contemporary social problems seen from a historical background?

ADHD is one of the most frequent diagnoses of children and adolescents nowadays (see, for example, Staufenberg, in press). There also is a high comorbidity between ADHD and other psychopathologies, for example, depressions (see, for example, Bharwaj and Goodyer, 2009: 178). Medical treatment has continously and dramatically increased since the 1990s. The prescription of methylphenidate (Medicinet, Concerta, Ritalin, and others) has increased from 0.3 million DDD (daily defined dose) in 1990 to 46 million DDD in 2007. In Germany 34 kg methylphenidate was sold annually in drug stores in 1993; in 2009 this had risen to 1,735 kg (an increase of 5,103%) (Bundesinstitut für Arzneimittel und Medizinprodukte [BfArM], 2010).

Mattner (2006), Amft (2006), and Gerspach (2006) give a short overview of the historical and societal context in which this increased use of Ritalin® and other psychopharmacological medication for children could be understood. Mattner (2006) elaborates that the search for neurophysiological reasons to explain socially deviant behaviour has a long tradition in European countries, particularly in Germany.[5]

Summarizing the history of this diagnosis in child psychiatry in the USA, Gilmore (2000) reports similar findings. George Still (1902: 266) first observed a group of children in his practice 'who showed a pattern of aggressiveness, resistance to discipline, excessive emotionality, little "inhibitory volition", "lawlessness", spitefulness, and cruelty: these children were also notable for their impaired attention, overactivity, and a defect in motor control'. This syndrome was attributed to an underlying neurological deficiency, and, consistent with the then current view of behavioural disorders, the influence of environment was largely ignored (Gilmore, 2000: 1,266–67). Interest in this disorder grew after the encephalitis outbreak of 1917–18, when many children, after their recovery from this illness, showed impairment in attention, regulation of activity, and impulse control, the now so-called 'postencephalitic behaviour disorder'. Laufer and Denhoff (1957) characterized a subgroup of these children as showing 'hyperkinetic impulse disorder', which was attributed to a postulated brain mechanism, namely 'poor filtering of stimuli'. These children were often treated with psychoactive drugs. Later, the term 'minimal brain damage' continued to be fashionable. In the 1960s the more modest term 'minimal brain dysfunction' was more widely used. Gilmore (2000) agrees with Mattner (2006) that both these diagnostic terms ultimately:

> yielded to scientific objections, as it became clear that many children and many syndromes were being lumped together without heuristic or prescriptive benefit under the umbrella of a pseudoscientific classification. As part of the growing trend towards descriptive, rather than etiological, classifications, the diagnostic wastebasket was broken down into observable and verifiable deficits.
>
> (Gilmore cited in Barkley, 1990: 10)

The specific 'hyperactive child syndrome' (Laufer and Denhoff, 1957) or 'hyperactive reaction of childhood' (DSM-II) reappeared as the official nomenclature for children with features of impulsive and aggressive behaviour and poor attention spans. While demonstrable brain damage could produce this syndrome, the majority of children so diagnosed were without known injury. Nonetheless, brain mechanisms responsible for these behavioural 'lags' were postulated, and prognosis was felt to be good on the basis of developmental maturation; that is, puberty was viewed as a watershed after which there was a good likelihood of resolution. Environmental factors were de-emphasized (Gilmore, 2000: 1,267–68). According to Gilmore particularly, the research done by Virginia Douglas and her group at McGill University led to the development of a paradigm which renamed the syndrome as 'attention deficit disorder' by the time that DSM-III was published in 1980. In the following years, environmental toxicity—food additives or technical over-stimulation—was also seen as relevant for ADD and the learning disabilities of these children. Learning disabilities were formally recognized by the US government with the Public Law 94–142 in 1975. Children diagnosed with ADD—as one form of learning disability—were offered a multimodal treatment approach, which included medication, special classroom programmes, dietary management, and parent counselling. In the 1980s—on the basis of newer studies—the classification of ADD without hyperactivity was dropped in DSM-III-R and renamed as the syndrome of Attention-Deficit/Hyperactivity Disorder, linking it with Oppositional Defiant Disorder and Conduct Disorder under the Disruptive Disorders in Childhood. It has been retained as such in DSM-IV.[6]

Gilmore (2000) mentions that in the past few decades, ADHD has achieved validity as a discrete diagnostic entity through epidemiological characterization (that is, it shows strong hereditary patterns and clusters with other specific psychiatric disorders) and through an increasing number of promising neuroanatomical studies that further differentiate sub-populations (Cantwell, 1996). Research into neurotransmitters has also burgeoned, although it has so far failed to yield the anticipated solution. In a ten-year review of the disorder for the *Journal of the American Academy of Child and Adolescent Psychiatry*, Dennis Cantwell (1996: 979) emphasizes that ADHD is 'one of the most important disorders that child and adolescent psychiatrists treat', and that it is a robust disorder with a high prevalence and a serious lifetime morbidity that responds best to multimodal intervention. He asserts unequivocally that 'psychosocial factors are not thought to play a primary etiological role', although (presumably secondary) negative mother–child interactions are commonly observed (Cantwell cited in Gilmore, 2000: 1,269). A similar position is taken by Barkley (2002), one of the most frequently quoted experts in the field of ADHD:

> The central psychological deficits in those with ADHD have now been linked through numerous studies using various scientific methods to several specific brain regions (the frontal lobe, its connections to the basal ganglia, and their relationship to the central aspects of the cerebrellum). Most neurological studies find that as a group those with ADHD have less brain electrical activity and show less reactivity to stimulation in one or more of these regions. And neuro-imaging studies of groups of those

> with ADHD also demonstrate relatively smaller areas of brain matter and less metabolic activity of this brain matter than is the case in control groups used in these studies. These same psychological deficits in inhibition and attention have been found in numerous studies of identical and fraternal twins conducted across various countries (US, Great Britain, Norway, Australia, etc.) to be primarily inherited. The genetic contribution to these traits is routinely found to be among the highest for any psychiatric disorder (70–95% of trait variation in the population), nearly approaching the genetic contribution to human height. One gene has recently been reliably demonstrated to be associated wiht this disorder and the search for more is underway by more than 12 different scientific teams worldwide at this time.
>
> (Barkley cited in Staufenberg, in press: 40)

Mattner (2006) and many other authors question these conclusions (for example, see Timimi and Leo, 2009). Mattner attributes such 'biological explanations for psychosocial problems of AD/HD children' to historical and social factors. He quotes, for example, Crary (1999), who showed in detail that only during the beginning of the 19th century, the 'industrial century', did it become necessary for children as well as adults to develop the capability to 'show attention in a disciplined way', 'to concentrate', and to comply with a joint process of production (without destructive and aggressive conflicts). Only since then have 'attention', 'concentration', and the capability to 'sit still for hours in learning situations in school or at work' become socially required virtues. Mattner therefore concludes: 'Probably the epidemic increase of psychopathologies in children with AD/HD indicates in a seismographical way the sufferings and problems of children in our postmodern times, which escape in our analyses from a purely neurobiological perspective' (2006: 18). In a similar line of argument, Amft (2006) has postulated that Ritalin® and other medicines can—without any doubt—be of help for some children suffering from ADHD, particularly given certain social conditions at school that allow for the de-escalation of conduct problems. At the same time, he warns of the neglect of family, social, and environmental factors:

> Without any doubt the application of Ritalin® and other psychopharmacological medication has a highly seductive character

> because they are very efficient, fast in their effects, not very costly and can adapt 'difficult children' to the everyday requirements of schools in our Western societies ... According to this argumentation it seems even unethical not to hand out these medicines to children with AD/HD ... Such a radically biological explanation of social problems of children does not consider the influence of factors of the so-called 'changed childhood' ('veränderte Kindheit') in our Western societies with its well-known features of broken families, early emotional neglect of children, the 'clash of civilizations and values', the influence of media as well as the complex realities of growing up in a globalized multicultural world etc.
>
> (Amft 2006: 119ff., translation by the authors; on this topic, see also Garlichs and Leuzinger-Bohleber, 1999, Ahrbeck, 2007)

Therefore, Mattner, Gerspach, and Amft all issue a plea for critical and differentiated analyses of the multiple fields of problems that children in post-industrial societies grow up with (see Sennett, 1998), and on this subject we agree with these authors; in talking about ADHD, social and cultural factors should be taken as seriously as the findings from modern neurobiology and brain research.

3 *Controversional theoretical positions with immense implications for treatments of ADHD children*

To summarize briefly:

The heated discussions of different explanations and treatments of ADHD children seem to have two poles:

I. ADHD is seen as a primarily genetically determined illness of certain brain regions and functions which can be efficiently treated by medication like methyphenidate and amphetamines. Environmental factors may play an additional but not a primarily important role and should be measured 'objectively' (like e.g. the influence of smoking to the embryo and a possible vulnerability to ADHD due to this factor). Anthough the authors often talk about a 'multimodal form of treatment', medical treatment is at the heart of the interventions.

II. ADHD is seen as a complex pattern of behaviour due to multiple factors determined by different individual, biographical (psychodynamic) determinants. Prenatal factors, social conditions under which children are growing up, as well as problematic or even traumatic experiences within early relationships or a mismatch of temperament between the primary caregiver and the baby are seen as mainly influential although genetic and biological factors (like temperament) also may play an important role. Interventions or therapies are thus mainly focusing on the individual biographical and social factors. A combination with medication may be necessary in the sense of an emergency strategy but not as a cure for the factors producing ADHD.

These positons mostly determine the strategies which are offered to ADHD children and their families in order to help them cope with their problems. In the following section we are illustrating just two different intervention strategies, which are based on these different poles in the understanding of ADHD.

3.1 Multimodal treatment of ADHD (a combination of cognitive behavioural and psychopharmacological treatments)

Lehmkuhl and Döpfner (2006), two of the best-known contemporary empirical researchers into ADHD in Germany, refer to the guidelines of the American Academy of Child and Adolescent Psychiatry. They appeal for a cautious professional approach to the diagnosis and an understanding of the pathogenesis of ADHD based on a *'biopsychosocial model'*. They illustrate this view with a diagram illustrating the interaction between 'causal' determining factors and resulting processes on different levels like the level of biochemistry and neurophysiology, neuropsychology, symptoms, interactions, and comorbidity.

The primary determining factors are seen in a genetic disposition which leads to dysfunctions of the neurotransmitter system (for example, dopamine system) and other cerebral dysfunctions. Possible additional factors could be substances in the food of the child or brain injury. These causal factors lead to disturbances in the regulation system of the self (lack of impulse control, and so forth), in working memory, the regulation of affects, motivation and attention, the automatization of language, and the development of sequences of actions. All these processes then lead to the hyperkinetic symptoms (attention deficit, impulsivity, hyperactivity). These symptoms in turn lead to an increase in negative interactions with people important to the child. Unfavourable factors in school and in the family may additonally (but not causally) increase the problems. Comorbid symptoms such as deficits in academic achievements, aggressive behaviour, and emotional distrurbances are the consequences of these processes.

In their treatment they include exclusively psychopharmacological and cognitive behavioural methods, sometimes in combination with a form of counselling offered to the parents of children with ADHD, which also follows cognitive behavioural principles. Their *Kölner Mutimodale Therapiestudie* was well received by insurance companies, medical institutions, and the media. Therefore, in many medical journals in Germany as well as in many public reports on television, one can read or hear that 'the combination of cognitive behavioural therapy and medication is the only scientifically proven treatment for ADHD children'. Sometimes one encounters the opinion that psychodynamic treatments with this group have to be considered unethical, as the method has not been 'scientifically proven' according to the criteria of evidence-based medicine.

3.2 A multidimensional, psychoanalytic approach concerning the genesis, the psychodynamics, prevention, and treatment of children suffering from ADHD

In contrast to the opinions held in behavioural therapy and psychiatry, just briefly outlined above, it is emphasized in psychoanalytic publications that attention deficit and hyperactivity are *symptoms* which may at the most be summed up as *syndromes* but which should not be considered together as a *full-blown clinical condition*, even if it turned out that a genetic disposition actually exists. There are no clear borders between 'normal' and 'pathological' forms of hyperactivity and attention deficit. As is generally known, children with ADHD are capable of addressing certain tasks with their full attention and concentration if they are really interested in them. Therefore, a psychoanalytic approach does not attempt the 'objective measurement and evaluation' of the symptoms of hyperactivity and attention deficit, but aims rather to understand the various personality structures underlying these symptoms, as well as grasping something of the dynamics of the emotional relationships in the families and educational institutions which may trigger ADHD. We have observed different structural levels in children identified as having ADHD, and a wide range of divergent object relations, which is why monocausal aetiology cannot be assumed (Leuzinger-Bohleber, Staufenberg, and Fischmann, 2007). As is generally known, many genetic researchers have pointed out that even a genetic disposition does not 'linearly' generate a phenotype of behaviour, but that it takes certain environmental conditions and specific situations (in the case of childhood psychopathology, usually very complex early experiences in relationships) to trigger certain gene constellations and thus to activate them (see, for example, Stassen *et al.*, 2004a, 2004b; see also contemporary discussion in the field of epigenetics, for example, Hill, 2009, Goldberg, 2009, Soumi, 2010). In the meantime, there have been many empirical clues that a baby's temperament plays an important role in the aetiology of ADHD, especially if there is a clash of temperament with the primary attachment figure (usually the mother) (see, for example, Emde and Fonagy, 1997; Stern, 1995; Beebe and Lachman, 2002; Carey, Fonagy, and Leuzinger-Bohleber in this volume). It may be a risk factor if a bubbly baby has a relatively quiet mother, above all because this mother will probably have difficulty in adequately empathizing with her child and regulating its affects. However, it has turned out to be empirically very difficult to capture differences in temperament in an unequivocal way.

Psychoanalytic retrospective studies indicate that the tolerance of the primary attachment figure for the baby's outbursts, as well as his or her ability to soothe, hold, and 'contain' the outbursts, play a central role in the genesis of ADHD (see Bürgin, 2005; Bürgin and Steck, 2007; Dammasch, 2006; Fonagy and Target, 2003; Leuzinger-Bohleber *et al.*, 2006, Leuzinger-Bohleber, 2009, Sugarman, 2010, Salomonsen, 2004, 2006). It has been shown that the complex early interactions between mothers and children with ADHD are often characterized by over- or under-stimulation and intrusive or neglecting maternal behaviour (see Beebe and Lachmann, 2002; Green, 2005). Often, the babies seemed to have little choice other than to motivate their mothers to deliver the most basic care by showing hyperactive and over-stimulated behaviour, a pattern which is probably generalized later on.

To summarize, despite their theoretical differences, all contemporary psychoanalytic schools share the basic belief that stable psychic structures can only develop in adequate and empathic early object relations. These need to include a well-functioning regulation of drive impulses and affects in the mother, enabling the same to be built up in the infant, as well as secure inner borders between self and object representations. Moreover, more recent psychoanalytic publications stress—apart from a sensitive and empathic mother—the relevance of an early relationship for the child with the father (in the sense of early triangulation; see Bürgin, 1998; Klitzing, 2002), as well as the father showing emotional support for the mother (see inter alia Herzog, 2001; Metzger, 2000; Dammasch, 2000; Hopf, 2007). ADHD children seem to have experienced inadequately stable primary relationships. They were not able to develop sufficiently secure inner structures of these developmentally vital kinds, and they are deficient in the ability of self-regulation (see case studies by Dammasch, 2006; Leuzinger *et al.*, 2006). Furthermore, they did not have enough compensatory relational experiences to enable 'interactive repair' for experiences of deprivation or the 'lack of a primary attachment figure' (see Klitzing, 2002: 883; Häußler and Hopf, 2002; Heinz, 2002; Lüpke, 2004; Green 2005, 2006; Hopf, 2009; Laezer in prep).

Authors committed to *empirical attachment theory* have presented analogous findings and concepts. There has been evidence in many studies that maternal sensitivity is an important factor in the prediction of the so-called attachment categories in the first year of life (see, for example, Grossmann *et al.*, 1989). Ainsworth *et al.* (1978) showed in their empirical studies that mothers reacting sensitively to their children's signals during their first year of life—that is, both promptly and sufficiently accurately—tended to have children who show *secure attachment behaviour* in the so-called Strange Situation (a standardized situation to investigate attachment behaviour). There is evidence from some studies that children with secure attachment behaviour develop ADHD less frequently during their years at elementary school (see, for example, Lüpke, 2006; Salomonsen, 2006; Staufenberg, in press).

Fonagy and Target (2002) consider the development of reflective or mentalization capacities to be a vital pillar of social cognitive competence in children, joining with the regulation of attention and emotion expression to enable the child to behave in developmentally appropriate, socialized ways. Difficulties in all three areas are characteristic problems of ADHD children; '[i]ncapabilities in these self-regulatory skills lie at the heart of a specific, genetically linked neurological syndrome AD/HD' (Carney, 2002: 300). Understanding such deficits and trying to modify them in the psychoanalytically based treatments of children suffering from ADHD is a goal for psychoanalysts of all psychoanalytic schools (see also Haubl, 2009; Hopf, 2007; Myssior and Mahado, 2008; Nelson, 2002; Reichert, 2010; Salomonsen, 2006; Sugarman, 2010).

Staufenberg (in press) and colleagues have even developed a 'manual for treating ADHD children' integrating the different psychoanalytical approaches just mentioned. This manual was applied in a comparative therapy outcome study on the results of psychoanalytic compared with cognitive-behaviroal/medication treatment already mentioned (see, for example, Laezer, in press).

Thus, in Germany, the psychoanalytic and psychodynamic treatment of children with ADHD is still the most frequent (see, for example, fakt KBV). But we urgently need more emprical studies showing whether these treatments are effective and *'nachhaltig'* (longlasting) even according to the criteria of evidence-based medicine. At the Sigmund-Freud-Institute we are just performing such a study comparing the results of psychoanalytical compared with cognitive-behavioral/medical treatments of ADHD (see, for example, Laezer *et al.*, 2010; Laezer in press). This extraclinical study takes the position that it has always been true to the core of psychoanalytic conceptualization that the symptoms of a child should be analysed as the products of complex unconscious and conscious factors, idiographic biographical factors on the one hand and specific genetic, biological, and neurobiological determinants on the other. Therefore, we agree with many contemporary authors that psychoanalysis—as a theory as well as a treatment method—has a lot to offer for understanding children with ADHD—and could even, once enriched by awareness of the biological determinants, be seen as the most comprehensive method and the treatment of choice (for example, Carney, 2002; Bürgin, 2005; Bürgin and Rothstein, 2002; Gilmore, 2002; Leuzinger-Bohleber, 2009; Sugarman, 2006; Zabarenko, 2002). But our clinical findings are not sufficient any more in the current debates on ADHD mentioned above: we need to prove them with sound empirical comparative empirical studies; a great challenge for contemporary psychoanalysis, but one which—if possible to meet—can be instructive.

Let us turn to another important topic of ADHD in the last section of our introduction: prevention and early intervention.

4 Prevention and early intervention: Some psychoanalytic and neurobiological considerations on psychosocial disintegration

The above psychoanalytic concepts on the aetiology of ADHD as well as the enormous significance of prevention and intervention in the first years of life are in line with interdisciplinary findings, especially from neurobiology. In a number of psychiatric and psychoanalytic papers, neuroscientific research which seems to be relevant to the understanding of ADHD is summarized (see, for example, Barkley, 1997; Levin, 1997; Gilmore, 2000; Rothstein, 2002; Salomonsson, 2004, 2007). Zabarenko (2002: 415ff.) mentions three research areas which are immediately relevant for ADHD: i) research on attention and executive control; ii) learning and neural plasticity; and iii) memory.

Another promising theoretical approach is a contemporary understanding of 'embodied memory and problem solving', supporting our thesis that the intensive psychoanalytic treatment of ADHD children has important advantages to add to exclusively medical treatment (see Leuzinger-Bohleber and Pfeifer, 2002, 2006; Pfeifer and Scheier, 1999; Pfeifer and Bongard, 2007; Fuchs, Sattel, and Henningsen, 2010). In the field of so-called 'Embodied Cognitive Science', results of biologically oriented memory research have been taken into account which prove that the computer metaphor which still forms the basis of many theories on memory is fundamentally wrong (for example, when we talk about 'stores' contained in the long-term memory and from which knowledge is transferred to the short-term memory, or a 'defect' in the neurotransmitter system which has to be 'restored' by psychostimulants). Living systems are forced to adapt constantly to a continuously changing environment. In this process, knowledge from earlier situations is used but has to be 're-written' again and again and adapted to the new situation. Therefore, memory is nowadays understood as an active, creative process of the whole organism based upon sensory-affective coordination processes and associated 'automatic', constantly adapting, re-categorizing processes. Thus, memory does not imply purely cognitive processes but is always 'embodied' (see also Leuzinger-Bohleber, 2008).

Thus, it can be assumed that even if certain genetic dispositions exist, specific early 'embodied' interaction experiences in object relations must have taken place which 'trigger' the development of attention deficit and hyperactivity. These early pathological experiences may in turn only be modified or corrected permanently, and in the sense of self-regulation of the infantile organism by means of new 'embodied' experiences, and not by medication supposed to adjust a particular malfunction in the brain. *In other words, neurobiologically and psychically failed developments may largely be corrected or at least softened by suitable, adequate, 'corrective' experiences with one's objects and the environment.* Although we agree that more research is still needed, we assume that such corrective opportunities are largely not produced by the medical treatment of ADHD children, although it is acknowledged that suppressing disruptive symptoms may create a better context for positive interactions.

Jaak Panksepp (1998), a leading neurobiologist and brain researcher into emotional development, adds more grounds for a similar position dealing with ADHD children. To summarize some of his arguments briefly, recent brain-imaging data have revealed that the major difference in the brains of individuals with ADHD is in the frontal areas.

At the gross structural level, brains of children diagnosed with ADHD exhibit a 5% reduction of overall size. There are also some neurochemical differences (Soltano, 1998), but none of them is sufficiently large to permit us to conclude that the differences constitute a medically significant abnormality. The neural differences in ADHD children have recently been formulated by Barkley (1997) and are summarized in Figure 1.

> According to this view, the fundamental problem in AD/HD is not a deficit in attention, but an abnormally low level of behavioural inhibition, a global function that allows better reflection, imagination, empathy and creativity. These abilities promote behavioural flexibility, better foresight and a more mature

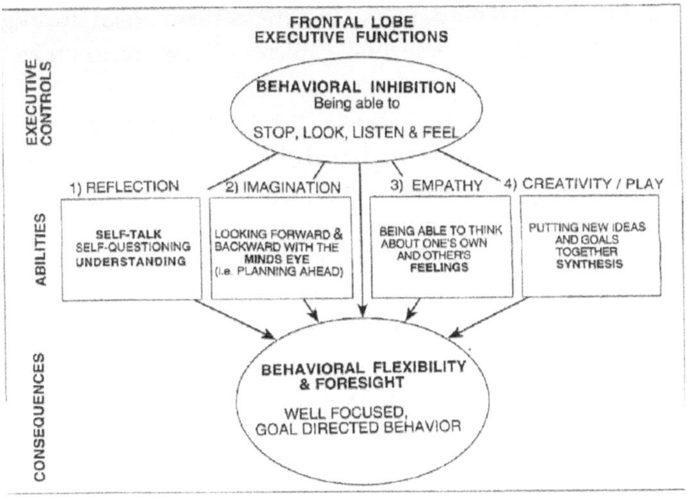

Figure 1. A synoptic interpretation of the frontal lobe functions that may be deficient in attention deficit hyperactivity disorder (adapted from Barkley, 1997).

> regulation of behaviour. If we accept the existence of a frontal lobe contribution to AD/HD, we still must consider whether there are environmental or physical ways to improve such frontal lobe functions permanently.
>
> (Panksepp, 1998: 93)

Medical treatment offers the 'physical' possibilities. Without any doubt, short-term behavioural improvements occur with psychostimulants. The problem is, as many studies have shown, that the long-term effects have rarely been evident. When medication is terminated, ADHD symptoms typically return, suggesting that the children are not learning to manage their lives better. Evidence for long-term improvements of cognitive functions and other abilities remains practically non-existent (for a summary of such work, see Barkley, 1997; Panksepp, 1998: 93). Panksepp then argues that the short-term benefits of the treatment with psychostimulants would be acceptable if they did not have any negative physical consequences (which have been argued to include a small decrease in the rate of physical growth; a relatively rare incidence of seizure, tics, mania, and delusional tendencies; and the controversial finding of a range other difficulties when these children grow up, such as drug abuse).

Due to methodological problems, the long-term effects of treatment with psychostimulants can hardly be studied in human beings.[7] Therefore, Panksepp quotes animal studies. There is some evidence from these studies that psychostimulants decrease—instead of increase—neural plasticity; 'In general, dopaminergic arousal, as can be achieved with psychostimulants, tends to reduce glutamate-mediated neural plasticity' (Panksepp, 1998: 95). Panksepp thus pleads for a different strategy in the treatment of ADHD children in our societies: to create more possibilities for young children to develop the frontal lobe executive functions by playing, and in particular by playing so-called rough-and-tumble games:

> The urge to indulge in rough-and-tumble play is a birthright of the mammalian brain ... Social play may be an experience-expectant, or preparatory, process that helps programme higher brain areas that will be required later in life. Indeed 'youth' may have evolved to give complex organisms time to play and thereby to exercise that natural skills they will need as adults. We already know that as the frontal lobes mature, frequency of play goes down ... Might access to rough-and-tumble play promote frontal lobe maturation?
>
> (Panksepp, 1998: 95–96)

To sum up, like many contemporary brain researchers, Panksepp postulates a user-dependent emergence of brain organic changes in hyperactivity and attention deficit. Particularly for children born with a (probably genetically determined) impulsive temper and character, the possibility of engaging in active exploration of their environment and in rough-and-tumble play seems to be essential in order to develop frontal lobe executive functions. If—for various reasons—children do not have sufficient possibilities to engage in such exploration and play (due to their early object relations, traumatic experiences, or simply environmental factors such as the absence of a playground for small children) they may develop ADHD. Medication probably does not help to compensate for this deficit in the frontal lobe executive functions. Organic brain (just like psychological) changes can only take place 'user-dependently', that is, in new playful and explorative situations, and are particularly effective if combined with intense, positive emotional relationship experiences (see also Damasio, 1994, 2003; Passolt, 2004; Hüther, 2006; Dawirs *et al.*, 1992; Moll *et al.*, 2000; Leuzinger-Bohleber, Roth, Buchheim, 2008; Doidge, 2007; Leuzinger-Bohleber, Röckerath, and Strauss, 2010; Fuchs, Sattel, and Henningsen, 2010).

These considerations are very consistent with psychoanalytic concepts of the development of disturbances such as ADHD, as will be discussed in several papers of this volume. The following short case examples, mostly taken from the *Frankfurt Prevention Study*, may illustrate this point.

5 Some short case studies

One aim of the *Frankfurt Prevention Study* was to contribute to a differentiation of the ADHD diagnosis by looking at it from a psychoanalytic point of view. As briefly discussed above, ADHD seems to have become a 'fashionable diagnosis'. All over the world, 10 million children are treated with amphetamines after having been diagnosed with ADHD. In Germany, 400,000 young people receive regular medication for this problem—and that number is increasing. The estimated prevalence rate at the age of 6 to 18 years is between 2 and 6% (BMGS, 2002).

We have been able to gather numerous and extensive single case observations as well as statistical data from the original sample of 500 children in our prevention/intervention group. Discussing our observations, we have found different subgroups of the children who had been diagnosed with ADHD according to the criteria of the Döpfner and the Conner Scales (both instruments are based on DSM-IV criteria). In other words, on a descriptive level, all the children suffered—according to DSM-IV—from ADHD. Nevertheless, it does not seem very helpful for a deepened understanding of these children to stick to a 'meaningful discrete diagnostic entity' (Gilmore, 2000: 1,258). From a psychoanalytic perspective, a more dynamic, precise perception of each child's idiosyncratic psychological and psychosocial situation offers, in our view, a better base for adequate treatment.

Therefore, we would like to outline some of these distinctions subsumed under the syndrome ADHD by defining different subgroups. As discussed above, from a psychoanalytic, dynamic point of view, we can always observe a complex interchange of many factors determining the individual picture of ADHD. Nevertheless, in the following subgroups, some of these factors seemed to dominate and were thus picked out in order to characterize the specific subgroup. All the examples (except example 1) illustrating the subgroup are taken from our sample in the *Frankfurt Prevention Study*. (As an illustration of VII 'Growing up with a depressed primary object', we will refer to the summary of the child analysis with Nora in the paper of Marianne Leuzinger-Bohleber in this volume.)

I Children with a brain organic problem

Michael, a 5-year-old only child, is the 'enfant terrible' of his kindergarten: he is involved in constant aggressive conflicts and absorbs his teachers for more or less the whole day. If they do not keep him under observation, the probability is high that he will hurt himself or another child:

> Often he does not intend to do so—but Michael is clumsy. He seems not to be able to perceive and evaluate situations adequately. He is throwing things at other kids, destroys their toys and drawings or, as happened last Wednesday, he once more fell off the climbing frame in the garden and had to be brought to the doctor.
>
> (Mrs M.)

His teachers agreed that Michael did not have any problems if he was alone with one of them in a dyadic situation, for example, when he was playing in the room with one member of staff:

> In such a situation he is able to concentrate and to sit still for at least 10 minutes. He is a nice and cute little boy when you have him alone. In contrast, he is terrible in a group situation. He constantly seems to be overwhelmed with stimuli. During the morning hours, he becomes more and more clumsy, restless and

> aggressive. Our institution can hardly deal with him anymore. We have to take care of another 18 kids in his group.
>
> (Teacher A)

In the psychological assessment, Michael's mother talked about the difficult, even traumatic, birth of Michael. He probably suffered from a lack of oxygen. He had a low Apgar asphyxia index and already showed severe eating and sleeping disturbances in the first months of his life. After the medical examinations U2, U3, and U4 (regularly carried out in Germany at X months by paediatricians, the results of which are documented in a special file for each child), the doctor told the parents that they should arrange a neurological assessment for Michael to test if an early intervention programme should be initiated to overcome Michael's retarded sensory motor development. The parents did not follow this advice. During the assessment interview, the mother said: 'My husband had exactly the same problems when he was a baby—he was a clumsy, crying infant—these are problems of his family. Michael will grow out of them and overcome them without extra help.' Only when her husband died suddenly six months later from a heart attack did she change her mind and became willing to accept therapeutic help for herself and Michael.

Looking back on the one year of psychoanalytic therapy with Michael (twice a week), it seemed most likely to me (M.L.-B.) that an organic component played an important role in Michael's ADHD symptoms, although he had never undergone detailed neurological testing (functional magnetic resonance imaging [FMRI], and so forth). However, in psychological tests, some indicators supporting this hypothesis could be found. In the HAWIK (Hamburg Wechsler Intelligence Test) he had a score of 102. In the Göttinger Formrepreoduktions-Test, a test which compares children with a diagnosed brain organic problem with two samples, one of 'normal' children and one of children with probable organic brain pathology, Michael´s probability score was 42. This means that he had a score at the 42nd percentile of children with an organic brain disorder; 58% of this group would achieve better results.

One major focus of the psychoanalytic therapy was to understand unconscious fantasies in the context of the traumatic loss of the father in the midst of Michael's oedipal developmental phase. His enormous guilt feelings and his 'magic conviction' that he had caused the death of his father could finally be understood and worked through in therapy. Michael had very low self-esteem, thinking that he was 'an ugly, uncontrollable, destructive monster'. This self-representation was partially due to his ADHD problems. He seemed to realize that he was different from the other kids. 'I cannot control my body and often just do things and hurt others without really wanting to' he said during a session. In this context, it was important for him that I tried to explain to him possible early roots of his problems according to the well-known consequences of 'so-called minimal brain dysfunction', as it had been discussed in Europe at that time (see the historical overview above). I told him:

> You are not a 'monster', as you fear ... you just have gone through some very special problems as a baby. Your body has not forgotten these experiences and still has more problems than those of other children to control some situations ... We will try to understand together what your body wants to tell you. Afterwards you will better be able to control your body, thoughts and feelings.

I cannot go into any details of the therapeutic process here but only want to mention that it also seemed essential that I worked with Michael's mother, too. I tried to help her to understand Michael's behaviour better in order to deal with him in a more adequate way (she was also in psychotherapy trying to overcome the traumatic loss of her husband and her resentful feeling 'that he has left me alone with this difficult child ...'[8]). The teachers of the kindergarten also helped the mother to structure the day for Michael in the sense of supporting or even compensating for his partially underdeveloped ego functions, trying to overcome his difficulties in controlling and regulating his affects and needs (clear daily structure with regular changes between concentration and relaxation phases for Michael, protection from being flooded with stimuli in group situations, TV consumption, undergoing psychomotor training, playing tennis, and so forth).

This combination of psychoanalytic therapy and counselling of the mother enabled Michael to start normal elementary school successfully and to 'develop in a normal way, intellectually and socially—for example, in respect of my friends and my girlfriend', as he said in a follow-up interview as an 18-year-old adolescent.

Nowadays, perhaps medication would be advised in a case such as Michael's. From a psychoanalytic perspective, it was impressive how Michael, as an 18-year-old adolescent, talked about his own achievements: 'I am proud that I made my way despite the early death of my father and my brain problems due to my birth.' To achieve these developments without the help of medication seemed to be essential for his self-esteem.

Stuart Hauser and his co-workers (2006) published a similar case: Pete, a boy who also had an ADHD diagnosis and severe behavioural problems during latency and early adolescence. The astonishing resilience of this boy is considered by these authors to be mainly connected with his capability of seeing his own contribution to his conduct problems in childhood and adolescence (see the Preface to this volume). Psychoanalytic therapies work on insights on precisely this topic and thus probably contribute to the resilience of children with ADHD.

II Children with early emotional neglect

Robert, a 5-year-old boy is—like Michael—hardly tolerable for his kindergarten. Due to his aggressive and destructive behaviour he is socially isolated, has not one single friend and usually plays alone. He is unable to concentrate for more than five minutes and seems to suffer from enormous anxieties. He is in constant motion and cannot sit still; one teacher characterized him as a 'a classical fidgeter—not one single meal passes without him making a mess somehow …'

Robert is the only son of an unemployed, 21-year-old, woman, Mrs X, who has a severe alcohol problem. Robert's father left his mother after a short and dramatic relationship before Robert was even born. The mother resents psychologists because, as she says, she was diagnosed as 'manic-depressive' by a psychiatrist who hospitalized her for several months. Mrs X tells the psychologist (Gerlinde Goeppel, a member of our research team) that she has broken off contact with her parents because 'both of them are alcoholics and maltreated me terribly as a child'. She now lives on social welfare, is socially isolated, and in danger of becoming an alcoholic. Robert though, she says, 'is all I have—the only thing that makes sense of my life …' After several talks with Gerlinde Goeppel, she is willing to accept psychological help, but after the kindergarten's summer break she does not return: she has moved away.

Our team, as well as the kindergarten teachers, were very concerned about the situation and Robert's future. He belonged to the group of 40 children who, in our view, would have needed psychotherapeutic help urgently but for whom the parents did not accept professional support. Robert's ADHD symptoms seemed to be connected to severe emotional neglect. His early object relations probably did not enable him to develop a secure attachment or a stable inner affect regulation.

In contrast, the parents of 17 children coming from a similar social background accepted help for their ADHD child because we could offer them that therapy in the kindergartens (the therapists were available to treat these children twice a week in special rooms at the kindergartens). One of the most impressive child therapies was reported extensively by Christina Waldung (Waldung *et al.*, 2006). We summarize some of her findings here. Peter (5 years old) is also a child who suffered from severe early emotional neglect and who developed ADHD symptoms.

In supervision with me (L-B), a teacher reported furiously that Peter had spat in her face. 'This is beyond the acceptable—I don't want to have him in my group anymore—I've tried so hard with him—and now this—I will not tolerate this—I am so disappointed …' I suggested in the supervision: 'Of course I don't want to excuse his behaviour, but perhaps Peter wanted to tell you something and has chosen you as his most beloved person in the kindergarten as the one to spit at. Let's try to understand his behaviour first and then talk about how to deal with it …'

After this intervention, another teacher of the supervision group remembers that the female cook recalled that Peter, who had been sent away, came to the kitchen and said: 'You know, sometimes I just do not want to live anymore …' We take his message very seriously. The headteacher of the kindergarten called Peter's father and discovered that Mr E had just lost his job as a taxi driver because of his diabetes. The mother is severely mentally ill and had repeatedly left the family. Mr E had tried to keep the family together, being 20 years older than his wife and more stable than her. Two older children had been taken into a children's home soon after starting school. Both of them had had severe conduct problems and were diagnosed with ADHD. In supervision, we ultimately understood that Peter tried to unconsciously communicate his despair to his most beloved teacher. He probably feared that his family situation would now definitely collapse and that he would be taken away to a children's home like his two siblings. I (L-B) tried to explain in supervision: 'If you have such an unbearable expectation as a child—it is well known that these children try to actively provoke something in order that they, at least, can have the fantasy that it was themselves who are responsible for the "punishment" instead of just being the passive, helpless victim ...' Fortunately, the father finally accepted psychoanalytic therapy for Peter. Peter has been in therapy for nearly three years and was able to be successful in normal elementary school. The therapist also worked intensively with both parents. The mother was sent to a mental hospital after Peter's birth for several months. She is in constant treatment by a psychiatrist but often does not take her pills. She has left the family again and again and had several affairs. Mr E, who once lost a former wife, which was a traumatic experience for him, fights to keep the family together and does not want 'to lose his last child'. The regular contact with the therapist helped him to overcome his depression due to his unemployment and to realize how important his fatherly role is in bringing up Peter.

Peter is a highly intelligent boy. At the beginning of therapy he was absorbed by the fantasy that if he were a girl he would not have the ADHD difficulties and 'my mother would love me more ...' He already showed transvestite symptoms, wanted to be a girl, and hated typical rough-and-tumble games. After these fantasies had been understood and worked through in therapy, the transvestite symptoms disappeared: he now seems to show 'normal male development'. Another infantile fantasy was that he had to save the marriage of his parents by lying between them in the marital bed whenever the mother returned to the father's home. Only after having understood the wishes and fears underlying these fantasies was he able to accept his own room and sleep alone.

Of course, he still has conduct problems at school. His mother was hospitalized again shortly after Peter began school. Because she was put under medication again, she suddenly wanted to have medication (Ritalin®) for Peter, too. Fortunately, we cooperated well with the University Clinic for Child and Adolescent Psychiatry to whom Peter was referred. Therefore, we could prevent the child therapy from being terminated. The psychiatrist convinced the parents that Peter does not need Ritalin® but does require a continuation of his psychotherapy.

For a long time the therapy focused on Peter's sudden aggressive outbursts, which had been a serious problem at school. These outbursts were often triggered by feelings of impotence and helplessness, which Peter could not stand, probably because they unconsciously reminded him of his early traumatic experiences with his primary objects.

Now (2009): more than two years after the termination of the psychotherapy Peter is able to concentrate in class. He is better socially integrated and no longer so hyperactive. Peter and his parents still have a long way to go, but we are convinced that the psychoanalytic therapy helped to strengthen the boy's resilience.

All the children in Peter's family were diagnosed with ADHD. Peter's development may illustrate that even if there should be a genetic component, psychotherapy could still help to change the ADHD symptoms by understanding the traumatic early relationships (for the theoretical considerations, see above).

III ADHD and trauma

Johi, 4½ years old, is called 'the little professor' by his peers in kindergarten because he often seems to be absent-minded, daydreaming, and unable to concentrate on anything. Sometimes he is also involved in aggressive conflicts with other children because he suddenly interrupts their play and disturbs them. He is hardly able to sit still—he seems in constant motor tension:

> He is a nice and lovely little boy but does not seem to be able to take into account any rules or agreements. Often I have the feeling that he just does not understand what I am telling him. Sometimes he forgets to take off his jacket and seems very surprised when I tell him that he still has his jacket on ...
>
> (Teacher B)

Several teachers reported in supervision that Johi was already able to read when he entered kindergarten aged 3½ years. His parents, intellectuals from an African country, had to flee under dramatic circumstances when Johi was 1 year old. They are convinced that Johi is exceptionally intellectually gifted and thought about sending him to a kindergarten for highly talented children. Only when the teachers told them about Johi's serious social problems did they stop pursuing the question of his intelligence. They declined the offer of having Johi's intelligence tested and for Johi's difficulties to be talked over with the Study psychologist. It may be that Johi is severely absorbed by the 'secrets' in his family due to their massive traumatization (the family lost several members in the civil war; the father was in prison; the mother probably a victim of sexual violence). Therefore, we have the hypothesis that the early capacity to read could also have compensatory functions: an unconscious attempt to cope with the trauma. His daydreaming and his dissociative state could also be seen in this context.

Johi was not the only child with ADHD symptoms who came from a severely traumatized refugee family. In some kindergartens in Frankfurt there are many children from families who fled from their countries. Often the kindergarten team knows little about the traumatic family history. In the supervisions we sometimes encouraged the teachers to try to talk with these families, because in some cases the kindergarten seems to be the only 'social meeting place' for these families. In some cases it was possible to initiate child or family therapies for these children or to refer them to a counselling centre for refugees in Frankfurt.[9]

IV ADHD and culture

Ahib, 5 years old, is the third son of a Pakistani family. In a sudden outburst of rage he kicked the stomach of a 4-year-old girl so violently that she had to be taken into hospital. The teachers commented in a resigned way:

> We have no idea what else we can do, we have tried everything—all three brothers had been extremely aggressive, hyperactive, and weak in their achievements ... but the parents stuck to their opinion that their sons do not have any problems at home and

> are highly talented. They came to Germany so that all of them should become medical doctors ... We can only wait until the school reacts and sends them to a special school for children with low intelligence and conduct problems. Ahib is already hardly tolerable in our institution. Since his little sister was born he particularly often attacks little girls ... Nearly every day we have difficulties with him ...
>
> (Teacher D)

Ahib's family comes from an Eastern country with a culture widely unknown to the teachers. According to the reports of the mother, the children in her native village mostly grow up in the streets. The boys in particular have to learn to assert themselves in their peer group. 'They have to learn to fight in order to survive ...' This cultural background as well as the problems with language (they hardly speak German) may contribute to the conduct problems of these boys. All of them could be diagnosed as suffering from ADHD.

Frankfurt, as many other cities in Western Europe, has become a multicultural city. To mention just one example, in one kindergarten with 103 children only three had a German passport. Twenty-seven different nations with many, many different cultures and languages were represented in this institution. What a challenge for teachers working in such a kindergarten![10] To diagnose many of these children as suffering from ADHD and to treat them with medication would suggest denial of one of the most urgent problems in our Western society: the need for social integration and the prevention of so-called 'parallel societies'.

V ADHD and extraordinarily talented children

Five-year-old Dominik became more and more problematic in his kindergarten due to a change of teaching policy introduced 1½ years ago by a new director. The new director introduced a more hierarchical, relatively rigid, educational model, with closed groups of children and a more or less structured schedule. 'The children should be educated in a more strict and direct way,' the director explained to the parents. 'We offer opportunities to learn English, French, and Maths regularly—each day from 10 to 11. Therefore, all the children have to be in kindergarten at 9 o'clock.' Dominik, coming from an intellectual background with very creative parents, just hated these changes and complained that he did not want to go to kindergarten anymore but preferred to stay at home 'because I want to play and do my own things ...' In kindergarten, he got involved more and more in aggressive conflicts, was rebellious in the lessons he had to attend, did not concentrate and was not able to sit still. Finally, the teachers recommended having him assessed for ADHD.

The tests showed that Dominik was extraordinarily talented with an IQ of about 132 (Kramer Intelligence Test). He understood French fluently and was already able to read in his fifth year of life. He also had an extraordinary level of skill in mathematical problem-solving. He surprised the psychologist by his vivid fantasy and creativity. He loved to draw but also to invent stories with Lego® and so on. When the psychologist asked him why he did not want to attend the English and Maths lessons in kindergarten, he said: 'It is just boring—I hate it—I want to do my own things.' After discussing the results of the psychological testing, the parents decided to take Dominik to another kindergarten with more open space in the educational agenda. Dominik liked to go there, played for hours with another very talented and creative child and lost all of his ADHD symptoms.

Dominik is one example of a child who may be diagnosed with ADHD but who is actually highly talented and responding to an environment ill-suited to accommodate this. They develop concentration problems and aggressive behaviour because they are forced into educational programmes which seem 'just boring' to them. ADHD may be—in these rare cases—seen as a manifestation of an unconscious protest against a denial of the idiosyncratic intellectual or emotional capacities of these children. Therefore, one should also, when diagnosing ADHD, consider the problems of such children in the context and atmosphere of their educational institutions and teachers.

VI ADHD and mourning or depression

Rahel, a 5-year-old girl, is not able to concentrate. She often sits in a corner in her group of children, sad and withdrawn. She seems to be in another world. Sometimes these withdrawals suddenly turn into aggressive and hyperactive behaviour (one reason why she also belongs to the group of ADHD children according to the criteria of our study). 'In such states she seems to be without any centre in herself, in constant tension and movement and looking for conflicts and aggressive interactions with other kids' (Teacher C).

Rahel had been a 'normal child' until, a year previously, her mother was diagnosed with lung cancer. She had to undergo radiotherapy and chemotherapy, without success. She died 6 months ago.

In supervision we discussed the hypothesis that the ADHD symptoms of Rahel could be seen as a kind of manic defence against unbearable feelings of despair, anxiety, and mourning. It turned out that Rahel's father had already lost his first wife because of cancer. She left him with two children, who are now 16 and 18 years of age. Rahel has a younger brother of 3 years. In supervision, the teachers report that she sometimes draws herself as her little brother's substitute mother, an indication of her identification with the dead mother. Her destructive and aggressive behaviour could also be connected to unconscious guilt feelings and fantasies that her oedipal strivings could have been one reason for her mother's death.

After several months and several consultations with the teachers of the kindergarten, Rahel's father was willing to accept psychoanalytic help for his family and for Rahel. Rahel is now in psychoanalytic treatment with an experienced colleague. Her ADHD symptoms have already decreased in the past four months since she started treatment.

This may seem like an exceptional example, although we would like to mention that Rahel was not the only child in the sample of the *Frankfurt Prevention Study* who developed ADHD symptoms after an unbearable life event. Sometimes the supervisors had to prompt the kindergarten teachers to ask the parents straight away what had happened in the family in order to understand a sudden change in the behaviour of a certain child. In some cases, the parents tried to hide the severe events, particularly if they were connected with the break-up of their marriages or similar (potentially shaming) events.

In the context of this paper we can only offer short summaries of these fully documented clinical cases of the *Frankfurt Prevention Study*. However, we hope that they have illustrated one of the major theses of this volume: ADHD is not a unitary condition, but has to be understood as the (symptomatic) product of an idiosyncratic complex intertwining of many factors and determinants.

6 *Clinical, conceptual, and empirical psychoanalytic research on ADHD and other disturbances of early development: Overview on the contributions of this volume*

As may be clear, we are convinced that interdisciplinary dialogue between psychoanalysts and other psychotherapists, child psychiatrists, brain researchers, educational, and social scientists and also between parents, teachers, and other professionals is absolutely necessary to deepen our understanding for possible origins, preventions, and interventions, helping children suffering from so-called 'attention deficit hyperactivity disorder' (ADHD), and related developmental disturbances. In this volume you will find papers illustrating this dialogue.

In *Part II* of this book *papers from non-psychoanalytical as well as from psychoanalytic research* are included: Two of the leading child psychiatrists in Germany, Gerd Lehmkuhl (Cologne) and Annette Streek-Fischer (Göttingen),[11] as well as one of the leading researchers on temperament, William Carey from Philadelphia (Discussant: Jorge Canestri, Rome) are contributing to this volume. Gerd Lehmkuhl discusses the dialogue between child psychatrist and child psychoanalysts and summarizes:

What are the conclusion and the overall perspective? Child psychiatrists ought to ask themselves how neuroscientific results can represent the inner world of their patients, which methods can better detect the experiences, feelings and self-concepts and how early attachment experiences can effect the cognitive and emotional development. And child psychoanalysts? They should be inspired by the versatile and complex developmental models in order to reassess the importance of the environment for intrapsychic processes.

> If mentalization disorders can be caused not only by negative attachment experiences, but also by biological processes, this has an important effect on treatment procedures, especially regarding the work with parents.

> Moreover, many factors suggest that mentalization and autobiographical memory are not completed at a certain point of time, but are part of a long-some course of development having consequences for treatment planning.
>
> (This volume)

In his paper, William Carey takes into consideration another element; he emphasizes as the main focus of his thesis that: 'the current neglect of normal temperament differences has resulted in an overdiagnosis of CNS-based psychopathology and an overuse of medication'. This situation, which appears to be extremely worrying in the USA according to the data provided by the author, is unfortunately not very different in Europe. The author rightly reminds us that there are temperamental differences in children. (The term 'temperament' is not common in psychoanalysis, but the concept can be easily traced. Carey defines temperament as 'the characteristic way with which the child experiences and responds to environmental stimuli'.)

In his discussion, Jorge Canestri mentions how Carey's observation of early 20th-century psychology, in contrast with that of previous centuries, emphasized the dominant importance of the environment, with a few exceptions, among them that of Freud, who wrote in *Analysis terminable and interminable* (1937): 'each individual ego is endowed from the beginning with its own peculiar dispositions and tendencies'. The author of *Coping with children's temperament* attributes to the 'general professional and public unfamiliarity with our growing knowledge about normal temperament differences' an important responsibility for producing this state of affairs.

The discussant, Jorge Canestri, underlines that a great deal of contemporary psychoanalysis, by excessively accentuating the effect of the environment and not acknowledging what Freud attributed to 'nature', is no less responsible. The match therefore seems to be between a so-called 'organic' type of psychiatry that is blind to the relationship between natural gifts and environment, and a psychoanalysis that, by neglecting the Freudian concept of complementary series, ends up by never including X in its equations, X being one of the firm assumptions of the father of psychoanalysis. For a long time it appeared that X—that is, the inborn factors, dispositions, and tendencies—were not known and it was therefore useless to include them. Today it is not possible, or advisable, to continue along this line, especially when we see the effects that this positioning of 'organicism' against 'environmentalism' can provoke.

In Part II we have also included some clinical papers, in spite of the well-known criticism of *clinical research in psychoanalysis* as well as the tradition of *case histories* in psychoanalysis, criticism increasing within the zeitgeist of evidence-based medicine. In spite of all these objections, Adelheid Staufenberg, Luisa Busch de Ahumada, Jorge L. Ahumada, Marianne Leuzinger-Bohleber, Annette Streek Fischer, and Angela Joyce take up this tradition in their papers. They do not pretend to present 'conclusive, objective findings', but rather to communicate complex and detailed clinical observations and some conceptualizations based on them. We are convinced that some of these observations can only *be told and not measured*. Most of the findings and insights of psychoanalysis are based on this kind of naturalistic, observational 'field research', the often years-long clinical work with our patients.

The tradition of communicating these findings by narratives is meeting with a new interest in contemporary educational fields and social sciences, and even in some fields of the neurosciences and Embodied Cognitive Science within academic psychology. In contrast to the presentation of results of empirical studies, we are often inspired by arts and literature while writing narratives, fields which remind us that in human communication there is no such thing as a single 'objective truth'. What we see and understand in a complex human interaction could be compared with carefully looking through a kaleidoscope—the patterns which we discover in complex clinical data often depend very much on the (unconscious) focus we choose. Again and again we recognize different information structures in complex phenomena. Of course, as Charles Hanly elaborates in his paper in *Part III*, the interpretations of our observations should not be contradictory but rather should supplement each other, looking at the same information from different perspectives and being prepared to falsify some of our hypotheses after precise multi-perspective observations. This is one of the specificities of our science ('Wissenschaft') which we have to explain in an assertive way in interdisciplinary discourse. On the other hand, as, for example, Horst Kächele (2008) has often reminded us, this specificity should never become an 'excuse' not to open up our research field to the observation, the understanding, and the critical perspectives of non-psychoanalytic scientists, particularly if they engage with the detailed clinical observations of the results of our psychoanalytic treatments, for example, with ADHD children. Therefore—thanks to the collaboration with the departments of Fritz Poustka (Frankfurt) and Emil Branik (Hamburg)—the research team at the Sigmund-Freud-Institut is now able to conduct an *empirical comparative outcome study on psychoanalytic therapies (group I), behavioural/pharmacological (group II), and 'normal' (pharmocological) psychiatric treatments of hyperactive children (group III)* (see www.sigmund-freud-institut.de and Laezer *et al.*, 2010; Laezer, in prep).

As will be discussed in *Part II* and *Part III* of this volume, psychoanalytic researchers always have to cope with a specific tension: on the one hand we have to argue that our specific research topic, unconscious fantasies and conflicts, are not directly observable and thus need the very specific research methodology of psychoanalysis, using the *precise observation and understanding* of free associations, dreams, slips of the tongue, and so forth, as well as of transference and counter-transference reactions in the psychoanalytic sessions. Psychoanalysis has also developed specific criteria of 'truth' in order to evaluate certain hypotheses or falsify others—in close cooperation with our analysts within the psychoanalytic setting. This genuine psychoanalytic form of research cannot be replaced by any other form of research, but only supplemented, a point which Björn Salomonsson takes up in his discussion of Peter Fonagy´s paper. The results of clinical research can often only be communicated by narratives. On the other hand, psychoanalytic researchers are confronted with the requirements of scientific communication such as the need for transparency of data and of the different steps of interpretations based on these observations, the falsifiability of hypotheses, the accessibility to criticism from the outside, the systematic control of subjective factors, and so forth.

As our Research Sub-committee has discussed in a recent paper (Leuzinger-Bohleber and Fischmann, 2006), innovative research in the field of conceptual research depends on its capacity to integrate a rich spectrum of clinical and conceptual knowledge as well as the current state of the findings of interdisciplinary studies relevant to the specific concept. Psychoanalytic concepts have to prove to be 'externally coherent' (Strenger) with this interdisciplinary state of the art. This is a challenge as well as an enormous opportunity. We will mention just one example from the contemporary dialogue between psychoanalysis and the neurosciences.

Bradley Peterson discussed one of the most basic questions of psychoanalytic developmental research in his contribution at the Joseph Sandler Conference:[12] the question of the chicken and the egg. Do ADHD children suffer from a genetically determined defect in the neurotransmitter regulation in their brains? Or are the findings of some deviations in brain functioning themselves the results of early and the earliest interactions with the environment (starting during pregnancy) as, for example, Jaak Panksepp postulates? Precisely these questions are also intensively debated in the field of Embodied Cognitive Science (see, for example, Pfeifer and Bongard, 2007) and in the discourse on neural plasticity (see for example, Doidge, 2007). It is extremely interesting also to look at some of the neurobiological studies. Let us take one example.

Mirescu, Peter, and Gould (2004) published a study, 'Early life experience alters responses of adult neurogenesis to stress' in *Nature Neuroscience*. They report that the separation of baby rats from their mothers directly after birth has severe long-term effects on their behaviour and neuroendocrinological circuits. These rats become more anxious, more sensitive to stress, react in a more aggressive way, and are limited in their exploration and learning behaviour. Analogously, could these findings hint at possible long-term effects of early traumatization in ADHD children as well? At any rate, the results of this study support the insights of the classical hospitalization studies of René Spitz as well as other studies on the effects of early separation by Bowlby, the Robertsons and others (see also Leuzinger-Bohleber, Roth, and Buchheim, 2008; Suomi, 2010). To integrate these interdisciplinary findings into our psychoanalytical concepts of early development and its disturbances seems to be a fascinating and promising task for future research.

Peter Fonagy's paper illustrates the fact that such integrations are not only a vision for the future. He combines knowledge from his clinical experiences with severely traumatized children with empirical findings from different fields such as attachment research and neurobiological brain research, and integrates all of these insights into fascinating conceptualizations on the influence of early development and its disturbances.

Although the relationship between clinical, conceptual, empirical, and interdisciplinary research is touched on in *Part II* of this volume, taking the example of ADHD as just mentioned, we will go into this issue on a more general level in *Part III*, and Charles Hanly, Jorge L. Ahumada, and Doria Medina will raise some of the sophisticated epistemological problems connected to these debates. Anna Ursula Dreher and Ilse Grubrich-Simitis will deepen the aforementioned aims, characteristics, and specifics of conceptual research in psychoanalysis.

We want to *conclude this introduction* by stressing the following points: a psychoanalytic perspective on ADHD focuses on the different underlying structures of the personality due to the idiosyncratic life history of a child with its early internal object relations, traumatizations, ego- and self-development and its specific limitations, as well as former and current external object relations. Our diagnostic and clinical experiences reveal a wide range of structural and object-relational levels in such children: *there is no monocausal aetiology*. ADHD children often might have shown a genetically based over-reactivity and hypersensitivity to various stimuli as infants, which the caregivers were not able to understand. The infant's consequent failure to regulate drive impulses and affects results in a disruption of what Bürgin (2005) called the 'narrative function', depleting the ego of the secondary-process functions underlying a sense of coherence of the self. We think that children of one subgroup of ADHD share such early 'mismatched' object relations combined with insecurity in attachment, causing vulnerability to flooding with stimuli and stress (see Panksepp, 1998; Hüther, 2006). Following this line of thought, these early experiences in object relations have left deficiencies concerning *attention,* seen as a highly complex ego function which develops in a specific relational context, and is influenced by genetic factors, early emotional exchanges, temperament, micro traumata, and so forth (see also Sugarman, 2006: 238). Attention regulation is in turn one of a set of related fundamental ego capacities also including affect regulation and mentalization (social cognition); a weakness in any of these would be expected to undermine the strength of the others.

Another perspective on the failure of developing early regulation and control was elaborated by Panksepp (1998): particularly for children born with a (probably genetically determined) impulsive temper and character, the opportunity to engage in active exploration of their environment and in rough-and tumble-games seems to be essential in order to develop frontal lobe executive functions. If they do not find 'good enough' environmental conditions for such games and exploration then they may develop ADHD.

There is separate evidence that medical treatment might have a shadowy side, restricting the neuroplastic compensations of the brain of ADHD children, as well as perhaps restricting growth overall. A first careful study by Randa *et al.* (2005: 284) showed in a 'population composed of twelve children treated with therapeutic doses of methylphenidate' that in 'all participants treatment induced a significant ... increase of chromosome aberrations, sister chromatic exchanges and micronuclei frequencies respectively ($P = 0.000$ in all cases). These findings warrant further investigations of the possible health effects of methylphenidate in humans, especially in view of the well-documented relationship between elevated frequencies of chromosome aberrations and increased cancer risk.' (See also Seeman and Machias, 1998.)

In our view, medication should only be given after a careful neurological, psychiatric, and psychological investigation. It should be reserved for children in whom no psychotherapeutic or pedagogic intervention seems to be available or shows signs of being successful. This caution is consistent with many psychiatric, neurological, and psychoanalytical authors who warn of early medical interference with the growing brain. On the other side of course is the hope that pharmacological regulation of a neurochemical abnormality would allow more normal growth of brain and psychological capacity. Independent studies on the long-term effects of medication are urgently needed, and in the meantime great caution is appropriate.

Of course, much more clinical and empirical research is needed on all aspects of this serious spectrum of disorders. Nevertheless, given the current 'state of the art', we reach the following conclusion: taking into account neurobiological, (unconscious) biographical as well as societal factors, we are convinced that contemporary psychoanalysis—due to its richness of conceptualization and clinical experience—offers a unique window on the complexities of ADHD. Besides, more than other psychotherapeutic approaches, psychoanalysts offer suitable 'corrective' experiences in the therapeutic relationship with these children and thus the possibility to 'correct' or at least to soften failed early development. Thus, psychoanalytic treatment should be considered *one of the promising therapeutic choices* for treating children with ADHD.

We hope to illustrate this thesis with the different contributions in this volume.

Notes

1. A. Staufenberg (in print) showed in a systematic literature review that hardly any psychoanalytic papers on ADHD could be found before 2000 in German-speaking psychoanalytical journals.
2. The study was supported financially mainly by the Zinnkan Foundation, but also by the Research Advisory Board (RAB) of the International Psychoanalytical Association, the Hertie Foundation, and the Polytechnische Gesellschaft, Frankfurt.
3. André Green (1999) talks about the 'dead mother' in a particular context. In his own biography his mother suddenly became depressed after a family tragedy. For him, in his second year of life, this was like losing her: she was 'emotionally dead' for him, not capable any more of participating in lively, affective, and resonant dialogue with him.
4. We do not aim to give a complete overview of the current literature on ADHD. A Google search for ADHD currently finds around 740,000 hits and many panels and blogs on this topic. We will concentrate on a small selection of the studies and literature available. At the University of Kassel Dr. Luise Laezer and a group of students have installed an elctronic documentation data bank for ADHD literature (see http://h1322887.stratoserver.net/login.php). We also should mention the 'European Network on Hyperkinetic Disorder' (EUNETHYDIS) founded in 1990 as well as the different 'Leitlinien ADHS' (medical guidelines for treating ADHD children) in Germany. Similar clinical guidelines exist in other countries.
5. In the 1980s 'Minimal Cerebral Dysfunction' (MCD) was widespread (see Mattner, 2006). It was seen as being closely connected with oppositional defiant disorder. This connection could already be observed in the 1950s. At that time, German authors discussed *'Encephalopathische Psychopathie'* (encephalopathic psychopathology), *'Hirnorganisch-psychisches Achsensyndrom'* (brain-organic axis syndrome) and *'Frühkindliches exogenes Psychosyndrom'*

(infantile exogene psychosyndrome). In Switzerland one used the term *'Frühkindliches Psycho-organisches Syndrom'* (POS) (infantile psycho-organic syndrome) (Ruf-Bächtinger, 1987). Berger (1977) talked about *'Teilleistungsstörungen'* (partial disturbances of functionings) or *'Teilleistungsschwächen'* (partial weakness infunctioning).

6. Rothstein (2002: 392) summarizes the diagnostic criteria briefly as follows: 'According to DSM-IV criteria, "Attention Deficit/ Hyperactivity Disorder" (AD/HD) is diagnosed if *four* conditions are met. One is either *a persistent pattern of inattention or hyperactivity-impulsivity* more frequent than is typical for the patient's age. A second is that *some of the symptoms must have been present before the age of seven*. Third, the *symptoms must be observed in at least two settings*, such as at home and at school or work. Finally, clear evidence is required of *compromised social, academic, or occupational functioning*.'

   There have been basic critiques concerning the descriptive classification manuals as DSM–IV, one reason why Mayes and Howitz (2005) published an alternative *Psychodynamic Diagnostic Manual* (PDM). The information contained in the PSM was collected by a collaborative task force which included members of the American Psychoanalytic Association, the Division of Psychoanalysis (Division 39) of the American Psychological Association, the American Academy of Psychoanalysis and Dynamic Psychiatry, and the National Membership Committee on Psychoanalysis in Clinical Social Work. Unfortunately PSM is not very well known in Europe and could not prevent the contribution of DSM-IV and ICD-10 to a marginalization of psychoanalysis in psychiatry. The field of ADHD is just one example of this marginalization (see also McWilliam, 2009).
7. An exception is the study by Randa *et al.* (2008) (see below).
8. The clinical team were convinced that child analysis at a higher frequency would have been an optimal treatment for Michael. Unfortunately, this was not possible for financial reasons. The mother preferred to go into therapy as well after the traumatic loss of her husband. Her therapy turned out to be a great help for her as well as for Michael—from our perspective, it was one reason for Michael's good development in spite of the limitations of his own therapy.
9. For these children, public kindergartens have a particularly important task to integrate these families socially, touching, as we all know, one of the most urgent problems of our Western societies (compare also children described in other subgroups; see Göppel, in press).
10. In a much less dramatic sense, we also had this problem in my native country, a mountain valley in Switzerland (Glarus) in the 1970s, when

a lot of families from Sicily moved into this canton. The children had, due to their different cultural background, such a different temperament compared with the native Swiss population that Swiss teachers, being used to the mild-tempered Swiss children, who were easy to handle, raised the question of whether the Italian children suffered from a 'minimal brain dysfunction'. Of course, the diagnosis of ADHD is not neutral but always risks a certain cultural bias.

11. Another chid psychiatrist, Fritz Poustka, gave one of the major papers of the Sandler Conference. Unfortunately his paper could not be included in this volume.
12. Unfortunately, it has not been possible to include his paper in this volume.

Bibliography

Ainsworth, M., Blehar, M., Waters, E. and Wall, S. (1978). *Patterns of Attachment: A Psychological Study of the Strange Situation.* Hillsdale: Erlbaum.

Amft, H. (2006). 'ADHS: Hirnstoffwechselstörungen und/oder Symptom einer kranken Gesellschaft? Psychopharmaka als Mittel einer gelingenden Naturbeherrschung am Menschen.' In: Leuzinger-Bohleber, M., Brandl, Y. and Hüther, G. (eds) *ADHS—Frühprävention statt Medikalisierung: Theorie, Forschung, Kontroversen.* Göttingen: Vandenhoeck & Ruprecht. pp. 70–90.

Amft, H., Gerspach, M. and Mattner, D. (2004). Kinder mit gestörter Aufmerksamkeit. ADS als Herausforderung für Pädagogik und Therapie. 2. *Auflage.* Stuttgart: Kohlhammer.

Barkley, R. (1990). *Attention Deficit Hyperactivity Disorder: A Handbook for Diagnosis and Treatment.* New York: Guilford Press.

Barkley, R. (1997). *AD/HD and the Nature of Self-control.* New York: Guilford Press.

Beebe, B. and Lachman, F.M. (2002). *Infant Research and Adult Treatment: Co-constructing Interactions.* Hillsdale/London: The Analytic Press.

Berger, E. (ed.) (1977). *Teilleistungsschwächen bei Kindern.* Bern: Huber.

BMGS (Bundesministerium für Gesundheit und soziale Sicherung) (2002). *Pressemitteilung vom.* 27.12.2002. Available from: http://www.bmgs.bund.de/archiv/presse_bmgs/presse2002/m/213.htm

Bhardway, A. and Goodyer, I.A. (2009). 'Depression and allied illnes in children and asolecents. Basic facts'. *Psychoanalytic Psychotherapy,* 23(3): 176–84.

Bürgin, D. (1998). *Triangulierung: Der Übergang zur Elternschaft.* Stuttgart: Schattauer.

Bürgin, D. (2005). Presentation, Panel, 'Attention Deficit Hyperactivity Disorder and Trauma', 44th Congress of the IPA, Rio de Janeiro, Brazil. 28 July.

Bürgin, D. and Steck, B. (2007). 'Psychoanalytische psychotherapie und ADHD-trias (impulsivitat, hypermotorik und aufmerksamkeitsstorungen)'. *Praxis der Kinderpsychologie und Kinderpsychiatrie*, 56: 310–32.

Busch de Ahumada, L.C. (2005). Presentation, Panel, 'Attention Deficit Hyperactivity Disorder and Trauma', 44th Congress of the IPA, Rio de Janeiro, Brazil. 28 July.

Cantwell, D. (1996). 'Attention Deficit Disorder: A Review of the Past Ten Years'. *Journal of the American Academy of Child and Adolescent Psychiatry*, 35: 978–87.

Carney, J.K. (2002). 'Prologue'. *Psychoanalytic Inquiry*, 22: 299–307.

Caspi, A., Sugden, K., Moffitt, T.E., Taylor, A., Craig, I.W., Harrington, H, McClay, J., Mill, J., Martin, J., Braithwaite, A. and Poulton, R. (2003). 'Influence of Life Stress on Depression: Moderation by a Polymorphism in the 5-HTT Gene'. *Science*, 301: 386–89.

Cierpka, M. and Schick, A. (2006). 'Das Fördern von emotionalen Kompetenzen mit FAUSTLOS bei Kindern'. In: Leuzinger-Bohleber, M., Brandl, Y. and Hüther, G. (eds) *ADHS—Frühprävention statt Medikalisierung: Theorie, Forschung, Kontroversen*. Göttingen: Vandenhoeck & Ruprecht. pp. 286–301.

Crary, J. (1999). *Suspension of Perception*. Cambridge: MIT Press.

Damasio, A.R. (1994). *Descartes' Error*. New York: Putnam.

Damasio, A.R. (2003). 'Feelings of emotion and the self'. *Annals of the New York Academy of Sciences*, 1,001: 253–61.

Dammasch, F. (2000). *Die innere Erlebniswelt von Kindern alleinerziehender Mütter: Eine Studie über Vaterlosigkeit anhand einer psychoanalytischen Interpretation zweier Erstinterviews*. Frankfurt a.M.: Brandes & Apsel.

Dammasch, F. (2006). ADHS—endlich hat das Kind einen Namen: Psychoanalytische Gedanken zur Bewegung des ruhelosen Kindes und zur Bedeutung von Ritalin®. In: Leuzinger-Bohleber, M., Brandl, Y. and Hüther, G. (eds) *ADHS—Frühprävention statt Medikalisierung: Theorie, Forschung, Kontroversen*. Göttingen: Vandenhoeck & Ruprecht. pp. 189–221.

Dawirs, R.R., Teuchert-Noodt, G. and Kacza, J. (1992). 'Naturally occurring degrading events in axon terminals of the dentate gyrus and stratum lucidum in the spiny mouse (Acomys cahirinus) during maturation, adulthood and aging'. *Developmental Neuroscience*, 14: 210–220.

Doidge, N. (2007). *The Brain that Changes Itself: Stories of Personal Triumph from the Frontiers of Brain Sciences*. New York: Viking.

Dornes, M. (1999). 'Bindungstheorie und Bindungsforschung—eine Herausforderung für die Schule?' In: Garlichs, A. and Leuzinger-Bohleber, M. (eds) *M. Identität und Bindung. Die Entwicklung von Beziehungen in Familie, Schule und Gesellschaft*. Weinheim/München: Juventa Verlag. pp. 161–73.

Emde, R.N. and Fonagy, P. (1997). 'An emerging culture for psychoanalytic research?' *International Journal of Psychoanalysis*, 78: 643–51.

Faraone, S.V., Perlis, R.H., Doyle, A.E. et al. (2005). 'Molecular Genetics of Attention-deficit/hyperactivity Disorder'. *Biological Psychiatry*, 57: 1,313–23.

Fischer, G. and Riedesser, P. (1998). *Lehrbuch der Psychotraumatologie*. München/Basel: Reinhardt.

Fonagy, P. and Target, M. (2002). 'Neubewertung der Entwicklung der Affektregulation vor dem Hintergrund von Winnicotts Konzept des "falschen Selbst"'. *Psyche—Z Psychoanal*, 56: 839–62.

Fonagy, P. and Target, M. (2003). *Psychoanalytic Theories: Perspectives from Developmental Psychopathology*. Stuttgart: Klett Cotta.

Fonagy, P. (2006). 'Der Interpersonale Interpretationsmechanismus (IIM)'. In: Green, V. (ed.). *Emotionale Entwicklung in Psychoanalyse, Bindungstheorie und Neuowissenschaften*. Gießen: Psychosozial Verlag. pp. 141–65.

Fuchs, Th., Sattel, H.C. and Henningsen, P. (eds.) (2010). *The Embodied Self. Dimensions, Coherence and Disorders*. Stuttgart: Schattauer.

Garlichs, A. and Leuzinger-Bohleber, M. (1999). *Identität und Bindung: Die Entwicklung von Beziehungen in Familie, Schule und Gesellschaft*. Weinheim/München: Juventa Verlag.

Gerspach, M. (2006). 'Zum Verstehen von Kindern mit Aufmerksamkeitsstörungen'. In: Leuzinger-Bohleber, M., Brandl, Y., and Hüther, G. (eds) *ADHS—Frühprävention statt Medikalisierung: Theorie, Forschung, Kontroversen*. Göttingen: Vandenhoeck & Ruprecht. pp. 91–110.

Gilmore, K. (2000). 'A psychoanalytic perspective on attention-deficit/hyperactivity disorder'. *Journal of the American Psychoanalytic Association*, 48: 1,258–93.

Gilmore, K. (2002). 'Diagnosis, dynamics, and development: Considerations in the psychoanalytic assessment of children with AD/HD'. *Psychoanalytic Inquiry*, 22: 372–91.

Goldberg, D. (2009). 'The interplay between biological and psychological factors in determining vulnerability to mental disorder'. *Psychoanalytic Psychotherapy*, 23: 236–47.

Göppel, G. (in press). *Children in Urban Areas of Social Conflict—Prevention and Intervention of Behavior Disorders in Kindergartens*.

Green, A. (1986). 'The dead mother'. In: Green A. (ed.) *On Private Madness*. London: The Hogarth Press. pp. 222–53.

Green, V. (2005). *Emotional Development in Psychoanalysis: Attachment Theory and Neuroscience. Creating Connections*. London: Brunner-Routledge.

Grossmann, K.E., August, E.P., Fremmer-Bombik, E., Friedl, A., Grossmann, K., Scheuerer-Englisch, H., Spangler, G., Stephan, C. and Suess, G.J. (1989). 'Die Bindungstheorie: Modell und entwicklungspsychologische Forschung'. In: Keller, H. (ed.) *Handbuch der Kleinkindforschung*. Berlin: Springer. pp. 31–35.

Haubl, R. (2009). 'Medikamentierte Wut: Wie Jungen mit einer AD(H)S um Selbstkontrolle ringen'. *Forum der Psychoanalyse*, 25: 255–68.

Hauser, S.T., Allen, J.-P. and Golden, E. (2006). *Out of the Woods: Tales of Resilient Teens*. London: Harvard University Press.

Häußler, G. and Hopf, H. (2002). 'Psychoanalytische Theorien'. In: Bovensiepen, G., Hopf, H., and Molitor, G. (eds) *Unruhige und unaufmerksame Kinder: Psychoanalyse des hyperkinetischen Syndroms*. Frankfurt a.M.: Brandes & Apsel. pp. 20–42.

Heinz, J. (2002). 'Nervosität der Moderne'. In: Bovensiepen, G., Hopf, H. and Molitor, G. (eds) *Unruhige und unaufmerksame Kinder: Psychoanalyse des hyperkinetischen Syndroms*. Frankfurt a.M.: Brandes & Apsel. pp. 315–40.

Herzog, J.M. (2001). *Father Hunger: Explorations with Adults and Children*. Hillsdale/London: The Analytic Press.

Hill, J. (2009). 'Developmental perspectives on adult depression'. *Psychoanalytic Psychotherapy*, 23, 209–12.

Hopf, H. (2007). 'Zwischen empathie und grenzsetzungen—Uberlegungen zur Psychodynamik und Behandlungstechnik bei psychoanalytischen Therapien von hyperkinetischen Störungen'. *Praxis der Kinderpsychologie und Kinderpsychiatrie*, 56: 333–55.

Hopf, H. (2009). '"Ich fühlte mich nicht allein in der schweren Situation ...": Supervision der psychoanalytischen Behandlung eines neunjahrigen Jungen mit der facharztlichen Diagnose ADHS'. *Kinderanalyse*, 17: 335–65.

Hüther, G. (2006). 'Die nutzungsabhängige Herausbildung hirnorganischer Veränderungen bei Hyperaktivität und Aurmerksamkeitsstörungen: Einfluss präventiver Maßnahmen und therapeutischer Internventionen'. In: Leuzinger-Bohleber, M., Brandl, Y. and Hüther, G. (eds) *ADHS—Frühprävention statt Medikalisierung: Theorie, Forschung, Kontroversen*. Göttingen: Vandenhoeck & Ruprecht. pp. 222–37.

Kawai, T. (2009). 'Union and Separation in the Therapy of Pervasive Developmental Disorders and ADHD'. *Journal of Analytical Psychology*, 54: 659–75.

Klitzing, K.V. (2002). 'Früher Entwicklung im Längsschnitt: Von der Beziehungswelt der Eltern zur Vorstellungswelt des Kindes'. *Psyche—Z Psychoanal*, 56: 863–87.

Laezer, L., Gaertner, B., Werner, I., Weisenburger. and Leuzinger-Bohleber, M. (2010): 'Therapievergleichsstudie von psychoanalytischen und kognitiv-verhaltenstherapeutisch/medikamentösen Behandlungen von hyperaktiven Kindern'. Poster presented at the Joseph Sandler Research Conference, February, 2010

Laezer, L. (in prep). Wirksamkeit psychotherapeutischer Behandlungen bei Kindern mit ADHS und der Störung des Sozialverhaltens—Psychoanalyse, Verhaltenstherapie und psychiatrische Behandlung im Vergleich. Habilitationsstudie an der Universität Kassel.

Laufer, M. and Dehnhoff, E. (1957). 'Hyperkinetic behavior syndrome in children'. *Journal of Pediatrics*, 50: 463–74.

Lehmkuhl, G. and Döpfner, M. (2006). 'Die Bedeutung multimodaler Therapieansätze bei Kindern mit Aufmerksamkeitsdefizit-/Hyperkativitätsstörungen'. In: Leuzinger-Bohleber, M., Brandl, Y., and Hüther, G. (eds) *ADHS—Frühprävention statt Medikalisierung: Theorie, Forschung, Kontroversen*. Göttingen: Vandenhoeck & Ruprecht. pp. 118–33.

Leuzinger-Bohleber, M. and Pfeifer, R. (2002). 'Remembering a depressive primary object? Psychoanalysis and Embodied Cognitive Science: A dialogue on memory'. *International Journal of Psychoanalysis*, 83: 3–33.

Leuzinger-Bohleber, M., Dreher, A.U. and Canestri, J. (eds) (2003). *Pluralism and Unity? Methods of Research in Psychoanalysis*. London: IPA.

Leuzinger-Bohleber, M. and Pfeifer, R. (2006). 'Recollecting the past in the present: Memory in the dialogue between psychoanalysis and cognitive science'. In: Mancia, M. (ed.) *Psychoanalyis and Neuroscience*. Milano: Springer. pp. 63–95.

Leuzinger-Bohleber, M., Brandl, Y., and Hüther, G. (eds) (2006). *ADHS—Frühprävention statt Medikalisierung: Theorie, Forschung, Kontroversen*. Göttingen: Vandenhoeck & Ruprecht.

Leuzinger-Bohleber, M., Brandl, Y., Hau, S., Aulbach, L., Caruso, B., Einert, K.-M., Glindemann, O., Göppel, G., Hermann, P., Hesse, P., Heumann, J., Karaca, G., König, J., Lendle, J., Rüger, B., Schwenk, A., Staufenberg, A., Steuber, S., Uhl, Ch., Vogel, J., Waldung, Ch., Wolff, L. and Hüther, G. (2006). 'Die Frankfurter Präventionsstudie. Zur psychischen und psychosozialen Integration von verhaltensauffälligen Kindern (insbesondere ADHS) im Kindergartenalter—ein Arbeitsbericht'. In: Leuzinger-Bohleber, M., Brandl, Y. and Hüther, G. (eds) *ADHS—Frühprävention statt Medikalisierung: Theorie, Forschung, Kontroversen*. Göttingen: Vandenhoeck & Ruprecht. pp. 238–69.

Leuzinger-Bohleber, M. and Fischmann, T. (2006). 'What is conceptual research in psychoanalysis?' *International Journal of Psychoanalysis*, 87: 1,355–86.

Leuzinger-Bohleber, M., Staufenberg, A. and Fischmann, T. (2007). 'ADHS—Indikation für psychoanalytische Behandlungen? Einige klinische, konzeptuelle und empirische Überlegungen ausgehend von der Frankfurter Präventionsstudie'. *Praxis der Kidnerpsychologie und Kinderpsychiatrie*, 56: 356–85.

Leuzinger-Bohleber, M., Rother, G. and Buchheim, A. (Hg.) (2008). *Psychoanalyse, Neurobiologie, Trauma*. Stuttgart: Schattauer.

Leuzinger-Bohleber, M., Fischmann, T. and Läzer, L. (2008). 'Triangulierung—ein zentrales Konzept der Frankfurter Präventionsstudie?' In: Dammasch, D., Katzenbach, D. and Ruth, J. (Hg.). *Triangulierung. Lernen, Denken und Handeln aus psychoanalytischer Sicht*. Frankfurt a. M.: Brandes & Apsel. pp. 131–65.

Leuzinger-Bohleber, M., Röckerath, K. and Strauss, L.V. (Hg.) (2010). *Depression und Neuroplastizität. Psychoanalytische Klinik und Forschung*. Frankfurt: Brandes & Apsel.

Levin, F.M. (1997). 'Discussion of Mark Solms' "Why consciousness?"' *Journal of the American Psychoanalytic Association*, 45: 732–39.

Lüpke, H.V. (2004). 'Hyperaktivität zwischen "Stoffwechselstörung" und Psychodynamik'. In: Passolt, M. (ed.) *Hyperaktivität zwischen Psychoanalyse, Neurobiologie und Systemtheorie. 2. Auflage*. München/Basel: Reinhardt. pp. 99–116.

Lüpke, H.V. (2006). 'Der Dialog in Bewegung und der entgleiste Dialog: Beiträge aus Säuglingsforschung und Neurobiologie'. In: Leuzinger-Bohleber, M., Brandl, Y. and Hüther, G. (eds) *ADHS—Frühprävention statt Medikalisierung: Theorie, Forschung, Kontroversen*. Göttingen: Vandenhoeck & Ruprecht. pp. 169–88.

Mattner, D. (2006). 'ADS—die Biologisierung abweichenden Verhaltens'. In: Leuzinger-Bohleber, M., Brandl, Y., and Hüther, G. (eds) *ADHS—Frühprävention statt Medikalisierung: Theorie, Forschung, Kontroversen*. Göttingen: Vandenhoeck & Ruprecht. pp. 51–69.

McWilliams, Nancy (2009): Some Thoughts on the Survival of Psychoanalytic Practice. *Clinical Social Work Journal*, 37: 81–83.

Metzger, H.-G. (2000). *Zwischen Dyade und Triade. Psychoanalytische Familienbeobachtungen zur Bedeutung des Vaters im Triangulierungsprozeß*. Tübingen: Edition diskord.

Moll, G.H., Mehnert, C., Wicker, M., Bock, N., Rothenberger, A., Rüther, E. and Hüther, G. (2000). 'Age-associated changes in the densities of presynaptic monoamine transporters in different regions of the rat brain from juvenile life to adulthood'. *Developmental Brain Research*, 119: 251–57.

Myssior, S. and Machado, Z. (2008). O que sera da atividade das criancas? (Notas sobre a hiperatividade). *Percurso Revista de Psicanalise*, 21: 75–80.

Nelson, C.A. (2007): 'What would Superman do?' In: Rubin, L. (ed.) *Using Superheroes in Counseling and Play Therapy*. New York: Springer. pp. 49–67.

Panksepp, J. (1998). *Affective Neuroscience: The Foundation of Human and Animal Emotions*. New York: Oxford University Press.

Panksepp, J. (2001). 'The long-term psychobiological consequences of infant emotions'. *Neuro-Psychoanalysis*, 3: 149–79.

Passolt, M. (ed.) (2004). *Hyperaktivität zwischen Psychoanalyse, Neurobiologie und Systemtheorie*. 2. Aufl. München/Basel: Reinhardt.

Pfeifer, R. and Bongard, J. (2007). *How the Body Shapes the Way We Think: A New View of Intelligence*. Cambridge: MIT Press.

Pfeifer, R. and Scheier, C. (1999). *Understanding Intelligence*. Cambridge: MIT Press.

Randa, A. et al. (2005). 'Cytogenetic Effects in Children Treated with Methylphenidate'. *Cancer Letters*, 230: 284–91.

Reichert, Y. (2010). 'Psychoanalytisch-familientherapeutische Behandlung eines Kindes mit ADHS vor dem Hintergrund von elterlicher Verlusttraumatisierung, Regulationsstorung und transgenerationaler Ubertragung'. *Kinderanalyse*, 18: 74–93.

Riedesser, P. (2006). 'Einige Argumente zur ADHS-Kontroverse in der Kinder—und Jugendpsychiatrie'. In: Leuzinger-Bohleber, M., Brandl, Y. and Hüther, G. (eds) *ADHS—Frühprävention statt Medikalisierung: Theorie, Forschung, Kontroversen*. Göttingen: Vandenhoeck & Ruprecht. pp. 111–17.

Risch, N., Herrell, R., Lehner, Th., Liang, K., Eaves, L., Hoh, J., Griem, A., Kovacs, M., Otto, J. and Ries Merikangas, K. (2009). 'Interaction between the serotonin transproter gene (5-HTTLPR), stressful life events, and the risk of depression. A meta-analysis'. *JAMA*, 23: 2,462–71.

Romanos, M., Freitag, C., Jacob, C. et al. (2008). 'Genome-wide Linkage Analysis of ADHD Using High-density SNP Arrays: Novel loci at 5q13.1 and 14q12'. *Molecular Psychiatry*, 13: 522–30.

Rothstein, A. (2002). 'Plea for a balanced conception of AD/HD and 1st diagnosis and treatment'. *Psychoanalytic Inquiry*, 22: 391–412.

Rothstein, A. and Glenn, J. (1999). *Learning Disabilities and Psychic Conflict: A Psychoanalytic Casebook*. Madison: International Universities Press.

Ruf-Bächtiger, L. (1987). *Das frühkindliche psychoorganische Syndrom*. Stuttgart: Thieme.

Rutter, M. (2009). 'Gene-Environment Interactions. Biologically vaid pathway or artifact?' *Arch Gen Psychiatry*, 66(12): 1,287–89.

Salomonsson, B. (2004). 'Some psychoanalytic viewpoints on neuropsychiatric disorders in children'. *International Journal of Psychoanalysis*, 85: 117–36.

Salomonsson, B. (2006). 'The Impact of Words on Children with ADHD and DAMP: Consequences for Psychoanalytic Technique'. *Int. J. Psycho-Anal.*, 87:1029–1047.

Schulte-Körne, G. and Allgaie, A.-K. (2008). 'Genetik depressiver Störungen'. *Zeitschrift für Kinder- und Jugendpsychiatrie und Psychotehrapie*, 36 (1): 27–43.

Seeman, P. and Machias, B.K. (1998). 'Anti-hyperactivity medication: methylphenidate and amphetamine'. *Molecular Psychiatry*, 3: 386–96.

Sennett, R. (1998). *The Corrosion of Character: The Personal Consequences of Work in the New Capitalism*. New York: Norton.

Soltano, M.V. (1998). 'Neuropsychopharmacological mechanisms of stimulant drug action in attention-deficit hyperactivity disorder: A review and integration'. *Behavioural Brain Research*, 94: 127–52.

Stassen, H., Begleiter, H., Beirut, L., Culverhouse, R., Hinrichs, T., Porjesz, B., Rice, J., Scharfetter, C. and Reich, T. (2004a). 'Oligogenic approaches to the predisposition of alcohol dependence: A genome-wide search on 255 families'. *Neurology, Psychiatry and Brain Research*, 11: 13–22

Stassen, H.H., Bridler, R., Hell, D., Weisbrod, M. and Scharfetter, C. (2004b). 'Ethnicity-independent genetic basis of functional psychoses: A Genotype-to-phenotype approach'. *American Journal of Medical Genetics*, 124: 101–12.

Staufenberg, A. et al. (2006). *Manual zur psychoanalytisch-psychotherapeutischen Behandlung psychosozialer Integrationsproblemen bei Kinder. Die Fraunkfurter Präventionsstudie)*. Unpublished.

Staufenberg, A. (in press). Psychoanalytische Behandlungen von hyperaktiven Kindern. Eine Katamnesestudie. Will be published 2011, Frankfurt: Brandes u. Apsel

Stern, D. (1995). *The Motherhood Constellation: A Unified View of Parent-infant Psychotherapy*. New York: Basic Books.

Still, G.F. (1902). 'Some abnormal psychical conditions in children'. *Lancet*, 1: 1,008–12; 1,077–82; 1,163–68.

Sugarman, A. (2006). 'Attention Deficit Hyperactivity Disorder and Trauma'. *International Journal of Psychoanalysis*, 87: 237–41.

Sugarman, A. (2010). 'Convergences and Divergences in Treatments of So-Called ADHD Children'. *International Journal of Psychoanalysis*, 91: 395–98.

Suomi, S. (2006). 'Risk, Resilience and Genex Environment Interactions in Rhesus Monkeys'. *New York Academy of Science*: 52–62.

Waldung, C., Göppel, G. and Wolff, L. (2006). 'Ein Fallbeispiel (Die Frankfurter Präventionsstudie)'. In: Leuzinger-Bohleber, M., Brandl, Y., and Hüther, G. (eds) *ADHS—Frühprävention statt Medikalisierung: Theorie, Forschung, Kontroversen*. Göttingen: Vandenhoeck & Ruprecht. pp. 256–62.

Zabarenko, L.M. (2002). 'AD/HD, Psychoanalysis and neuroscience: A survey of recent findings and their applications'. *Psychoanalytic Inquiry*, 22: 412–32.

PART II

EARLY DEVELOPMENT AND ITS DISTURBANCES

CHAPTER TWO

Attachment, trauma, and psychoanalysis: Where psychoanalysis meets neuroscience

Peter Fonagy

Why do we do this to each other?

Trauma is puzzling: a couple of deeply puzzling vignettes to start us off. James is currently in prison for armed robbery. His father was frequently violent towards James, in the name of punishment. On one occasion, at the age of nine, James was punished for stealing. This is how James later described that incident:

> he put the gas cooker on, right, and um— I will always remember this, he put a hand on top of the gas cooker, and roasted our hands (your hand) yeah, my hand, and uhm—the next day I went to school with gloves on, because they [were] really, really bad ...

James' reactions to these and dozens of similar experiences is telling: 'I used to have a drink and sleep and when I wake up I was a different person.' When asked to describe if he ever felt upset, James is completely unable to understand the question. 'When I was young I never really got upset because I had everything I wanted really and when you get everything that you want you don't really get upset.'

When asked how his childhood experiences might have affected his adult personality, he responds totally without insight: 'I cannot explain, I can't, it's not even up there for me to explain.'

In case you think that James is a special case, let me introduce you to Stuart, also a robber, and also violent and dangerous. Stuart was brought up by his mother and a succession of stepfathers; he was traumatized particularly by his second one. In Stuart's and his mother's mind, his stepfather just wanted to 'straighten him out'. If he behaved badly he would be beaten when his father came home, and every night afterwards for a period of a week. Once Stuart was caught shoplifting and was brought home by the police. This is what followed: 'He tied me to the bed ... and he got a screwdriver, and he was stabbing me in the hands with it, because they [the hands] were what stole ... and I was just laughing at him, 'cause I was ... I don't know ... And then he went downstairs, and he got a hammer and nails, and he nailed one of my hands to the board of the bed, like. Just stuck a nail straight through my hand, like. Like, so I was howling, I couldn't move, and the blood was ... and I was screaming then. I had to cry then, I couldn't handle it. And after they had done it, my hands went numb, so I couldn't feel it. And I looked at my hands, and I started laughing at myself. And I felt I was going mad, like, cause I was going "Ha ha", you know, and I was thinking, *"I had done that."*'

When upset, as with many severe trauma victims, Stuart attacks himself, hitting the walls with all his considerable force: 'The amount of times I've broken my hands, my arms, you know. Five times, in six months. Different arms.' Like other abused children, Stuart expressed gratitude to his stepfather for hardening him, enabling him to take violence from others.

When Stuart was 12 his stepfather threatened to shoot him and had to be disarmed by the police. His mother then arranged for Stuart to be taken into care, explaining that this was for his own protection.

Two weeks before the interview, this stepfather, long estranged from his mother, committed suicide. At the inquest into this death, his mother screamed across the courtroom that it was all Stuart's fault: '... she starts screaming in the court. And then I went; I flipped my lid there. I jumped out of the dock. I grabbed a hold of her by the hair, like, and I was banging her head off. The police had to get me off her.'

Stuart, like the others we interviewed, shows a bizarre lack of understanding of what makes him, his mother, his stepfather, or indeed anyone else, tick. When I asked about the effects of his attachment trauma on his adult personality, he admits to 'going over the top' but also says, 'I mean, I am not a danger to anyone; I am a danger to myself, not other people.' He seems genuinely unaware of how other people experience his violent outbursts. In prison, not only the guards but also his fellow inmates are scared of him. You will not be surprised to hear that his behaviour in prison often gets extremely severe punishments from the system.

A psychoanalytic development phenomenology of the response to attachment trauma

I will begin by describing the trauma-related loss of the capacity to conceive of mental states.

Often in adults with a history of childhood attachment trauma there seems to be an acquired failure to conceive of how people think and/or feel. We call this a failure of mentalization. Mentalization is a concept originally introduced by French psychoanalysts[1] (Luquet, 1981, 1987; Marty and De M'Uzan, 1963) working with psychosomatic patients. They noted a lack of symbolization of mental states in such individuals, a lack of freedom in free association, and a characteristic way of thinking too close to sensations and primary unconscious fantasies.

We define mentalization following a tradition in philosophy of mind established by Brentano (1973/1874), Dennett (1978), and others, as a form of mostly preconscious *imaginative* mental activity, namely, interpreting people's actions in terms of 'intentional' mental states. It is *imaginative* because we have to imagine what other people might be thinking or feeling; an important indicator of the high quality of mentalization is the awareness that we do not actually know what is in someone else's mind. The same kind of imaginative leap can be required to understand one's own mental experience, particularly in relation to emotionally charged issues or irrational (perhaps unconsciously driven) reactions. Some philosophers of mind have suggested that psychic determinism (the discovery that human actions could be more completely understood by ascribing unconscious wishes and beliefs in addition to conscious states) was

Freud's greatest contribution (Hopkins, 1992; Wollheim, 1999). To adopt this stance, to conceive of self and others as having a 'mind', the individual needs a symbolic representational system for mental states. Although mentalization probably involved numerous contact systems, it is commonly associated with activation in the middle prefrontal areas of the brain—probably the paracingulate area.

The difficulty of traumatized patients in understanding themselves and others struck us forcibly over 15 years ago while treating borderline women and violent men (Fonagy, 1989). A later study of the psychoanalytic treatment of 30 young adults with violent and suicidal behaviour, led by Anne-Marie Sandler at the Anna Freud Centre, reinforced these conclusions (Gerber, 2004; Perelberg, 1999).[2] 83% were in analysis (29% psychotherapy).

What does it look like when trauma brings about a temporary collapse of mentalization? James describes thinking: 'I keep doing these crazy things. Why am I doing these things? I was confused. I used to just sit down for hours sometimes and drive myself mad, thinking. And I just didn't get anywhere. It used to wind me up.' Research has shown that the capacity for mentalization is undermined in most people who have experienced trauma. Children cannot learn words for feelings (Beeghly and Cicchetti, 1994), and traumatized adults have more difficulty recognizing the intent behind facial expressions. (Fonagy *et al.*, 2003).

The equation of inner and outer is a second aspect of the phenomenology. The collapse of mentalization in the face of trauma entails a loss of awareness of the relationship between internal and external reality (Fonagy and Target, 2000). Modes of representing the internal world re-emerge that developmentally precede an awareness that thoughts, feelings, and wishes are part of the mind. The child aged two to three, not yet experiencing their mind as truly representational, assumes that what they think exists also in the physical world. This generates a lack of flexibility which we have termed 'psychic equivalence': mental states are equated with physical reality (Fonagy and Target, 1996; Target & Fonagy, 1996). Not only is there an omnipotence of subjectivity ('I know what is right') but also everything that is out there is felt to be known ('You can't tell me anything'). This of course leaves no room for alternative perspectives.

The three-year-old's acute fear of a fantasy (the tiger under their bed and such) is highly compelling. Post-traumatic subjective experience (the flashback) is similarly compelling, resistant to argument, and, until it becomes mentalized, feels dangerous. Often, survivors of trauma simply refuse to think about their experience because thinking about it means reliving it. They may show marked psychic equivalence even in other, different, contexts. James talked about writing letters: 'When you write to someone, it's like, you're going in that letter, you put your hand in the letter, or your whole body's in the letter. And when they open the letter, the words, you are the words so you know, it's like you're outside, but you're still in, still in prison.' Aspects of psychic equivalence overlap with descriptions of paranoid-schizoid forms of thinking, particularly as formulated by Wilfrid Bion (1963) in the *Elements of Psychoanalysis* (Hobson *et al.*, 1998), and the symbolic equation as formulated by Hanna Segal (1957).

Separation from reality is the third aspect of the phenomology of attachment trauma. The pretend mode is a developmental complement to psychic equivalence. Not yet able to conceive of internal experience as mental, the child's fantasies are dramatically divided off from the external world. Small children cannot simultaneously pretend (even though they know it is not real) and engage with normal reality; asking them if their pretend gun is a gun or a stick spoils the game.

Following trauma and the constriction of mentalization we see the intrusion of the pretend mode, particularly in dissociative experiences. In dissociated thinking, nothing can be linked to anything—the principle of the 'pretend mode', in which fantasy is cut off from the real world, is extended so that nothing has implications (Fonagy and Target, 2000). The compulsive search for meaning (hyperactive mentalization), what James describes as 'driving himself mad', is a common reaction against the sense of emptiness and disconnection that the pretend mode generates. Patients report 'blanking out', 'clamming up', or remembering their traumatic experiences only in dreams. The most characteristic feature of traumatization is the oscillation between psychic equivalence and pretend modes of experiencing the internal world.

'I believe it when I see it,' is a further pre-mentalistic aspect of psychic reality. It is the re-emergence of a teleological mode of thought. This mode of understanding the world antedates even language. Infants as young as nine months of age are able to attribute goals to people and to objects that seem to behave purposefully, but these goals are not yet truly mental, they are tied to what is observable. The return of this teleological mode of thought is perhaps the most painful aspect of a subjectivity stripped of mentalization.

Following trauma, verbal reassurance means little. Interacting with others at a mental level has been replaced by attempts at altering thoughts and feelings through action. Most trauma, certainly physical and sexual abuse, is by definition teleological. It is hardly surprising that the victim feels that the mind of another can only be altered in this same mode, through a physical act, threat, or seduction. Stuart described his feelings about being sent to live in a hostel at the age of eleven as follows: 'I tried to make them understand that I was upset so I was throwing things quite a lot. I threw my bed out of the window. I broke all the windows in the room. The only way I could make them understand that I did not like it.' It is not just those who are severely traumatized like Stuart who find physical modes of expression more persuasive than words—words which are all too easily experienced as meaningless within a pretend mode. Following trauma we all need physical assurances of security.

A neuroscientific-attachment theory understanding of the loss of mentalization associated with trauma

Attachment theory and trauma

Attachment theory and research offer a useful starting point for understanding the impact of trauma. *Trauma triggers the attachment system.* As John Bowlby pointed out, it inhibits exploration and activates affectional bonds (Bowlby, 1969). We feel distressed and we want to be hugged. The 7/7 incidents triggered the need to belong to a community in Londoners; as 9/11 did in New York, and 3/11 did in Madrid. Crisis most challenges those whose capacity for relationship is weakest, while a history of secure attachments increases the chances of responding to trauma in relatively adaptive ways. Why?

Classical attachment and some object relations theories contend that templates of relationships are established in infancy and are enacted in later development (Bretherton and Munholland, 1999; Crittenden, 1994; Sroufe, 1996). Early traumatic experiences establish such early relationship expectations, and later ones activate and interact with them. A child of parental conflict whose attachments have been disrupted and their sense of security undermined, perhaps often expects to be rejected. Such a child might dismiss a helper in much the same way as the infant in the strange situation feels she cannot afford to turn to the caregiver for comfort.

This is a simplistic model from a psychoanalytic perspective. For example, to understand adult violence as a mere repetition of attachment trauma fails to reflect the extent of the devastation wreaked on a child's psychological integrity. To understand this devastation we have to go back in time, not just through the child's life, but right back through two million years of human evolution now illuminated by a combination of fossil and neuroscientific investigations.

The evolution of the social brain

The most generally accepted model of how humans evolved was proposed by Richard Alexander (1989). It suggests that our exceptional intelligence evolved not to deal with the hostile forces of nature but rather to deal with competition from other people. This occurred only after our species had achieved relative dominance over its environment. At that point it seems we became our 'own principal hostile forces of nature' (Alexander, 1989: 469).

All species face competition from within, but humans are special in the role that social groups[3] play in achieving success in this type of competition. There was a kind of 'evolutionary arms race' among ever more effective social groups (Flinn *et al.*, 2005). This effectiveness depended on skill in social cognition, which has much in common with the psychoanalytic concept which we have called mentalization, the symbolic representation of mental states: to know, to understand other people also allows one to outsmart them.[4] As the intelligence of the opposition increased so did the requirement for ever greater ability for communication, imaginative social and emotional understanding, and the anticipation of others' reactions—capacities finely honed in most psychoanalysts!

The brain and self and other awareness

Brain studies and fossil records suggest that self-awareness most likely evolved in order to aid other awareness. Closely associated with evolutionary changes in social intelligence were changes in human brain structure. There was a modest proportional expansion (about 10%) in parts of the prefrontal cortex (Semendeferi and Damasio, 2000), with an increased richness of interconnections between neurones in these areas. There are unique features of human neuroanatomy that underpin social interpretation such as increased lateralization. There was a disproportionate expansion of the right prefrontal cortex and the frontal pole (Holloway, 1996; Zilles *et al.*, 1996). These areas of the brain have been shown by imaging studies to be involved in self-awareness, the ability to remember personal experiences, and to project oneself into the future (Tulving, 2002). Self-awareness enables us to modify the way we wish to present ourselves, and also to mislead. The right prefrontal cortex may be there 'to allow us to see ourselves as others see us so that we may cause competitive others to see us as we wish them to' (Alexander, 1990: 7). Thus the original evolutionary function of subjective experiences such as daydreams and fantasies might have been to allow individuals to form goals, carry out plans, and integrate these within a seamless knowledge of one's life history (Levine, 1999).

It seems that self-awareness and awareness of the mental states of others are closely linked, certainly in terms of the brain areas involved. Mentalization was there not mainly to facilitate collaboration and positive relationships but to facilitate social survival. Mentalization serves competition: more like the antlers of a reindeer (used to fight other reindeer) than the eyes of the hawk (used to find prey).

What are the implications of this for our understanding of attachment trauma?

Attachment and the arms-race of mentalization

As the mind needs to adapt to variable conditions, the capacity for mentalization is prepared but not fixed by genetics. Increased sophistication in social cognition evolved hand in hand with greater helplessness in infancy, the prolongation of childhood, and the emergence of intensive parenting (Geary and Huffman, 2002; Hrdy, 2000; Siegal and Varley, 2002). Evolution, it seems, has charged attachment relationships with ensuring the full development of the social brain. The child discovers minds in his objects as he tries to find himself as thinking and feeling in their actions. The child's capacity to represent mental states symbolically has long been assumed by psychoanalysts to be acquired within the primary object relationship. The idea is clearest in Bion, but is implicit in Fairbairn, explicated in Winnicott, restated in Kohut, and rediscovered with new emphases by relational writers such as S. Mitchell.[5] The work I have been referring to allows us to see how and why brains have evolved to nurture this capacity within the parent–infant relationship. This is why the disruption of early affectional bonds not only sets up maladaptive attachment patterns but also undermines a range of capacities vital to normal social development.

The neurobiology of attachment

Recent neuroimaging studies cast an intriguing light on the association of attachment with the development of mentalization. The neurobiology of attachment is now fairly well understood.[6] In brief it seems that changes in attachment behaviour, such as falling in love, which are stimulated by social/sexual activity, entails the activation of an oxytocin and vasopressin sensitive circuit within the anterior hypothalamus (MPOA) linked to the VTA and the nucleus accumbens shell (Insel, 2003). Functional Imaging studies indicate specific activation of the same pathways in the brain of somebody seeing their own baby or their partner, as compared to another familiar baby or someone else's partner (Nitschke *et al.*, 2004).

Bartels and Zeki (2000, 2004), in two separate imaging studies, reported that the activation of areas mediating maternal and/or romantic attachments appeared simultaneously to suppress brain activity in regions associated with making social judgements and mentalizing. This suggests that being in an intensely emotionally attached state inhibits mentalizing and the capacity accurately to see the attachment figure as a person.

These findings are extremely important. Taking the evolutionary perspective just elaborated, competition requires thinking about motives, but attachment involves trust. To be attached to someone is to be predisposed to trust them, to assume that their motives are known and benign. The phrase 'love is blind' must exist in a number of languages. As attachment suppresses mentalization, the mental states of the attachment figures will perhaps always remain somewhat enigmatic. Perhaps psychoanalysis provides a much-needed opportunity for clarification and elaboration of the thoughts and feelings of attachment figures in the past and present precisely because the 'heat' has moved from them to the analyst in the transference.

The configuration described by Bartels and Zeki has critical developmental implications. To acquire the capacity to think about mental states is likely to be facilitated by attachment, because it makes for a safe context for making mistakes. Missing out on early attachment experience (as for the Romanian orphans) creates a long-term vulnerability from which the child may never recover—the capacity for mentalization is never fully established, leaving the child vulnerable to later trauma and unable to cope fully with attachment relationships (O'Connor *et al.*, 2003; Rutter and O'Connor, 2004). More importantly, trauma, by activating attachment, will cause the suppression of the capacity for mentalization. This of course is greatly exacerbated when the trauma is attachment trauma. It is to three related clinical aspects of this issue that we now turn.

The hyperactivation of the attachment system is the first of these. Attachment is normally the ideal 'training ground' for the development of mentalization because it is safe and non-competitive. This biological configuration, which is so adaptive in the context of normal development, becomes immensely destructive in the presence of attachment trauma. Attachment trauma hyperactivates the attachment system because the person to whom the child looks for reassurance and protection is the one causing fear. The devastating psychic impact of attachment trauma is then the combined result of the inhibition of mentalization by attachment and the hyperactivation of the attachment system by trauma. This context demands extraordinary mentalizing capacities from the child, yet the hyperactivation of the attachment system will have suppressed the limited capacity that they have.

The coincidence of trauma and attachment creates a biological vicious cycle. Trauma normally leads a child to seek safety in being close to the attachment figure. This generates a characteristic dependency on the maltreating figure, with the real risk of an escalating sequence of further maltreatment, increased distress, and an ever greater inner need for the attachment figure. The inhibition of mentalization in a traumatizing, hyperactivated attachment relationship is always likely to lead to a prementalistic psychic reality, largely split into psychic equivalence and pretend modes. The memory of the trauma feels currently real so that there is a constant danger of re-traumatization from inside. The traumatized child often begins to fear their own mind, needing the attachment figure even more. The inhibition of mentalization is often an intrapsychic adaptation to traumatic violent attachment. The frankly malevolent mental state of the abuser terrifies the helpless child. The parents' abuse undermines the child's capacity to mentalize, because it is no longer safe for the child, for example, to think about wishing, if this implies recognizing their parent's wish to harm them.

A further complication follows because the child with attachment trauma who phobically avoids the mind of the parent cannot use the other as mirror to understand the self, and diffusion of identity and dissociation can be the conscience. Even more pernicious is the state when, desperate for some kind of self-awareness, psychic reality comes to be experienced through incorporating the other as part of the self. Recall Stuart's description of how after feeling numb he looked at his hands, and started laughing at himself: 'I was going "Ha ha", you know, and I was thinking, "*I had done that.*"' Of course this process, taking the perspective of the other intent on destroying him, is very similar to what Anna Freud described as the process of identification with the aggressor.

The second aspect concerns arousal, the 'biology of being frazzled'. The impact of trauma on mentalization is intermittent. Sometimes the disappearance of mentalization is to do with the intensification of an attachment relationship, for example in the course of an analysis. At other times, being stressed (for example, touching on a sensitive issue) can trigger what feel like wild, unjustified reactions. Six years ago, in a hallmark paper in Science entitled 'The biology of being frazzled', Amy Arnsten (1998) explained why (see also on this subject Arnsten *et al.*, 1999; Mayes, 2000). At the risk of simplifying highly complex pioneering neuroscientific work, Arnsten's Dual Arousal Systems Model delineates two complementary, independent arousal systems: the prefrontal and posterior cortical and subcortical systems (Arnsten, 1998; Arnsten *et al.*, 1999; Mayes, 2000). The system that activates frontal and pre-frontal regions inhibits the second arousal system that normally 'kicks in' only at quite high levels of arousal, when pre-frontal activity goes 'offline' and posterior cortical and subcortical functions (for example, more automatic or motor functions, not thinking so much as running) take over.

The switch-point between the two arousal systems may be shifted by childhood trauma. Undoubtedly, as mentalization involves the prefrontal cortex, this accounts for some of the inhibition of mentalization in individuals with attachment trauma, in response to increases in arousal that would not be high enough to inhibit mentalization in most of us. 'I just snap. You know what I mean. It's like a switch. But I don't like it. I hate it. But I just can't help myself for doing it.'

In the light of this phenomenon it is important for analysts to monitor the traumatized patient's readiness to hear comments about thoughts and feelings. As arousal increases, in part in response to interpretative work, traumatized patients cannot process talk about their minds. Interpretations of the transference at these times, however accurate they might be, are likely to be way beyond the capacity of the patient to hear. The clinical priority has to be to reduce arousal so that the patient can again think of other perspectives (mentalize).

Finally, and clinically most significant, is projective identification, which becomes a matter of life and death.

Bion's (1963: 3) first element in his elements of psychoanalysis is 'the essential feature of Melanie Klein's conception of projective identification ... the dynamic relationship between container and contained'. Edith Jacobson (1954) and Donald Winnicott (1956) independently noted that the internalization of the representation of another before the boundaries of the self are fully formed undermines the creation of a coherent sense of self. The infant is forced to internalize the other not as an internal object but as a core part of their self. If the caregiver fails to contain the infant's anxieties, metabolize them, and mirror the self state, the infant, rather than gradually constructing a representation of their internal states through mirroring and 'normal' projective identification, is forced to accommodate the object, an alien being, within their self-representation.

Of course these introjections in traumatized individuals are coloured by the traumatic context in which they occur.[7] What is internalized as part of the self is a caregiver with terrifying intentions. This can generate momentary experiences of unbearable psychic pain when the self feels attacked literally from within and almost overwhelmed by an experience of 'badness' that is impossible to mitigate by reassurance. Experienced in the mode of psychic equivalence the feeling of badness translates directly into 'actual badness' from which, in a teleological mode of functioning, self-destruction might appear the only escape. In our view, this state is commonly the trigger for acts of self-harm and suicide, often associated with attachment trauma.

The only way the person can deal with such introjects is by constantly externalizing these alien parts of the self-structure into a container. Through projective identification the persecutory parts are experienced as outside. It is then essential that the alien experiences are owned by another mind, so that another mind is in control of the parts of the self set upon its own destruction. The need for projective identification is a matter of life and death for those with a traumatizing part of the self-structure, but the constellation creates a dependence on the object that has many features of addiction. But we know that the triggering of the attachment system (by the need to have a proximal container for traumatized, alien parts of the self) could further suppress mentalization. This reduces the chance of either alternative solutions being accepted or a non-teleological (non-physical) solution being found.

The following verbatim extract from a patient illustrates the experience of externalizing the alien self better than I could describe it. He was traumatically sexually abused by his stepfather and brothers. He was now making a living as a male prostitute. 'The more you experience, the more immune you become to anything. If you get lured into a gang of queers and then, you're abused, you don't fear queers no more. You just probably revenge against them. Cause you can turn your mind, into their activity and use it against them. I'm not getting into fights or anything like that, but I do happen to get into people's heads and hurt them, do you know what I mean?'

Clinical implications

So what should be the object of psychoanalysis with such patients?

The traumatized individual comes to seek psychoanalytic help for more than simply dealing with the adversity that they have experienced. The devastation of psychic function that attachment trauma leaves in its wake impairs capacity to cope *with all* the 'ordinary' vicissitudes of mental life: unconscious conflicts over aggression; oedipal desires and defences mounted against them; narcissistic vulnerabilities; conflicts in relation to ambivalently cathected objects, and so forth. All the inescapable pains of the human condition are experienced with the immediacy of the open wound unprotected by the skin provided by mentalization. While some of these derivatives will interact with trauma suffered, the intensity of the associated feelings should not mislead the analyst into thinking that these later conflicts are the underlying cause of the patient's mental anguish. They have been amplified and prolonged by the patient's difficulty in mentally processing any painful experience.

The overall aim of treatment of trauma patients is thus to help them to establish a more robust, mentalizing self so that they may mentalize trauma and conflict and develop more secure relationships. Mentalizing gives a buffer between feeling and action, necessary if impulses are to be caught before they become overwhelming, and motivations of self and other can be monitored and understood. Enhancing mentalization bridges the gap between affects and their representation, especially with current mental states. This is not necessarily via work on the trauma itself. Psychoanalysis fosters mentalization in relation to the patient's self, not just in relation to his trauma. It entails finding or recovering mentalization through a developmentally appropriate process—finding one's psychological self through the mind of a benign attachment figure.

But how should we help a patient with memories of attachment trauma to become more able to mentalize about these experiences?

Recovering memories of trauma

Research on memory shows that childhood memories are very fallible, but the gist of experience recalled is mostly accurate (Christianson, 1992; Heuer and Reisberg, 1992; Riccio *et al.*, 1994), particularly for traumatic events (Usher and Neisser, 1993). Although episodic memory does not develop until age five, children can probably encode and store many experiences that they are unable to describe. This does not mean though that systematic reconstruction of such experiences would necessarily be helpful in the treatment of trauma. The reason for this is because trauma—in particular early trauma—interferes with autobiographical memory (Teicher *et al.*, 1994), probably through hippocampal damage (Bremner *et al.*, 1993). In the absence of its integrative function, patients are likely to be left with fragmented images and emotions that they are unable to combine with their life narrative or self-schema.

The frontal lobes appear to play a key role in monitoring the source of a memory image, including distinguishing true and false memories; prior expectations can create an unusually vivid set of ideas or images. The hyperactivation of the attachment system in individuals with trauma and the likely associated inhibition of mentalizing may compromise knowing where an image has come from. Any pressure by a therapist to recreate and revive memories would be likely to introduce a further bias and inaccuracy. The therapist must be aware that the cognitive functions normally available to prevent confusion between fantasy and memory will be specifically compromised in traumatized individuals. Nevertheless, I believe that reconstruction is essential to the therapeutic process because:

i. it provides a means to bring the patient's mind into contact with what it has previously found intolerable;
ii. it provides a place where threat to the ego and therapeutic goal are reasonably balanced;
iii. it generates a coherent self-narrative assuming a historical continuity of self which may itself be of therapeutic value (Holmes, 1998; Schafer, 1980; Spence, 1994); and
iv. most importantly, it can help in the primary task of the recovery of mentalization. It is this last point that I would like to illustrate with a clinical example.

Clinical illustration

Miss C had originally presented with a mixture of quite severe anxiety and depression, and a history which included a psychotic episode and abuse from a psychotic stepfather. The abuse was severe enough for extensive social services involvement and a realistic risk of the eleven-year-old Miss C being taken into care.

The trauma was cumulative. As well as being physically, but not explicitly sexually, abusive, her stepfather systematically humiliated her. For example, she recalled having to stand by her bed at night reciting her homework, knowing that any mistake would be followed by physical punishment.

Not surprisingly, in Miss C's analysis memories acquired great significance. At one level she experienced her work with me as a masochistic submission to a mad and cruel man, demanding that she remember her past in great detail no matter how painful and humiliating. Also unsurprising was her reaction to this submission, which consisted of an enraged regression into an, at times, infantile state of withdrawal. For days, sometimes weeks, she would not speak to me. She came to the appointments on time and seemed to value her time on the couch, but during the sessions with me made no response to invitations to free associate or even to answer direct questions. She seemed to have cut off awareness of being in the room with me.

While remembering was fraught, the present was unbearable. The longest periods of silence invariably followed any attempt I made to link the painful experiences she recalled to the current relationship with me. For example, she had brought a memory of a time when she had gone to bed hoping that her stepfather had forgotten about the testing that evening. She had been careful to keep especially quiet to make sure that she did not inadvertently draw attention to herself. She recalled her terror when he burst into her room some time after she had gone to sleep. He demanded an explanation for her daring to go to bed without having been tested. I gently made the intervention that she was equally fearful of how I might at times act in ways or say things that she did not anticipate, and that being silent was therefore the only way that she could feel safe in the analysis. She acknowledged what I said with a vague shrug and said nothing for the rest of the session. She was also more or less totally silent at the session after.

With hindsight it is clear to me that she experienced my interpretations in a psychic equivalence mode. Even though gently put, the analogy in the transference to her stepfather's behaviour seemed to be an actual threat of my behaving in unpredictable ways, and an implicit demand on her not to move or draw attention to herself. The current relationship with Miss C was not an appropriate entry point into her inner world.

What turned out to be most useful was what seemed like direct work with her experiences of trauma. She found it helpful when we talked about her terror of her stepfather; his moodiness; the way his gestures or facial expressions could indicate to her what to expect; the way the beatings felt; where her mother was and what she might have been thinking when the abuse occurred; her ways of trying to comply with his wishes; and the tricks she was proud of developing that she used to distract him from his wish to maltreat her. The remembering as it occurred in this analysis took quite some time—in fact most of the first year of Miss C's treatment. The remembering took the place of an analysis—as classically described. During this time there was an increased understanding of her traumatic experience but little apparent understanding of her. Yet the impact on her was clearly positive and, as a year passed, she engaged with her treatment and the difficulties with her work also began to ease.

I brought this case to show that our emphasis on mentalization is not inconsistent with reconstruction. To this day I remain unconvinced about the accuracy of Miss C's memories of abuse. I would recall that she had presented the same incidents in quite different ways at different times. The whole idea of remembering was so fraught, so loaded with unmetabolized affects, that I felt continually drawn into the abuse. Even mild questioning of her silence fixed me in that role. Yet my tolerance of her silence was vital, ultimately enabling her to speak—as she was allowed to not 'do her homework'. But perhaps even more concretely, remembering allowed her to become able to mentalize her experiences.

She worked through the same memories, screen memories or real, again and again. But with each recollection she would be able to depict with slightly greater clarity her thoughts and feelings, and perhaps even more important, the putative thoughts and feelings of her tormenter. As she remembered what sounded like different accounts of the same events, I would realize that she was trying out different perspectives on the experience. When Miss C remembered waiting in her bed, listening in terror, trying to identify her stepfather's footsteps, she was not only remembering trauma but also making the imaginative leap of mentalization, putting herself into the mind of the eight-year-old girl listening to the sounds and remembering her constructions. When she recalled her stepfather's face contorted into a Kabuki grimace of rage, the therapeutic benefit was from stepping behind his mask and seeing the cruelty of a man struggling with his own internal demons; demons who probably persecuted him as mercilessly as he persecuted Miss C.

The experiences changed status from static pictures of the past, to moving and even talking pictures where Miss C's experience of herself and others was no longer either equated to the past or dissociated. In retrospect it seems clear that the memories of the trauma for Miss C paradoxically created the safest context for the recovery of mentalization. The benefit is not from the recovery of memories or even the discovery of specific states of mind that are contained within them, but rather it is in rediscovering *the mere fact of thought and feeling*, the layeredness of subjective experience. Miss C came to describe this stage of her treatment as 'remembering'. On one occasion she added, 'It's not enough to remember; you've got to make remembering count.'

The role of 'memory work' in psychoanalysis

While reconstruction of how things actually were in childhood may significantly contribute to therapeutic action, this does not mean that the outcome of reconstruction, the remembering of hypothetical autobiographical events, is the key. It is the process of re-working current experiences in the context of other perspectives, that is, enhancing mentalization, that I believe to be curative in what we do. The other perspectives may be from the patient's childhood, but they could be the analyst's current experience, or the way that the patient is experienced by others that are close to them in the present.

Conclusion

I have suggested that the psychological consequences of trauma, in an attachment context and perhaps beyond, entail a decoupling of mentalization and a re-emergence of non-mentalizing modes of representing internal reality. This is pernicious because the immediacy of a memory experienced in the non-mentalizing mode of psychic equivalence has the capacity to re-traumatize again and again. This further decouples mentalization and makes the experience ever more real. Trauma in the attachment context is most pernicious because the biological basis of attachment assumes trust. Part of this is the safety of not having to mentalize, of knowing that others are thinking for us, that we need not monitor our own and others' thinking. Trauma inevitably activates the attachment system. This activation (probably for evolutionary reasons) temporarily inhibits areas of the brain concerned with both remembering and mentalization. This is why mentalization comes to be so readily abandoned in the face of trauma, particularly attachment trauma. Unmentalized trauma endures and compromises mental functioning. Of course it also interferes with new relationships. The self being destroyed from within, by identification with the aggressor, is an imperative for projective identification, drawing the other closer and selecting relationships that will retraumatize. Thus the individual loses a possible route to be freed from the shackles of a traumatic past, constantly relived. To escape from the grip of trauma, the individual needs help to recover mentalization. Fortunately there are many routes to this; provided by psychoanalysis, remembering in the context of an enduring analytic relationship is one, but not the only one.

Bibliography

Alexander, R.D. (1989). 'Evolution of the human psyche'. In: Mellars, P. and Stringer, C. (eds) *The Human Revolution: Behavioural and Biological Perspectives on the Origins of Modern Humans.* Princeton: Princeton University Press. pp. 455–513.

Alexander, R.D. (1990). 'How did humans evolve? Reflections on the uniquely unique species'. *Museum of Zoology (Special publication no. 1).* Ann Arbor, MI: University of Michigan.

Arnsten, A.F.T. (1998). 'The biology of being frazzled'. *Science,* 280: 1,711–12.

Arnsten, A.F.T., Mathew, R., Ubriani, R., Taylor, J.R. and Li, B.-M. (1999). 'alpha-1 noradrenergic receptor stimulation impairs prefrontal corical cognitive function'. *Biological Psychiatry,* 45: 26–31.

Bartels, A. and Zeki, S. (2000). 'The neural basis of romantic love'. *Neuroreport,* 11 (17): 3,829–34.

Bartels, A. and Zeki, S. (2004). 'The neural correlates of maternal and romantic love'. *Neuroimage,* 21 (3): 1,155–66.

Beeghly, M. and Cicchetti, D. (1994). 'Child maltreatment, attachment, and the self system: Emergence of an internal state lexicon in toddlers at high social risk'. *Development and Psychopathology,* 6: 5–30.

Bion, W.R. (1963). *Elements of Psycho-analysis.* London: Heinemann.

Bloom, P. (2000). *How Children Learn the Meaning of Words*. Cambridge: MIT Press.

Bowlby, J. (1969). *Attachment and Loss, Vol. 1: Attachment*. London: Hogarth Press and the Institute of Psycho-Analysis.

Bremner, J.D., Scott, T.M., Delaney, R.C., Southwick, S.M., Mason, J.W., Johnson, D.R., *et al.* (1993). 'Deficits in short-term memory in posttraumatic stress disorder'. *American Journal of Psychiatry*, 150: 1,015–19.

Brentano, F. (1973/1874). *Psychology from an Empirical Standpoint*. London: Routledge.

Bretherton, K. and Munholland, K.A. (1999). 'Internal working models in attachment relationships: A construct revisited'. In: Cassidy, J. and Shaver, P.R. (eds) *Handbook of Attachment: Theory, Research and Clinical Applications*. New York: Guilford. pp. 89–114.

Christianson, S. (1992). 'Remembering emotional events: Potential mechanisms'. In:

Christianson, S. (ed.) *The Handbook of Emotion and Memory: Research and Theory*. Hillsdale, NJ: Erlbaum. pp. 307–40.

Crittenden, P.M. (1994). 'Peering into the black box: An exploratory treatise on the development of self in young children'. In: Cicchetti, D. and Toth, S.L. (eds) *Disorders and Dysfunctions of the Self: Rochester Symposium on Developmental Psychopathology, Vol 5*. Rochester, NY: University of Rochester Press. pp. 79–148.

Dennett, D.C. (1978). 'Beliefs about beliefs'. *Behaviour and Brain Sciences*, 4: 568–570.

Flinn, M., Geary, D. and Ward, C. (2005). 'Ecological dominance, social competition, and the coalitionary arms races: Why humans evolved extraordinary interlligence'. *Evolution and Human Behavior*, 26: 10–46.

Fonagy, P. (1989). 'On tolerating mental states: Theory of mind in borderline patients'. *Bulletin of the Anna Freud Centre*, 12: 91–115.

Fonagy, P., Stein, H., Allen, J. and Fultz, J. (2003). *The Relationship of Mentalization and Childhood and Adolescent Adversity to Adult Functioning*. Paper presented at the Biennial Meeting of the Society for Research in Child Development, Tampa, FL.

Fonagy, P. and Target, M. (1996). 'Playing with Reality: I. Theory of Mind and the Normal Development of Psychic Reality'. *International Journal of Psycho-Analysis*, 77: 217–33.

Fonagy, P. and Target, M. (2000). 'Playing with Reality III: The Persistence of Dual Psychic Reality in Borderline Patients'. *International Journal of Psychoanalysis*, 81 (5): 853–74.

Freud, A. (1936). *The Ego and the Mechanisms of Defence*. New York: International Universities Press.

Geary, D.C. (2005). *The Origin of Mind: Evolution of Brain, Cognition, and General Intelligence*. Washington, DC: American Psychological Association.

Geary, D.C. and Huffman, K.J. (2002). Brain and Cognitive Evolution: Forms of Modularity and Functions of Mind. *Psychol Bull*, 128 (5): 667–98.

Gerber, A.J. (2004). *Psychodynamic Psychotherapy for Severe Personality Disorders: A Quantitative Study of Treatment Process and Outcome*. Unpublished PhD Thesis, University of London.

Heuer, F. and Reisberg, D. (1992). Emotion, Arousal, and Memory for Detail. In Christianson, S. (ed) *The Handbook of Emotion and Memory: Research and Theory*. Hillsdale, NH: Erlbaum. pp. 151–80.

Hobson, R.P., Patrick, M.P. and Valentine, J.D. (1998). 'Objectivity in Psychoanalytic Judgements'. *Br J Psychiatry*, 173: 172–77.

Holloway, R.L. (1996). 'Evolution of the Human Brain. In: Lock, A. and Peters, C.R. (eds) *Handbook of Human Symbolic Evolution*. New York: Oxford University Press. pp. 74–116.

Holmes, J. (1998). 'Defensive and Creative Uses of Narrative in Psychotherapy: An Attachment Perspective'. In: Roberts, G. and Holmes, J. (eds) *Narrative and Psychotherapy and Psychiatry*. Oxford: Oxford University Press. pp. 49–68.

Hopkins, J. (1992). 'Psychoanalysis, Interpretation, and Science'. In: Hopkins, J. and Saville, A. (eds) *Psychoanalysis, Mind and Art: Perspectives on Richard Wollheim*. Oxford: Blackwell. pp. 3–34.

Hrdy, S.B. (2000). *Mother Nature*. New York: Ballentine Books.

Insel, T. (1997). 'A Neurobiological Basis of Social Attachment'. *American Journal of Psychiatry*, 154: 726–35.

Insel, T.R. (2003). 'Is Social Attachment an Addictive Disorder?' *Physiol Behav*, 79 (3): 351–57.

Jacobson, E. (1954). 'The Self and the Object World: Vicissitudes of their Infantile Cathexes and their Influence on Ideational Affective Development'. *The Psychoanalytic Study of the Child*, 9: 75–127.

Levine, B. (1999). 'Self-regulation and Autonoetic Consciousness'. In: Tulving, E. (ed.), *Memory, Consciousness and the Brain: the Talinn Conference*. Philadelphia: Psychology Press. pp. 200–14.

Luquet, P. (1981). 'Le changement dans la Mentalization'. *Revue Francais de Psychoanalyse*, 45: 1,023–28.

Luquet, P. (1987). 'Penser-Parler: Un apport psychanalytique a la theorie du langage'. In: Christie, R., Christie-Luterbacher, M.M. and Luquet, P. (eds), *La Parole Troublee*. Paris: Presses Universitaire de France. pp. 161–300.

MacLean, P. (1990). *The Triune Brain in Evolution: Role in Paleocerebral Functions.* New York: Plenum.

Marty, P. (1968). 'A Major Process of Somatization: The Progressive Disorganization'. *International Journal of Psycho-Analysis,* 49: 246–249.

Marty, P. (1990). *La Psychosomatique de l'Adulte.* Paris: Presses Universitaire de France.

Marty, P. and De M'Uzan, M. (1963). 'La Pens,e Op, ratoire'. *Revue Fran‡aise de Psychanalyse,* 27 (Suppl.): 1,345–56.

Mayes, L.C. (2000). 'A Developmental Perspective on the Regulation of Arousal States'. *Seminars in Perinatology,* 24: 267–79.

Miller and Cohen. (2001). In: 1905.

Nimchinsky, E.A., Gilissen, E., Allman, J.M., Perl, D.P., Erwin, J.M. and Hof, P.R. (1999). 'A Neuronal Morphologic Type Unique to Humans and Great Apes'. *Proc Natl Acad Sci U S A,* 96 (9): 5,268–73.

Nitschke, J.B., Nelson, E.E., Rusch, B.D., Fox, A.S., Oakes, T.R. and Davidson, R.J. (2004). 'Orbitofrontal Cortex Tracks Positive Mood in Mothers Viewing Pictures of their Newborn Infants'. *Neuroimage,* 21 (2): 583–92.

O'Connor, T.G., Marvin, R.S., Rutter, M., Olrick, J.T. and Britner, P.A. (2003). 'Child–parent Attachment Following Early Institutional Deprivation'. *Dev Psychopathol,* 15 (1): 19–38.

Panksepp, J. (1998). *Affective Neuroscience: The Foundations of Human and Animal Emotions.* Oxford: Oxford University Press.

Perelberg, R.J. (Ed.). (1999). *Psychoanalytic Understanding of Violence and Suicide.* London: Routledge.

Riccio, D.C., Rabinowitz, V.C. and Axelrod, S. (1994). 'Memory: When Less is More'. *American Psychologist,* 49: 917–26.

Rutter, M. and O'Connor, T.G. (2004). 'Are there biological programming effects for psychological development? Findings from a study of Romanian adoptees'. *Dev Psychol,* 40 (1): 81–94.

Schafer, R. (1980). 'Action and narration in psychoanalysis'. *New Literary History,* 12: 61–85.

Segal, H. (1957). 'Notes on symbol formation'. *International Journal of Psycho-Analysis,* 38: 391–97.

Semendeferi, K. and Damasio, H. (2000). 'The brain and its main anatomical subdivisions in living hominoids using magnetic resonance imaging'. *Journal of Human Evolution,* 38: 317–32.

Siegal, M. and Varley, R. (2002). 'Neural systems involved in "theory of mind"'. *Nat Rev Neurosci,* 3 (6): 463–71.

Sohn, L. (1985). 'Narcissistic organisation, projective identification and the formation of the identificate'. *International Journal of Psychoanalysis,* 66: 201–13.

Spence, D.P. (1994). 'The special nature of psychoanalytic facts'. *International Journal of Psycho-Analysis*, 75: 915–925.

Sroufe, L.A. (1996). *Emotional Development: The Organization of Emotional Life in the Early Years*. New York: Cambridge University Press.

Target, M. and Fonagy, P. (1996). 'Playing with Reality II: The Development of Psychic Reality from a Theoretical Perspective'. *International Journal of Psycho-Analysis*, 77: 459–79.

Teicher, M.H., Ito, Y., Glod, C.A., Schiffer, F. and Gelbard, H.A. (1994). 'Early abuse, limbic system dysfunction, and borderline personality disorder'. In: Silk, K. R. (ed.) *Biological and Neurobehavioral Studies of Borderline Personality Disorder*. Washington, DC: American Psychiatric Press. pp. 177–207.

Tulving, E. (2002). 'Episodic memory: from mind to brain'. *Annu Rev Psychol*, 53: 1–25.

Usher, J.A. and Neisser, U. (1993). 'Childhood amnesia and the beginnings of memory for four early life events'. *Journal of Experimental Psychology: General*, 122: 155–65.

Winnicott, D.W. (1956). 'Mirror role of mother and family in child development'. In:

Winnicott, D.W. (ed.) *Playing and Reality*. London: Tavistock. pp. 111–18.

Wollheim, R. (1999). *On the Emotions*. New Haven: Yale University Press.

Zilles, K., Dabringhaus, A., Geyer, S., Amunts, K., Qu, M., Schleicher, A., *et al.* (1996). 'Structural asymmetries in the human forebrain and the forebrain of non-human primates and rats'. *Neurosci Biobehav Rev*, 20 (4): 593–605.

Developmental risks and their sequelae: Effects on attachment and mentalization

Gerd Lehmkuhl

In a persuading and inspiring manner Peter Fonagy´s paper shows how psychoanalytic positions and perspectives can be innovatively defined and redeveloped. His specifications take on Eric Kandel´s demand to develop a shared framework for psychoanalysis and neurosciences in order to be able to investigate the effects of early mother–child interaction and the sequelae of different attachment representations with new methodologies, such as the development of mentalization processes. A number of studies prove that experiences of separation, stress, and deprivation in early childhood cause insufficient affect regulation and have a negative impact on brain maturation and on cognitive and emotional development.

Recently, in a comprehensive review, James Swain and co-workers (2007) have pointed out:

> 'Brain basis of early parent-infant-interactions: psychology, physiology and in vivo functional neuroimaging studies.'

They came to the following conclusion

The parent–infant bond, so central to the human condition, may also determine the risks of developing mood and anxiety disorders, and the potential for resiliency and protection against the development of psychopathology later in life, not to mention the far-reaching aspects of human attachment across individual behaviours and between cultures. Efforts to characterize this reciprocal interaction between caregiver and infant and to assess its impact have provided a powerful theoretical and empirical framework in the fields of social and emotional development.

This conclusion they based on a number of empirical cognitive neuroscientific results and raised the question of what extent a different attachment style of the mother has an impact on the brain development of their infants:

> Do mothers with insecure patterns of attachment respond differently to their infant cues? Are neglecting mothers unresponsive to these cues or do they fail to receive reward signals in the brain? Longitudinal research designs may help in this regard. In addition, it will be important to clarify the role of different neuroendocrine pathways and different genetic variations in mediating parenting brain activations (280).

In their opinion, systematic studies with well characterized different groups of parents could extensively contribute to our existing knowledge, especially if a number of child-stimuli parameter and psychometric instruments were included.

As in other areas of cognitive neuroscience, there will be debates regarding whether to use more ethologically sound but poorly controlled stimuli versus stimuli which is less generalizable but more tightly controlled. Both types of experiment will be needed to tease apart the basic apparatus of baby responsiveness and bond formations as well as the parts of the circuit that are actually at work in normal day-to-day parenting. This work will also require joint study of parents and infants to understand how their interactions contribute to their bond and infant outcomes.

According to Ruth Feldman (2007) the concept of synchronicity illustrates a central approach to interpersonal and self-regulating functions. Micro-analysis of parent–child interaction could essentially improve our understanding of pathological pathways.

Infants enter into the social world through the sensitive moment-by-moment adaptation of an attuned and caring adult during social interactions. Such interactions are adjusted to micro-shifts in infant affect and arousal, coalesce into patterned configurations of vocal, visual, and affective sequences, and organize the infant's biological rhythms and attentive states into a lived experience that highlights the present moment. As seen, this early experience is critical for the development of symbol use, empathy, emotional resonance, and self-regulation, and lays the foundation for the child's later capacity for intimacy throughout their life.

A clinical perspective conveys the results of the Mannheim children-at-risk study. Among other things they investigated the impact of mother–child interaction on the development and long-term prognosis of children being at high or as well as those being at low social risk. In this regard, the results of Laucht and coworkers (2004) are particularly interesting, whose study used a sample of babies with regulation disorders. Altogether, the mothers' behaviour was less sensitive and less responsive; they smiled less at their child and vocalized less with their child. Furthermore, the mothers were more stereotypical in their interactive behaviour and less stimulating. The babies, on the other side, smiled less at their mothers and were generally less reactive. The data analyses proved that a cumulation of stressors—such as a regulation disorder and negative disharmonic early interactions—later led to most psychological problems at ages eight and eleven.

Interestingly, the infants with regulation problems particularly had a negative prognosis in terms of increasing external symptoms during their development when the mothers behaved less reactively with them as babies. Dependent upon gender, controversial relationships were found: whereas little reactivity in the mother caused an increase of external problems in girls with multiple regulation problems in the course of their development, in boys this was caused by a high reactivity of the mother. This indicates that in girls a prognosis of early childhood regulation disorders is influenced by a depriving quality to the early mother–child interactions, and in boys an overstimulating quality.

In the Mannheim children-at-risk-study, mostly psychosocial stress factors of the family, such as a low level of education or the psychiatric illness of a parent, were meaningful for the long-term prognosis of external and internal problems. On the other hand these results do not allow for a linear causal explanation: variables of the child have an impact on the early formation of the interaction as well as the behaviour and stressors of the mother, meaning that the individual *Passung* ("fitting") is essential. This can be influenced by genetic and physical deviations of the child as well as an insufficient sensitivity and acceptance of the baby on the mother´s side. The example of children with early-onset autism demonstrates that certain basic requirements ought to be fulfilled in order to initiate a successful mentalization process. So far we still have insufficient knowledge of the extent, and in which areas, limitations arise on different levels of mentalization and how this could possibly be improved.

We are thus so far confronted with a complex situation regarding the understanding of different possible influences for better describing effective parenting. McLaughlin and Harrison (2006: 83) described this in their paper 'Parenting Practices of Mothers of Children with ADHD: The Role of Maternal and Child Factors' as follows:

One hundred and fifty Australian mothers of children diagnosed with ADHD were interviewed and asked to assess the severity of their child's disruptive behaviour, their own parenting sense of competence, perceptions of social isolation and parenting practices. The hypothesis was that severity of child disruptive behaviour, higher child age, 'only' child status, lower parental sense of competence and greater social isolation would be associated with the use of less effective parenting practices. The regression analysis indicated that the combination of these variables was significantly associated with parenting practices, accounting for 32% of the variance. Unique contributions were evident for severity of overall behavioural disturbance and parental sense of competence.

A recent article from Bradley and Corwyn (2008: 128) could also prove a relationship between maternal sensitivity and behavioural problems in children with temperamental difficulties.

When it comes to manifesting externalizing behaviour, children with difficult temperaments were more affected by the kinds of parenting they received than children with average and easy temperaments. Having opportunities for productive activity was associated with a significant reduction in externalizing behaviour problems for children with difficult and average temperaments, but not for children with easy temperaments. Likewise, it was only children with difficult temperaments who showed a significant reduction in externalizing behaviour when they were exposed to high levels of maternal sensitivity and harsh parenting. In effect, the findings show that children with difficult temperaments are differentially responsive to multiple aspects of their social and physical environments as regards the development of externalizing behaviour.

Concluding the author's dispute critically the effects of parenting programmes with respect to school children is summarized:

There appears to be a complex interplay between children's temperamental dispositions and their history of positive and negative experiences. Most programmes aimed at improving parenting practice do not appear to incorporate lessons from such a complex set of findings in a comprehensive or carefully targeted way, including adequate attention to developmental changes in self-regulatory capacities.

Also molecular genetic studies emphasize these complex interacting associations and the importance of cumulative developmental risks on different levels. Boys who were exposed to prenatal smoking and who had a specific genetic type of the dopamine transporter gene (DAT1-allel) more often developed hyperactive impulsive behavioural patterns (Becker *et al.*, 2007). The occurence of hyperactive behaviour based on a certain type of the DAT-transporter-gene on the condition of coexisting psychosocial risks proves the importance of gene-environment-interactions.

Fonagy´s and Target´s (2004) mentalization and psychosocial developmental model explicitly includes the results of behavioural genetics and moves towards an interdisciplinary approach; they show an understanding of how deviations in mother–child interactions are only one cause of mentalization problems, and how a biological vulnerability, such as an attention deficit, could limit the reflective functioning of the child. They emphasize that most developmental aspects—such as biological vulnerability—could be understood as a subtle bi-directional causation process. Vulnerability abets interpersonal conflicting situations and blocks the social, emotional, and cognitive abilities of the child. Thus on the one hand biological factors can constrict mentalization potential and, on the other, can participate in shaping an environment that blocks the development of a mature mentalization (Fonagy *et al.*, 2004). Examplarily Fonagy and coworkers describe this in a group of children who are characterized by intensive dramatic affects and a hunger for social contact. Self-harming behaviour, inability to tolerate separation, hyperactivity, and temper tantrums characterize their early development. They fulfil the criteria of attention deficit hyperactivity disorder; they seem anxious, depressed, irritable, and explosive. Little excitement and frustrations lead to an affect storm—to uncontrolled emotional disruptions that are disproportionate to the apparent trigger. Being highly self-centred these children oscillate between idealization and devaluation and, according to Fonagy, are an extreme type of an insecurely attached infant.

Bovensiepen (2002) gives a comparable description of the clinical symptoms with their possible psychodynamic backgrounds. As babies these children were deemed to be insecurely attached, fragmented, and constantly 'on the go'. According to Pozzi (2001) children with hyperactive disorders exhibit preoccupied and desorganized attachment representations. The attachment disorder is considered to be the essential cause together with an early deficit in motherly containment. Based on the presented empirical results the dichotomy of neurobiology and psychodynamic causation cannot be maintained. These results and their meaning, however, are interpreted and weighted quite differently. Leuzinger-Bohleber (2006: 46) marked this dilemma of a difficult dialogue between the representatives of different therapy schools and scientific disciplines as follows: 'We often do not speak a common language and share our scientific and professional opinions only rudimentary.'

The concept of mentalization could be an approach which might have the potential to connect the different professions. Therefore, however, it would be necessary to better evaluate the concept and to be able to measure it. On which condition do mentalization processes change over the course of development? How are they connected with the autobiographical memory? Do other risk factors exist beside the ones that were already mentioned? Are there protective conditions—as adoption studies with Rumanian orphans suggest? Can cognitive methods contribute to our knowledge of mentalization processes?

Clinical experience suggests a spectrum diagnosis in reference to ADHD. There is a variety of different shapes of symptoms and stress factors, and different combinations of biological and psychosocial risks. It is essential to differentiate every individual case and to not act on the assumption of a common genesis or a common psychodynamic appearance. The different etiological backgrounds can impact the developmental course quite differently. This is as well to bear in mind as the course of symptomatology itself. Often affected pre- and school children perceive themselves as vital, successful, emotionally happy, and full of self-consciousness. Within just a short time this self-image can essentially change through learning and social experiences in kindergarten, in school, or in the family. Even though relationship experiences and early mother–child interaction is of essential importance for the psychodynamic understanding of the genesis of hypercinetic disorders, recurring only on this aspect misses out other important ones. A multidimensional model of ADHD is supposed to correspond to a differentiated psychodynamic conception.

Markowitsch and Welzer (2005: 12) point out that the development of the autobiographical memory extends into early adulthood. The development of the autobiographical memory is based on a very subtle interaction of biological, psychological, social, and cultural processes which are interdependent. Strongly associated with the maturation of the brain the autobiographical memory ensures the synchronization of the individual with his or her social environment:

It assures that despite the elapsing time and despite the physical and psychological changes over the course of life we always deal with one and the same ego. The level of requirements and proficiency rises in an increasingly sophisticated world with more and more long and complex chain of activities corresponding to an autobiographical memory as sort of relais for psychosocial synchronization. This accounts for the prolonging duration of the education and development compared to former times.

Memory and mentalization evolve in a dialogue and therefore represent a social process that in a second step establishes metarepresentations. According to Singer (2006), this is the reason why we can postpone reactions to stimuli and can balance decisions. It is possible to establish inner models and to measure the expected success of actions against them. In this way we succeed in careful acting, in preventing dangers, and in developing creativity. Forming these internal models can be proved via functional imaging techniques.

So far, however, we still know too little as to how this inner process and these self-concepts emerge.

What are the conclusion and the overall perspective?

Child psychiatrists ought to ask themselves how neuroscientific results can represent the inner world of their patients, which methods can better detect the experiences, feelings, and self-concepts, and how early attachment experiences can effect the cognitive and emotional development.

And child psychoanalysts?

They should be inspired by the versatile and complex developmental models in order to reassess the importance of the environment for intrapsychic processes. If mentalization disorders could not only be caused by negative attachment experiences, but also by biological processes, this had an important effect on treatment procedures, especially regarding the work with parents. Moreover, many factors suggest that mentalization and autobiographical memory are not completed at a certain point of time, but rather are part of a long course of development having consequences for treatment planning.

Fonagy´s concept of mentalization is a major and indispensable contribution towards a convergence of professions. I hope that Kandel's (2006: 3) idea of 'biology within the framework of psychoanalysis' results in new findings.

Bibliography

Becker, K., El-Faddagh, M., Schmidt, M.H., Esser, G. and Laucht, M. (2008). 'Interaction of Dopamine Transporter Genotype with Prenatal Smoke Exposure on ADHD Symptoms'. *J Pediatrics*, 152 (2): 263–69.

Bovensiepen, G., Hopf, H. and Molitor, G. (2002, Hrsg.). *Unruhige und unaufmerksame Kinder. Psychoanalyse des hyperkinetischen Syndroms.* Frankfurt: Brandes & Appsel.

Bradley, R.H. and Corwyn, R.F. (2007). 'Infant temperament, parenting, and externalising behaviour in first grade: a test of the differential susceptibility hypothesis'. *J Child Psychol Psychiat*, 49 (2) : 124–31.

Feldmann, R. (2007). 'Parent-infant synchrony and the construction of shared timing; physiological precursors, developmental outcomes, and risk conditions'. *J Child Psychol Psychiat*, 48 (3/4) : 329–54.

Fonagy, P. (2008). *Bindung, Trauma und Psychoanalyse: Wo Psychoanalyse auf Neurowissenschaften trifft*. Frankfurt: Joseph Sandler Research Conference.

Fonagy, P., Gergely, G., Jurist, E.L. and Target, M. (2004). *Affektregulierung, Mentalisierung und die Entwicklung des Selbst*. Stuttgart: Klett-Cotta.

Kandel, E.R. (2006). *Psychiatrie, Psychoanalyse und die neue Biologie des Geistes*. Frankfurt: Suhrkamp.

Laucht, M., Schmidt, M.G. and Esser, G. (2004). *Frühkindliche Regulationsprobleme: Vorläufer von Verhaltensauffälligkeiten des späteren Kindesalters?* In: Papousek, M., Schieche, M., and Wurmser, H. (Hrsg.): *Regulationsstörungen der frühen Kindheit*. Huber, Bern. S. 339–56.

Leuzinger-Bohleber, M. (2006). *Persönlichkeitsstörungen und Depression. Schulenübergreifende Dialoge und Kontroversen*. In: Springer, A., Gerlach, A. and Schlösser, A.-M. (Hrsg.). *Störungen der Persönlichkeit*. Gießen: Psychosozial-Verlag. S. 15–52.

Markowitsch, H.J. and Welzer, H. (2005). *Das Autobiographische Gedächtnis. Hirnorganische Grundlagen und Biosoziale Entwicklung*. Stuttgart: Klett-Cotta.

McLaughlin, D.P. and Harrison, Ch.A. (2006). Parenting Practices of Mothers of Children with ADHD: The Role of Maternal and Child Factors. *Child and Adolescent Mental Health*, 11 (2): 82–89.

Pozzi, M.E. (2001). 'Ritalin für wen? Wie können wir das Bedürfnis nach Ritalin in der psychodynamischen Beratung von Familien mit Kindern unter fünf Jahren verstehen?' *Analytische Kinder—und Jugendlichenpsychotherapie*, Heft, 112 (32): 519–41.

Singer, W. (2006). *Vom Gehirn zum Bewusstsein*. Frankfurt: Suhrkamp.

Swain, J.E., Lorberbaum, J.P., Kose, S. and Strathearn, L. (2007). 'Brain basis of early parent-infant-interactions: psychology, physiology and in vivo functional neuroimaging studies'. *J Child Psychol Psychiat*, 48 (3/4): 262–87.

Attachment, trauma, and psychoanalysis: Where psychoanalysis meets neuroscience

Björn Salomonsson

Commentary on Peter Fonagy's paper including some personal remarks

Before discussing some points of your rich and challenging paper, I would like to sketch the background of our cooperation. I met you as a student in 2004, at the Research Training Programme-course in London, initiated by the International Psychoanalytic Association, where Linda Mayes and you directed the course. During that prolific week, you kindly invited me to link my research project on infants and mothers in Stockholm with your Parent Infant Psychotherapy project at the Anna Freud centre in London. Since then, I have been working with your research psychologist, Michelle Sleed. You have been enormously helpful and welcoming; from providing ideas about design, statistics, and the structure of our paper to lending me your collapsible bike. Thus, profiting from your vast knowledge and generosity has been a real treat, and you have taught me many and valuable things.

This is our common ground as researchers. As analysts, our backgrounds are more divergent. Your writings are influenced by an Anna-Freudian terminology and mode of thinking, to which you add from many other fields of your expert knowledge, such as developmental psychology, attachment theory, and neuroscience. I, on my part, am a psychoanalyst who tends to understand clinical processes in Post-Kleinian object relational terms, but who is also influenced by intersubjectivist and French semiotic thinkers. To this is added my psychoanalytic experience with infants and mothers according to Norman (2001, 2004).

My discussion tonight comes from the vantage point of a psychoanalyst at work. I will focus on how you use the attachment concept to substantiate your perceptions in research and psychoanalytic settings, alternately. As you demonstrate, attachment is a valid concept in systematic research. However, is it a valid *psychoanalytic* concept? That is my question. My hesitation does not diminish my fascination with the *neuroscientific* perspectives that you open up, for example, via the work of Bartels and Zeki. The fact that the same brain areas are activated in romantic and maternal love and that in both cases, there is a suppression of 'critical social assessment of other people and with negative emotions' (Bartels, 2004: 1,164) is indeed thrilling. You substantiate this, both with the everyday observation that 'love is blind', and with the neurochemistry findings of the activation of oxytocin circuits during these psychological processes. As we know, in several mammalian species oxytocin stimulates maternal behaviour and bonding to the offspring. Here, we learn that it is also activated in romantic love.

Now, let me have a *psychoanalytic* look at the relations between two romantic lovers, and mother and infant, respectively. Childcare, says Freud (1905: 223), offers the child unending sexual excitation because his mother regards him with feelings 'derived from her own sexual life: she strokes him, kisses him, rocks him and quite clearly treats him as a substitute for a complete sexual object'. Jean Laplanche (1997: 661) depicts a 'primary seduction' by which the mother transmits her 'enigmatic message' to the child, who thereby gets flooded with her unconscious desire, a desire which he, however, cannot comprehend. These psychoanalytic ideas parallel the fMRI-findings of Bartels and Zeki (2004); the glimmering eyes of the amorous couple and of the mother–baby dyad are not as far apart as our morality would prefer them to be, whether we locate this proximity by the psychoanalytic term 'the Unconscious' or by the neurological term 'the brain'. Similarly, the synaptic suppression of critical judgement according to Bartels and Zeki finds a counterpart in, in Meltzer's (1988: 8) words, that 'the percentage of "beautiful" mothers recorded in the course of psycho-analysis far exceeds the national average and that this appellation clearly refers back to childhood impressions'.

I deliberately said that the psychoanalytic formulations by Freud and so on *paralleled*, not *supported* or *substantiated*, Bartels's and Zeki's fMRI-findings. These researchers aim to find out 'what the two types of attachment [maternal and romantic love] have in common in neural terms' (p. 1155). I, however, see problems in linking concepts from three different fields of knowledge, that is, psychoanalysis, neuroscience, and attachment theory, in order to make one field support the other. Researchers need to correlate data with operationalized entities, and attachment is one such entity. However, formulating experiences within a psychoanalytic framework implies saying something else, for example, that the roots of a mother's love reach down into her unconscious desire. Such formulations have clinical implications. For instance, a mother might have conflicts around nursing because it unconsciously signifies to her forbidden desire or aggression. This might influence the baby who gets fussy at the breast. Whether you agree with such an interpretation or not, you probably agree that it is psychoanalytic; it claims that both partners are involved in unconscious and conflictual emotions and interactions. But is this the same as stating that the baby suffers from an attachment disturbance? If so, I fear that attachment becomes a concept wide enough to cover anything similar to 'human relations'.

Let me exemplify my argument with your moving accounts of James and Stuart, two men in despair. You link their childhood victimizations with their eruptive violence and inability to speak of their own feelings and understand those of others. You describe Stuart's present behaviour as 'the effects of his attachment trauma on his adult personality'. These men suffered trauma, for sure, but what does 'attachment trauma' imply? Traumatized early object relations? I could think of many characters that also suffered an 'attachment trauma', but who showed very different pictures. To sketch some examples; in Wagner's opera *Tristan and Isolde*, Tristan lets life's bright prospects be devastated by his infatuation with his foster father's wife Isolde. Consequent on his adultery, Tristan is deadly wounded. In the end, he lies waiting for Isolde to return and deliver him through death. In an act of impressive self-analysis, Tristan realizes that his infatuation with Isolde resulted from his lifelong and impossible yearning for the parents he lost at birth. He is possessed by an internal tune: *die alte Weise sagt mir's wieder: mich sehnen—und sterben*. That is, 'The ancient tune tells me once more: to desire—and die.' At birth, Tristan was taken care of by his mother's brother, the King, himself a widower. He grew up surrounded by death, and this was his trauma. As I have understood your use of the concept of attachment trauma, Tristan's case seems to belong to this category.

Looking for a case of a directly observed baby, I choose Benny, a boy two months of age. When his mother offers him the breast, he turns his head away and starts screaming. The closer he gets to the nipple, the more he pushes it away. The mother gets desperate. When I speak with Benny, in mother–infant psychoanalytic treatment, he follows me attentively. However, when he moves his gaze towards Mum, he follows me attentively with his eyes. She feels hurt and jealous, and tells me that by his third week of life the health visitor had told her that he hadn't gained enough weight. 'I felt like a no-good mother!' Since then, he has been refusing the nipple. Once again, I assume you would agree that this is a case of attachment trauma.

Tristan lost his parents at birth and was brought up by his uncle. He became a gentle and courageous, unhappy, and yearning young man. His mentalizing capacities seemed well developed, as witnessed by his empathy with his foster father's pain due to his own treachery. Benny's mother relation is clouded by her anxiety and his ambivalence at approaching her nipple. He alternates between contentment and fussiness. James and Stuart are brought up in violence and humiliation. Today, they are jail-birds, always on the alert to assault or be assaulted. All these cases contain many more and unmentioned factors, but to say that they all suffered early object relational trauma is to state their obvious and lowest common denominator. One could also name them 'attachment trauma' but I would ask you to clarify what new substance, from a psychoanalytic perspective, such a formulation adds. As a researcher, I see the value of an operationalized concept, like the one of attachment. As a clinician clothing my experiences in psychoanalytic terms, I find the concept too inclusive and not specific enough.

Thus, as a researcher, I sympathize with your conclusions, and as a psychoanalyst I am more prone to disagree. I will illustrate further from your analysis with Miss C. Ralph Greenson (1968) once wrote about the analyst's daily mistakes. Whereas he made mistakes everyday and openly discussed them, he wondered why colleagues were so reluctant to discuss them. Obviously, you would agree with Greenson's approach; you question your transference interpretations, like when you told Miss C that she feared that you, like her stepfather, might do or say things that she did not anticipate. When you shifted into empathically conveying how badly the stepfather had treated her, you got a better contact with her.

I, you, and all psychoanalysts, make mistakes every day, whatever theory we rely on. We get overwhelmed by the patient's demand to join in their story. In Joseph Sandler's (1993) words, through our 'role-responsiveness' we comply with a script that the patient pushes on to us. Or, to use Racker's (1957) terms, we concord or complement with these identifications. We become directive or defensive, and we rush into or avoid transference interpretations. We fear not to understand our patients, and we try to outsmart them. We get enmeshed in their projections and become confused, aroused, indifferent, tired …

In short, our own unconscious plays tricks on us and colours our counter-transference. In such situations, we might try to drive home an interpretation, although we might *feel* that we 'gently made the intervention that she was equally fearful of how I might at times act in ways or say things that she did not anticipate', as you told Miss C, and as I, too, might have told her. Obviously, we all make mistakes. But can we step back and get a look at what is going on? That is the psychoanalytic challenge, that of scrutinizing our counter-transference and trying to understand whom the patient experiences us to be.

Therefore, as you see, I have no reason to argue about your handling of Miss C. My perspective is rather how you use attachment theory to substantiate your technical changes. You rely on the concept of mentalization (Allen and Fonagy, 2006) to advocate a renewal of technique for certain mental disturbances; not until you have helped the patient mentalizing is it meaningful and helpful to interpret what they fear and wish, whether in the transference or with other people. The analyst should first monitor the traumatized patient's 'readiness to hear comments about thoughts and feelings', as you put it. I completely agree. You state that 'the clinical priority has to be to reduce arousal so that the patient can again think of other perspectives (mentalize)'. I agree with this perspective, too, and I would like to remind all of us that this has been part of good psychoanalytic technique since the arrival of ego-psychology.

However, let us not underestimate the conflictual aspect of mentalization. Suppose you had your interviewee Stuart in psychoanalysis instead. Just like in the interview he would tell you, his analyst, 'I am not a danger to anyone, I am a danger to myself, not other people,' or 'I grabbed a hold of her [mum] by the hair, like, and I was banging her head off. The police had to get me off her.' Stuart might *seem* unable to understand that his words affected you. However, as analysis proceeded you might discover that his inability was only half the story. He might also find it excruciating to think of you as a fellow with feelings, or as someone who is able to think and talk with an adversary instead of just punching his jaw. Such insights can be so painful as to numb his thinking capacities, which could appear like an inability to mentalize. This is not to say that I recommend such notions to be thrown into his face as premature interpretations.

Conclusion

To sum up; the title of your paper is 'Attachment, trauma and psychoanalysis: where psychoanalysis meets neuroscience'. The gist of my argument is this: before we find out where psychoanalysis could meet neuroscience, let us discuss in depth where attachment theory meets psychoanalytic theory. There might be several meeting points but, just like Siegfried Zepf (2006) wrote recently, the topic merits an investigation. I look forward to hearing your points of view, both now and in our future meetings at the Anna Freud Centre.

Notes

1. French psychoanalysts developed a notion of mentalization largely formulated from the economic point of view. Pierre Marty discussed mentalization as a protective buffer in the preconscious system which prevents progressive disorganization (Marty, 1968). He considers mentalization as connecting drive excitations and

mental representations and thereby creating both 'fluidity' and 'constancy' (Marty, 1990, 1991). Mentalization ensures freedom in the use of associations as well as ensuring permanence and stability. At the same time, Pierre Luquet (1981, 1988) discussed the development of different forms of thinking and the reorganization of inner experience alongside this development. In his chapter on a theory of language (Luquet, 1987) he distinguished primary mentalization (which we would consider the absence of RF) with secondary symbolic mentalization. While this form of mentalization was still seen as closely connected to sensory data and primary unconscious fantasies it was nevertheless also seen as representative of these processes and observable in dreams, art, and play. His third level was verbal thought, which he considered most distant from bodily processes. Similar ideas were proposed by André Green (1975), Hanna Segal (1957), and Joyce McDougall (1978), and more recently by Frosch (1995), Busch (1995), and Auerbach (1993; Auerbach and Blatt, 1996).

2. Incidentally, the statistical analysis of the results of these treatments was recently completed and underscored the effectiveness of the psychoanalytic approach. In this sample of young adult personality-disordered subjects who were sequentially assigned to psychoanalysis and psychodynamic psychotherapy, 63% improved significantly on a very conservative composite measure of psychiatric diagnosis, depression, and anxiety. Eighty-three per cent of those who were treated with psychoanalysis, in opposition to just 29% of those treated in psychotherapy, showed these improvements. Only 9% of subjects in psychoanalysis for whom post-termination follow-up data were available did not maintain the gains of treatment.
3. These are normally negotiated, dynamic, multilevel kinship groups.
4. The more cognitively, socially, and behaviourally sophisticated individuals are able to outmanoeuvre and manipulate other individuals to gain control of resources and to gain control of the behaviour of other people. But why such (in evolutionary terms) rapid development? Most evolutionary adaptations have a downside which makes them self-limiting (for example, an increase in the size of a reindeer's antlers will help in combating other males but only up to a point after which the laws of physics make it an obstruction and a handicap). There is no such constraint on social intelligence other than the possibility of totally destroying our ecology (Flinn *et al.*, 2005). The increasing coherence and organization of hominid groups and the ever more sophisticated cognitive capacities that

underpin these bring increasing ecological advantages rather than costs. A virtuous cycle was created of ever increasing ecological dominance and ever higher social intelligence and social complexity. Linguistic and social cognitive capacities were favoured because they enabled our ancestors to anticipate and influence social interactions with other increasingly intelligent humans.

5. Children develop a malleable system that enables them to adapt to the particular mental structures that have evolved within a cultural group as specific adaptations to that environment (Bloom, 2000).
6. It is linked to the mesocorticolimbic dopaminergic reward circuit which also plays a key role in mediating the process of physical (as well as emotional) addiction (Insel, 1997; MacLean, 1990; Panksepp, 1998). It is highly unlikely that nature created a brain system specifically to subserve cocaine and alcohol abuse. It is more likely that addictions are the accidental byproduct of the activation of a biological system that underpins the crucial evolutionary function of attachment (Insel, 1997; MacLean, 1990; Panksepp, 1998). Attachment, then, is an 'addictive disorder' (Insel, 2003).
7. Thus trauma contributes to the foregrounding of self-fragmentation (identity diffusion) because traumatized individuals can make use of discontinuities within the self to adapt to incomprehensible assault from someone connected to them by attachment bonds by 'identifying with the aggressor' (Freud, 1936). One individual, who had been sexually abused as a child and was in prison for rape, vividly described how this happens in answering a question about how his childhood experiences had affected his adult personality: 'I don't think none of its been a setback I think its all been everything has been more positive because its just like lets take, lets take slavery for example errm not from a racist point of view but from a realistic point of view you take a man and you make him work for you, you feed him what you don't want to eat you put him in places you wouldn't want your dog to live but yet still he makes that home his castle he makes gourmet meals out of your trash one mans trash is another mans treasure one man's nightmare is another man's pleasure see and when you have a situation and you know that you are not going to get out of it well you start feeling good in it quicker than you can imagine.'

Bibliography

Allen, J. and Fonagy, P. (2006). *Handbook of Mentalization-Based Treatment.* Chichester: John Wiley & Sons.

Bartels, A. and Zeki, S. (2004). 'The neural correlates of maternal and romantic love'. *NeuroImage.* 21: 1,155–66.

Freud, S. (1905). *Three Essays on Sexuality. S.E 7.*

Greenson, R. (1968). 'The Use of Dream Sequences for Detecting Errors of Technique'. In: (1978) *Explorations in Psychoanalysis.* New York: International Universities Press.

Laplanche, J. (1997). 'The theory of seduction and the problem of the Other'. *Int. J. Psychoanal.*, 78: 653–66.

Meltzer, D. (1988). *The Apprehension of Beauty.* Perthshire: Clunie Press.

Norman, J. (2001). 'The psychoanalyst and the baby: a new look at work with infants'. *Int. J. Psychoanal.*, 82 (1): 83–100.

Norman, J. (2004). 'Transformations of early experiences'. *Int. J. Psychoanal.*, 85: 1,103–22.

Racker, H. (1957). 'The Meanings and Uses of Counter-transference'. *Psychoanal. Quart.* 26: 303–57.

Sandler, J. (1993). 'On communication from patient to analyst: Not everything is projective identification'. *Int. J. Psychoanal.*, 74: 1,097–1,107.

Zepf, S. (2006). 'Attachment theory and psychoanalysis: some remarks from an epistemological and from a Freudian viewpoint'. *Int. J. Psychoanal.*, 87: 1,529–48.

CHAPTER THREE

Coping with children's temperament

William B. Carey, M.D.

Introduction

The main focus of this volume is 'Early Development and its Disturbances' with special emphasis on the 'psychoanalytic perspective on the development of Attention deficit/Hyperactivity Disorder (ADHD) and other psychopathologies'. My assignment is to discuss 'Coping with Children's Temperament' (Carey and McDevitt, 1995) as part of this complicated area. The main observation I would like to make is this: the current neglect of normal temperament differences has resulted in an overdiagnosis of CNS-based (central nervous system based) psychopathology and an overuse of medication. I shall propose that we must do better at recognizing children's temperaments and other normal behaviours and must help parents to cope with them appropriately rather than ignoring or pathologizing them.

Current status of overdiagnosis of ADHD, bipolar disorder, and other psychopathologies

In the USA estimates of the use of psychotropic medications indicate that 5–10% of our children are being so treated. In some areas the rate is greater than this and in some it is less. Several years ago a survey in three schools in Norfolk, Virginia, found that 17% of the students were diagnosed with ADHD and were being given stimulants. The highest rate in my personal acquaintance was two years ago in a prestigious private school for normal wealthy children not far from where I live, where the rate was an astonishing 35%. The USA remains the largest producer and consumer of Ritalin® (and similar products), accounting for 80% of the usage in the world.

There appear to be several important factors contributing to this alarming situation. My intention is to emphasize two of them. One is the general professional and public unfamiliarity with our growing knowledge about normal temperament differences. My other principal concern is with the faulty mental health diagnostic system presently available to us, which makes it easy for normal children to be overdiagnosed. Other factors include the faulty application of the system by practitioners.

Temperament differences in children

The term 'temperament' describes the largely inborn normal differences in behavioural style that make a major contribution to a child's normal daily behaviour. However, temperament differences can contribute to judgements of psychopathology when there is a poor fit between them and the environment and when the traits themselves are misinterpreted as abnormal.

Definition

The most concise definition of temperament is as 'behavioural style' or the characteristic way with which the child experiences and responds to environmental stimuli. It is the 'how' of behaviour rather than the 'what' (the abilities) or the 'why' (the adjustment or motivations). The term is used loosely with varying meanings in general speech and in the non-professional literature with such designations as the judicial or artistic temperament, but these terms probably refer more to other aspects of the overall personality than specifically to the reaction style.

History

The term 'temperament' is not a recent invention. The ancient Greeks and Romans, particularly Galen, developed the humoral theory of health and temperament. Their view was that the variable mixture in the individual of blood, yellow bile, black bile, and phlegm determined whether one would be sanguine, choleric, melancholic, or phlegmatic. Despite the complete lack of scientific evidence for this theory, it dominated thinking in European culture until the 19th century.

The psychology of the early 20th century shifted to the opposite extreme of emphasizing the dominant importance of the environment. Yet, a few prominent physicians generated theories of temperament as mediating between the individual and the setting: Sigmund Freud (1856–1939) had offered the observation that 'each individual ego is endowed from the beginning with its own peculiar dispositions and tendencies' (Freud, 1950). Ivan Pavlov (1849–1936), the Russian physiologist, not only taught us about conditioning but also developed a theory of normal nervous system types. Arnold Gesell (1880–1961) in New Haven, Connecticut, in addition to establishing the earliest tables of normal developmental milestones, described alpha, beta, and gamma temperamental types. The theories of these three and a few others were paid little attention then because they were ahead of their times.

Not until 1956 was a well constructed clinical investigation of temperament launched by Alexander Thomas, Stella Chess, and associates in the New York Longitudinal Study. They were the real pioneers who deserve the credit for having scientifically demonstrated the nature and clinical significance of these largely innate behavioural style traits. This was a major turning point in psychological theory. Both before and since then several developmental psychologists have proposed different sets of traits. However, because these alternative attempts have been derived more from computer analysis of selected data than from actual clinical observations, they have been less valuable for clinical work and are used almost exclusively for research (Chess and Thomas, 1984; Thomas, Chess, and Birch, 1968).

Traits and clusters

On the basis of discussions with parents and from their own observations, Thomas and Chess identified nine normal traits that they believed would predispose some children to being more likely to develop reactive behaviour problems in the first dozen years of life (see Table 1). These traits are: activity; rhythmicity/predictability; approach/withdrawal (the initial response to novelty or challenge); adaptability/flexibility; intensity (the usual amount of energy of responses, whether positive or negative); mood (the typical amount of friendly and positive reactions observed, as opposed to unfriendly and negative ones); persistence and attention span; distractibility; and sensory threshold/sensitivity. The New York group proposed that these traits themselves are all normal whether

Table 1. The nine NYLS dimensions of temperament.

1. *Activity: The amount of physical motion during sleep eating play dressing bathing and so forth.*
   a) Rhythmicity: The regularity of physiologic functions such as hunger sleep and elimination.
   b) Approach/withdrawal: The nature of initial responses to new stimuli such as people, situations, places, foods, toys, and procedures.
   c) Adaptability: The ease or difficulty with which reactions to stimuli can be modified in a desired way. Flexibility.
   d) Intensity: The energy level of responses, regardless of quality or direction.
   e) Mood: The amount of pleasant and friendly or unpleasant and unfriendly behaviour in various situations (overt behaviour; not assumed internal feelings).
   f) Persistence/attention span: The length of time that particular activities are pursued by the child, with or without obstacles.
   g) Distractibility: The effectiveness of extraneous stimuli in interfering with on-going behaviours.
   h) Sensory threshold: The amount of stimulation, such as sounds or light, necessary to evoke discernable responses in the child.

(Adapted from Thomas and Chess, 1977).

high or low, but the possibility of abnormality at the far extremes remained to be clarified.

These nine traits formed three clusters used for research purposes. The 'difficult' children were low in approach, adaptability, mood, and regularity, and conversely high in intensity. 'Easy' children showed the opposite. The 'slow-to-warm-up' children were like the difficult ones but were less intense, that is, they were essentially shy children. Their research project, which began in 1956 with 133 New York children, demonstrated that difficult and stwu children were much more likely than easy ones to develop reactive behaviour problems in the first 12 years.

Goodness or poorness of fit

However, it soon became apparent that there were no traits that were always conducive to problems or always conducive to satisfactory emotional and behavioural health. What mattered most of all was the 'goodness or poorness of the fit' between the traits presented by the child and the expectations and values of the parents or other caregivers. The compatibility or discord between them led to harmonious or stressful interactions and thus to healthy function or dysfunction in the child. For example, the inflexible and negative child might be at particular risk of a difficult adult interaction but equally important would be the understanding, tolerance, and management skills of the adult.

We must recognize that the child's temperament can actually change the impact of the environment:

1. by being more sensitive to some aspects of it than others
   i. by selecting different aspects of it with which to engage and react; and
   ii. by actually evoking changes in it.

Poor fit is not necessarily a sign of psychopathology but is often treated as such.

Origins and stability

Evidence from twin and adoption studies tells us that these temperament traits are about 50% genetically determined. The rest come from pre-, peri-, and post-natal non-genetic physical factors and from the psychosocial environment. Stability is small at first but increases with age, at least up until adolescence. However, temperament traits are never completely fixed or completely changeable.

Assessment

The New York group employed long and detailed interviews to obtain descriptions of the characteristics of their subjects. This process was too cumbersome for further applications. With a group of developmental psychologists, especially Sean McDevitt, I developed a series of five different parent questionnaires for ages one month through twelve years to facilitate the collection and rating of the same data content for research or consultative purposes. They can be completed by the parent in 20 to 30 minutes and scored by the staff of the professional person in about 10 minutes. A computer scoring system is even faster. For routine use by primary care paediatricians I have recommended the use of abbreviated interviewing when there is some concern but questionnaires for more complicated cases. Direct observation of the child can also help to complete the assessment.

Practical importance

The impact of the child's temperament on the parents, teachers, and others involved, and on the child his or herself, is great. The child's behavioural style influences how the caregivers feel about themselves and how they go about their parenting practices. The effects on the children are even greater:

i. physical: predisposing to certain problems such as accidents and child abuse, and affecting others, such as when greater attention is paid to the irritable, sick child;
ii. developmental: some modification of the timing and ease of achievement of walking, toilet training, acquisition of expressive language, and so forth;
iii. social behavioural adjustment: as demonstrated by Thomas and Chess;
iv. school performance: to be discussed shortly (see Keogh, 2003);
v. various other aspects of adjustment: such as self-regulation, emotional state, and coping skills; and
vi. symptoms of physical function such as disruptions to eating, sleeping, and elimination. (Table 2)

Table 2. BASICS profile of behavioural adjustment.

Area of behavioural adjustment emotions	*Concerns: behaviour, emotions, functions*
Behaviour competence in social relationships. Attachment. Skills, success, caring cooperation, involvement, reliance. Parents, siblings, peers, teachers, other adults.	Undersocialization: aggression, opposition, withdrawal.
Achievements: task performance and mastery in school, home, community. High or sufficient achievement, effort, motivation, and satisfaction	Poor achievement or failure. Excessive preoccupation with work or play.
Self-relations. Self-assurance. Self-esteem about academics, social worth, appearance, physical abilities. Self-care, good health and safety attitudes, practices, handling personal stress. Self-control or regulation, actions, feelings.	Poor self-esteem. Poor body image. Self-neglect, risk taking. Overconcern for oneself. Over-control inhibition or under-control impulsivity.
Internal status: feeling and thinking. Reasonable contentment. Thought clarity.	Anxiety. Depression. Thought disturbance (for example, obsessions).
Coping or problem-solving patterns. Direct and appropriate engagement Identifies problems; plans solutions; works on solutions; persists at solutions; revises solutions; gets help for solutions.	Ineffective, maladaptive problem solving with excessive use of denial, avoidance or repression.
Symptoms of physical function. Comfortable function.	Moderate to severe symptoms in eating, sleeping elimination gender unexplained physical complaints, repetitive behaviours.

Adapted from: Carey, W.B. (in press).

The matter of the probable role of temperament in attachment has been investigated but has been resisted by some who believe that parental care is the entire explanation for the outcome. However, a recent review of genetic factors in attachment seems to support a contribution from the child, which is likely to be temperament (Bakermans-Kranenburg and van Jzendoorn, 2007).

Management

When the parental concern is simply about an annoying temperament trait in a child who is not dysfunctional, the best strategy for the clinician is to recognize the traits as temperament and not dysfunction and to:

i. revise the caregiver's understanding and handling to improve the fit:
ii. suggest relief for the caregivers when necessary by environmental intervention; and
iii. refer to a mental health specialist for this concern only if there are complex reactive problems.

The most effective parent counselling has proven to be to help them to understand the nature of the specific temperament traits, to aid them in tolerating them better, and to manage them more skillfully with accommodation rather than with punitive discipline, psychotherapy, or medication.

Current status of knowledge and research

Before taking up a more detailed review of the impact of temperament on social adjustment and school performance, presented here are a few general thoughts about the current status of temperament research and diffusion of the information to the professions and to the general public. For 50 years convincing evidence has been accumulating that temperament exists, that it matters greatly clinically, and that the appropriate management is different from that of behaviour problems (Carey and McDevitt, 1995). Yet, the subject is not even mentioned in about half of the textbooks for child health professionals or in popular advice books for parents. Current research is being done almost entirely by academic developmental psychologists, who apparently are more interested in theoretical issues such as factor structures and predictions than in helping children and their parents deal with their concerns right now.

Relationship of temperament to ADHD and other psychopathology

Having described briefly what we know about temperament, the discussion focuses now in greater detail on what the relationship seems to be between it and psychopathology and in particular ADHD.

The current Diagnostic and Statistical Manual (DSM-IV-TR APA 2000) criteria for the ADHD diagnosis are familiar: 6/9 inattention symptoms or 6/9 hyperactivity-impulsivity symptoms ('that is maladaptive and inconsistent with developmental level') for at least six months with some starting before seven years, with impairment in at least two settings, and not due to some other cause.

The neurological explanation

The DSM does not say so explicitly but virtually all users assume that this is a 'neurodevelopmental disorder', and that some degree of intrinsic cerebral malfunction is present (Barkley, 1998). Stimulants and other drugs are widely recommended as a requirement to repair a supposedly defective nervous system and psychosocial treatments are widely neglected.

Psychological interpretations

The psychoanalytic view of ADHD, as I understand it, is that a deficiency of early relationships has failed to 'provide the child with sufficiently stable supporting ego functions' or has resulted in insufficient internalization of impulse controls. Early emotional trauma may have been involved. Preferred treatment is a 'corrective emotional experience' (Leuzinger-Bohleber, Fischmann and Laezar, 2008; Sugarman, 2006).

Role of temperament

Both the neurological and psychological explanations have some empirical support, more for the latter. However, we must ask how the child's temperament, which is caused by neither a cerebral abnormality nor by experience being reared, might be involved with the inappropriate diagnosis of ADHD. There are two principal ways in which this is happening.

1 Temperament–environment misfit

When there is a poor fit between the temperament and the adult management, a reactive behaviour problem may emerge. This resulting problem may be misinterpreted as being the result of a nervous system defect for which drug treatment is recommended.

Seven-year-old Sally in an example of this. She was a likeable but somewhat 'difficult' child who had nevertheless been well adjusted at home and in kindergarten and first grade because of the understanding and skilful handling by her parents and teachers. In second grade she was assigned to a class with a rigid, demanding teacher. While some parents thought that this new teacher was excellent for their disorganized children, the poor fit was not helpful for Sally. Sally did not pay sufficient attention to the teacher and follow her directions about class or homework. The teacher advised her parents to seek medical intervention for her problems including the possible use of medications. Clinical evaluation quickly revealed that she did not have ADHD or other psychopathology but just a poor fit with her teacher and a resulting reaction. There was a power struggle between an inflexible child and an inflexible teacher. The paediatric consultant advised the parents to have a conference with the inexperienced teacher to explain to her what kind of child she was, what management had worked for them at home, and that, although the teacher should not modify her requirements and expectations for achievement, she could be more flexible in allowing extra time for young children who do not make changes quickly or easily. With this plan in effect, her performance in school improved rapidly to her previous level. Her temperament continued the same but the behavioural disturbance disappeared. No DSM diagnosis was applied and no medication was needed or prescribed. Since a simple change in management brought such a dramatic improvement that one could readily discard the mistaken notion of brain malfunction. Years later Sally is working successfully as a teacher herself.

2 *Temperament itself pathologized*

Another common problem is that the temperament itself may be misdiagnosed as an abnormality. Since many teachers do not know about or recognize normal temperament variations, they may suggest a diagnosis of ADHD because they do not have at their disposal sufficient training or experience to arrive at the correct conclusion.

A good example of this is Steve, a five-year-old boy who was just finishing a year in a preschool childcare centre and who was getting ready to enter kindergarten. On the last day his preschool teacher confidently informed his mother that Steve had ADHD and should be taking Ritalin®. His surprised and skeptical parents sought a more informed opinion. His parents recognized that he had a challenging temperament but they had been able to manage him well enough to avoid reactive behaviour problems. A review of his situation by his paediatrician revealed that he was not overactive, inattentive, or dysfunctional. He was a child with the low adaptability and other characteristics of a 'difficult' child but who was being managed well and successfully by his parents. The preschool teacher found him to be unlike most of her other students and, being unaware of normal temperament variations, had assumed that his differences were due to ADHD. No pathological diagnosis was called for and no medication. When Steve started kindergarten soon after, his experienced teacher regarded him as normal.

3 *Temperament as a precursor to ADHD?*

The next question is whether the child's temperament can lead directly to an appropriate diagnosis of ADHD. The nebulous DSM criteria for ADHD complicate the discussion. Confusing the situation are the facts that the majority of those now getting the ADHD diagnosis have a 'comorbid' mental health condition, and the fact that half of all children are more active or less attentive than average, or both. Perhaps for these children their 'comorbid' behaviour or cognitive symptoms are the real underlying issue in children who just happen also to be more active or inattentive than average. Does that mean that those numerous children have ADHD?

On the other hand, if one uses a more stringent definition of ADHD as in the ICD-10 (WHO, 1992), then only 1–2% can be said to be affected (Schachar and Tannock, 2002). The ICD criteria are not just variations of normal, like 'often talks excessively' or 'often has difficulty awaiting turn' as in the DSM, but rather describe 'disorganized, ill-regulated, and excessive activity', which is 'often reckless and impulsive, prone to accidents', and so forth. For these few the extreme activity or inattention may be derived from something other than a normal temperament variation and may possibly be organic in origin, such as with trauma, lead poisoning, or infection. This question remains unresolved, awaiting the establishment of clearer diagnostic criteria.

Relationship of temperament to other psychopathology

Bipolar disorder is now being widely diagnosed in the USA. This newly fashionable condition is so loosely and confusingly defined that it is likely that many children who are normally active, intense, non-adaptable, or otherwise aversive, are being erroneously labelled as having mania and being introduced to drug treatment.

Also, the difference between Social Anxiety Disorder and poorly supported normal shyness has yet to be clarified. Medication for shyness is a questionable practice.

Summary about temperament

The main points to retain about temperament differences in children and psychopathology are that temperament–caregiver misfits may result in reactive behaviour problems, which may be misdiagnosed as being based on CNS abnormality, as with ADHD. The traits themselves may be misinterpreted as abnormal; and the contribution of temperament to correctly diagnosed ADHD (dysfunction related directly to overactivity or inattention) remains obscure largely as the result of the ambiguities of the ADHD definition.

Problems with the DSM diagnostic system

One should not leave this discussion of the connections between temperament and psychopathology without attempting to clarify the deficiencies of the DSM diagnostic system of the American Psychiatric Association. The current Fourth Edition is an improvement over the previous ones and all are better than the complete absence of any common language that existed just a few decades ago. One hopes that the Fifth Edition will advance the process further. The problems with this present version are part of our current difficulties with clinical and research diagnosis.

The DSM system, as a whole, rests on a static, categorical disease model, which often does not fit with observable reality. It is a catalogue of problems, which fails among other omissions to mention temperament and other normal behaviours. A better system, as proposed by Jensen *et al.* (2006), would be dimensional, adaptational, developmental, and contextual. Despite all of these shortcomings, there has been a generally uncritical acceptance of the DSM system by professionals using it, such as by the American Academy of Pediatrics. There is also extensive evidence that, at the practical level, diagnoses are frequently being applied without the required criteria being met.

Several other diagnostic schemes are available, such as the ICD-10 (WHO, 1992), DSM-PC (AAP, 1996), the DC 0-3 (NCIP, 2005). None of them have sufficient breadth or recognition of the child's assets and interactions to meet the needs of this confusing situation.

Specifically, the defects in the diagnostic criteria for ADHD are extensive. The ADHD behaviours are not clearly distinguishable from normal temperament variations. The role of the environment and interactions with it are completely ignored. There is no clear evidence that the symptoms defining ADHD, such as frequently talking excessively, are related to brain malfunction. The diagnostic questionnaires now in use are highly subjective and impressionistic. My presentation of these objections and several others at the 1998 NIH [National Institute of Health] Consensus Conference on ADHD (Carey, 2002) have been ignored by the leaders in the ADHD field.

To recapitulate this part of my paper, it seems that a substantial part of the confusion in diagnosis today is the failings of the current system.

Suggested changes to improve the situation

We all care deeply about the children entrusted to our care and to the parents and teachers who are trying to raise them as healthy human beings. What can we do to help?

We can promote a broader and deeper understanding of normal temperament and behavioural adjustment. Instruction about these matters should be included in the education of all child health and childcare professions. This information is readily available. Also, there has been suggested a summary of adjustment that is not just a list of problems but is a profile of six BASICS areas of function: Behaviour or social competence; Achievements; Self relations: self-esteem, care, and control; Internal status: feelings and thinking; Coping strategies; and Symptoms of physical function: eating, elimination, sleeping, and so forth. Attachment is included but there are other important measures of outcome. (See Table 2.)

Also required is clearer diagnostic criteria for what is abnormal, as just mentioned. The DSM is not sacred and needs a radical revision.

Furthermore, we need better public education. Of the industrialized nations, only in the USA and New Zealand can drug companies advertise directly to the public about their products requiring prescription from physicians. This mistaken policy has led many citizens to expect a 'quick fix'—a pill or combination of pills that will quickly make life beautiful again. The professional medical, psychological, and educational organizations should take the lead here.

Also needing revision are other problems contributing to the confusion, such as large payments from drug companies to physicians to get them to use and speak well of their products.

Conclusion

The central message of this paper is that the fully competent child physical and mental health professional needs a working knowledge of temperament differences and how to help parents to cope with them by better understanding and tolerating them, and by management based on accommodation rather than behaviour modification, punishment, psychotherapy, or medication. Only when parental accommodation is insufficient to resolve the 'poor fit', should professional intervention be considered appropriate.

This knowledge will help these persons to recognize normal variants, such as low adaptability, which usually needs only parent counselling to keep the child functioning well. It should enable the professional to distinguish that some psychopathology is the result of the stress from a poor fit between the temperament and the caregiver handling, which can usually be altered adequately by parent counselling, or, when severe, by psychiatric intervention, but not by medication. It should also help the clinician comprehend that these results of poor fits, and even just the temperament itself, are frequently being misdiagnosed as ADHD. Such a point of view will lead to the understanding that, although a very small number of children (perhaps 1–2%) are dysfunctional because of very high and pervasive activity or inattention alone, much of the present diagnosis of ADHD is probably incorrect and leads to an unjustified use of psychotropic medications.

Sources for recommended temperament questionnaires based on NYLS traits

For parent ratings: Behavioral/Developmental Initiatives, 14636 N 55th Street, Scottsdale AZ 85254, USA.

Tel.: 800-405-2313. Website: http://www.b-di.com (Dr. Carey helped to start the B-D I firm but is not an officer or owner of it.)

For teacher ratings: Roy P. Martin, Ph.D., 325 Aderhold Hall, University of Georgia, Athens, GA 30602, USA.

Bibliography

American Academy of Pediatrics. (1996). *The Classification of Child and Adolescent Mental Diagnoses in Primary Care: (DSM-PC) Child and Adolescent Version*. Elk Grove Village, IL.

American Psychiatric Association. (2000). *Diagnostic and Statistical Manual of Mental Disorders* 4th *edition.* (DSM-IV) Washington, D.C. DSM-IV-T.

Bakermans-Kranenburg, M. and van, I. Jzendoorn, M. (2007). 'Research Review: Genetic vulnerability or differential susceptibility in child development: the case of attachment'. *J. Child Psychol. Psychiat.* 48 (12): 1,160–73.

Barkley, R.A. (1998). 'Attention-deficit hyperactivity disorder'. *Sci. Am.* 279: 66–71.

Carey, W.B. (2002). 'Is ADHD a Valid Disorder?' In: Jensen, P.J. and Cooper, J.R. (eds) *ADHD: State of the Science: Best Practices.* Kingston, N.J., Civic Research Institute.

Carey, W.B. and McDevitt, S.C. (1995). *Coping with Children's Temperament: A Guide for Professionals.* New York: Basic Books.

Carey, W.B. (2009) 'Normal differences in temperament and behavioral adjustment'. In: Carey, W.B. and Crocker, A.C., *et al.* (eds) *Development-Behavioral Pediatrics*. 4th edn. Philadelphia: Elsevier.

Chess, S. and Thomas, A. (1984). *Origins and Evolution of Behavior Disorders from Infancy to Early Adult Life.* New York: Brunner/Mazel.

Freud, S. (1950). 'Analysis, terminable and interminable'. *Collected Papers*. 5: 316. London: Hogarth Press.

ICD [International Classification of Diseases] (1992). 10th edn. Geneva: World Health Organization.

Jensen, P.S., Knapp, P. and Mrazak, D.A. (2006). *Towards a new diagnostic system for child psychopathology*. New York: Guilford

Keogh, B.K. (2003). *Temperament in the Classroom*. Baltimore: Brookes.

Leuzinger-Bohleber, M., Fischmann, T. and Läzer, L. (2008). 'Triangulierung—ein zentrales Konzept der Frankfurter Präventionsstudie?' In: Dammasch, F. Katzenbach, D. und Ruth, J. (Hg.) *Triangulierung*. Lernen, Denken und Handeln aus psychoanalytischer Sicht. Frankfurt a. M.: Brandes & Apsel, pp. 131–65.

National Center for Clinical Infant Programs (2005). *Diagnostic Classification. Zero To Three. (DC: 0-3) 1994. Revised DC: 0-3R.* Washington DC.

Rutter, M. and Taylor, E. (eds). *Child and Adolescent Psychiatry.* 4th edn. Oxford, UK. Blackwell. pp. 399–418.

Schachar, R. and Tannock, R. (2002). 'Syndromes of hyperactivity and attention deficit'. In:

Sugarman, A. (2006). 'ADHD and trauma'. *Int. J. Psycoanal,* 87: 237–41.

Thomas, A. and Chess, A. (1977). *Temperament and Development.* New York: Brunner/Mazel.

Thomas, A., Chess, S. and Birch, H.G. (1968). *Temperament and Behavior Disorders in Children*. New York: NYU Press.

World Health Organization. (1992). *International Statistical Classification of Diseases and Related Health Problems* (10th Rev.). Geneva, Switzerland.

Books for parents

Carey, W.B. (with Jablow, M.) (1997). *Understanding Your Child's Temperament.* New York: Macmillan. Revised edition. Philadelphia: Xlibris.

Kurcinka, M.S. (1991) *Raising Your Spirited Child.* New York: HarperCollins.

Turecki, S. and Tonner, L. (1985) *The Difficult Child*. New York: Bantam.

DISCUSSION OF WILLIAM B. CAREY'S PAPER

Coping with children's temperament: Early development and its disturbances

Jorge Canestri

Being in agreement with William Carey's work in many ways, in my comment I will attempt to link his thoughts to some psychoanalytical concepts.

To begin with, Carey emphasizes the main focus of his thesis: 'the current neglect of normal temperament differences has resulted in an overdiagnosis of CNS-based psychopathology and an overuse of medication'. This situation, which appears to be extremely worrying in the USA according to the data provided by the author, is unfortunately not very different in Europe. The statements of some European psychoanalytical societies against the indiscriminate use of Ritalin® and other psychotropic drugs, also on very young children, have remained—as usual—unheard.

The author rightly reminds us that there are temperamental differences in children. The term 'temperament' is not common in psychoanalysis, but the concept can be easily traced. Carey defines temperament as 'the characteristic way with which the child experiences and responds to environmental stimuli', and he outlines a short but interesting history of the concept—from the Romans and Greeks to the research carried out by Thomas and Chess, from 1956 onwards (New York Longitudinal Study), resulting in nine normal traits and three clusters (difficult, easy, and slow-to-warm-up children).

Carey observes how early 20th-century psychology, in contrast with that of previous centuries, emphasized the dominant importance of the environment, with a few exceptions, among them that of Freud, who wrote in 'Analysis Terminable and Interminable' (1937: 393): 'each individual ego is endowed from the beginning with its own peculiar dispositions and tendencies'. The author of 'Coping with Children's Temperament' attributes to the 'general professional and public unfamiliarity with our growing knowledge about normal temperament differences' an important responsibility for producing this state of affairs.

I could say that a great deal of contemporary psychoanalysis, by excessively accentuating the effect of the environment and not acknowledging what Freud attributed to 'nature', is no less responsible. The match therefore seems to be between a so-called 'organic' type of psychiatry that is blind to the relationship between natural gifts and environment, and a psychoanalysis that by neglecting the Freudian concept of 'complementary series', ends up by never including X in its equations, X being one of the firm assumptions of the father of psychoanalysis. For a long time it appeared that X—that is, the inborn factors, dispositions, and tendencies—were not known and it was therefore useless to include them. I think that today it is not possible, or advisable, to continue along this line, especially when we see the effects that this contraposition between 'organicism' and 'environmentalism' can provoke. The author shows us how ignorance about inborn temperamental differences can lead to unfounded, incorrect, and harmful diagnoses.

What are we really discussing in this and in many other cases, if not the classical, and in many ways outdated, 'nature/nurture' controversy—a controversy that from the point of view of biologists is meaningless?

Let us take a step backwards. Just as 'temperament' does not appear in Freudian terminology (at the most, the term 'temperamental variations' is mentioned by Breuer in 'Studies on Hysteria, III', pp. 196–197), neither do 'nature/nurture'. Let us look at the terms used by Freud. Three terms occur frequently: 'disposition' (*Veranlagung*), 'constitutional or innate' (*Verfassungsmäßig; Angeboren; Natürlich*) and 'heredity' (*Erblichkeit; Vererbung*). Some terms conceptually linked to the previous terms are also used less frequently by Freud, such as *Verkommenheit*, that is, 'degeneracy', and *Tendenz*, that is, 'proclivity'. The real problem however is not the terminology but, rather, the conceptual content.

I will not present you with a long list of all the occasions on which Freud referred to disposition, constitutional factors, or heredity. I hope you will trust me if I tell you that we must begin with the letters to Fliess and finish with 'Analysis Terminable and Interminable'. In this latter work, Freud emphasizes how the economic, quantitative, and constitutional factor is the most neglected in psychoanalysis when dealing with studying the ego's struggle to restrain the drives. It is not superfluous to recall that the concept invented by Freud to account for the etiology of neuroses, that is, the concept of *complementary series*, included in the 'endogenous factor'—called *fixation*—both childhood experiences *and* hereditary constitution. This concept is in agreement with contemporary etiologic research that privileges *multi-factorial models of illness* that take due account of the complexity principle. As Robert N. Emde (1988: 69) states in his work 'Development terminable and interminable—1. Innate and motivational factors from infancy': 'Modern biology has been characterized as the biology of organized complexity, with modern developmental biology as the biology of increasingly organized complexity' (p. 24). The more we delve into the so-called 'nature/nurture' controversy, the more we understand the complexity of the nature/nurture relationship. However, it is possible to say that disposition can be considered as potentiality, that is, waiting for realization, unless we are faced with an illness of clearly genetic origin; but even in some of these cases, as in the well-known example of phenylketonuria, a diet free of phenylalanine, that is, adequate environmental cure, would avoid the development of the serious consequences deriving from the enzymatic defect. The influence of each dispositional and environmental element upon the other is constant and may transform the potential in form and substance. Nevertheless, it is not sufficient to describe a reciprocal and generic influence; it is necessary to go ahead with the research for specificity.

While apparently, in the nature/nurture polarity, the problematic and obscure term of the equation was 'nature'—Freud's X that it was impossible to access (let us not forget that genetics, as we know it, took its first steps in 1909)—the other term, interpreting 'nurture' as environment, did not seem to be much of an obstacle. But also in this case things turn out to be more complex than they appear. In the first place it would be wrong to consider the environment as a completely independent variable because, as R. Lewontin (2000) said, the environment of a living being might not only be the totality of independent and pre-existing problems to which the living beings have to find solutions inasmuch as living beings do not simply solve problems, but they also might create them. We do not always take into account that human beings, from a certain point onwards, condition their environment. Emde (1988: 26) is aware of this when he says that:

> ... behavioural development is seen in terms of reciprocal relationships between the developing infant and the environment; new behaviours which result from this reciprocity, in turn, influence both infant and environment, and such an iterative process continues as the complexity of organization increases.

The incidence of infantile behaviour on the environment conditions the response of the environment and provokes new responses that are in their turn conditioning. Carey insists that this is where the need derives for parents, teachers, and professionals to have knowledge of the inborn and *normal* temperamental variety of children, in order to guarantee an adequate and non-iatrogenic response.

Studies carried out on monozygotic twins compared with non-monozygotic twins, adopted siblings, or casual couples, have revealed that environmental effects that are not shared—for example the pre-natal developmental environment or the casual variations of the genetic pool—can prove to be more important than the shared ones. These results are of great importance in understanding mental pathology.

It is also important to mention that genes are activated or deactivated during development in constant interaction with the environment, and that this influence is manifested throughout the whole course of the individual's existence. Many researches could be mentioned here, but among them it is worth recalling the studies of S. Rutherford and S. Lindquist (1998, 2002) on the 'chaperon' proteins and on the expression of genetic potentialities that are mute or hidden until an environmental event exposes them. The example of

HSP proteins (Heat Shock Proteins 90) reveals the existence within the genome of *potentialites that are not expressed,* but are available for manifestation in certain environmental conditions and *at any age of the individual.* Gene effects vary with the environment in which development takes place and environmental effects vary with the genetic constitution of the organism growing up in that environment. Nature and nurture coexist in reciprocity and this reciprocity begins before birth and continues throughout life.

It is clear that the environment does not alter the nature of the genetic pool, but it does modify the nature of the information that the cells can consult, and consequently the proteins that they can produce. These are phenomena of differential consultation. Recent studies better clarify how environmental risk factors are moderated by genetic influences, showing the importance of gene-environment interactions in humans. Let us consider the example of the MAOA gene, the gene that encodes MonoAmine Oxidase A, the enzyme that degrades amine neurotransmitters, such as dopamine, norepinephrine, and serotonin. Caspi *et al.* (2002: 851–854) in 'Role of Genotype in the Cycle of Violence in Maltreated Children' studied a large sample of male children from birth to adulthood to determine why some children who are maltreated grow up to develop antisocial behaviour, whereas others do not. Functional promoter polymorphism in the MAOA gene was found to moderate the effect of maltreatment. Maltreated children with a genotype conferring high levels of MAOA expression were less likely to develop antisocial problems. They concluded that their findings may partly explain why not all victims of maltreatment grow up to victimize others, and they provided epidemiologic evidence that genotypes can moderate children's sensitivity to environmental insults. These results were confirmed by the successive report (Caspi, 2003) on the serotonin transporter gene and the effect on the occurrence of depressive disorder, whereby the susceptibility gene had little effect in the absence of environmental stress or adversity, but had a substantial effect in moderating the environmental risk effect. In other words, the adverse environment had little effect in the absence of genetic susceptibility, but had a big effect in its presence (Rutter, 2005: 3–18).

In conclusion we can say that genes, in the great majority of cases, do not cause disease directly, rather, they determine only the way an organism responds to the environment. As was predictable, the progress made in genetics and molecular biology has begun to give form to the X of the Freudian equation. Today hypotheses about the cause of a number of diseases have evolved from one-cause theory to the view that it is a complex, multi-factorial, disorder caused by the confluence of many different types of risk factors (that is, genetic, biological, environmental, and psychosocial) with every type having a small effect on the increasing vulnerability to the disorder through their additive and *interactive* effects. Environmental stimulation in several models of disease (for example, neurodegenerative) has demonstrated that therapy based on the principles of environmental enrichment might benefit disease sufferers. Neurosciences have also demonstrated that the reorganization of cortical pathways is possible not only in early childhood—even if adaptation to one's own early environment would be expected to have the greatest impact—but that the brain is able to incorporate the structure of experience in its own structure through the lifespan. West and King (1987: 549–562) coined the term 'ontogenetic niche' to emphasize that the organism develops within an ecologic and social setting which, like its genes, it shares with its parents, school, and peer group environment.

I think that when he writes that 'the child's temperament (we are speaking of normal variations) can actually change the impact of the environment', Carey aligns himself with the concept I have attempted to outline. The interaction between temperament (50% conditioned genetically, as the author reminds us) and the environment, may or may not fit, but this does not necessarily mean that a pathology is in action. The factors that influence the remaining 50% are, as Carey says, of a multiple nature (pre-, peri-, and postnatal non-genetic physical factors and psycho-social environment). He accurately describes both the effect that the temperament of the child has on the parents and teachers, and the effect that the feedback from the environment has on the child, which is certainly of much greater significance. His suggestions for a satisfactory management of the problem that may result as the consequence of an inadequate fit can certainly be shared without reserve by analysts.

Carey notes a dissociation between research on temperament at an academic level and the diffusion of such knowledge among professionals and the public in general. I have tried to point out a similar deficit in post-Freudian psychoanalytic culture concerning research that provides content to the Freudian X of the complementary series and to his multi-factorial models of illness.

Relative to psychopathology, and more specifically to ADHD, the diagnostic criteria of the Diagnostic and Statistical Manual (DSM-IV-TR APA 2009) are well known. Carey rightly underlines the shortcomings of the DSM: 'ADHA behaviours are not clearly distinguishable from normal temperament variations [and] the role of environment and interactions ... are completely ignored.' As can be seen, these two characteristics of the DSM openly contradict the position that I have tried to describe previously.

The hypothesis of a 'neurodevelopmental disorder' to which the DSM implicitly adheres, has 'some support' (Carey) coming from molecular genetics and some from neural imaging (fMRI [functional Magnetic Resonance Imaging]; PET [Positron Emission Tomography]; Spect [Single photo emission computed tomography]). Genetical studies worked on the DBH gene, the locus that encodes the enzyme dopamine-ß-hydroxylase, which converts dopamine in norepinephrine, on the association of DRD4 in children with comorbid conduct problems, and so on. Neural imaging analysed the frontal lobe, the basal ganglia, and the vermis (see for example, The ADHD Molecular Genetics Network, 2002; Faraone *et al.*, 2002, 2008; Holmes *et al.*, 2002). As far as I know, and as Faraone in his comment of an international meeting on ADHD says: 'Despite recent advances, more work is needed to better characterize heritable aspects of the ADHD phenotype as well as the actual candidate genes themselves.' This indicates that the evidence we have accumulated so far is poor and not very specific.

Psychoanalytical interpretation, linked to an early relationship failure to provide the child with sufficiently stable supporting ego functions, insufficiently internalized impulse controls, and early emotional trauma (Leuzinger-Bohleber, Fischman and Laezer, 2008 and Sugarman, 2006, quoted by Carey) appears to have, as Carey comments, a greater empirical basis. I will not dwell longer on these aspects, which we are more familiar with. It is sufficient simply to mention the recent panel at the Rio de Janeiro Congress and the report written by Sugarman (2006). As the report says, the panelists agreed on the contribution of early trauma. Bürgin states that ADHD may be considered as a syndrome, 'but never an illness, even if common genetic base is postulate'. And, in agreement with what was said above, that: 'Any possible genetic factor requires a specific situation and environment for its expression.' The work presented by Marianne Leuzinger-Bohleber follows the same lines, with recommendations that are extremely close to those of our author—supervision, education, psychological therapies, contact and training of parents, and cooperation with social and mental health organizations.

I believe, on the other hand, that it is important to emphasize Carey's insistence on the role that failure to acknowledge a child's temperament, with its normal variations, can play in the inappropriate diagnosis of ADHD. Carey traces two main modalities through which this can happen. The first concerns the misfit between temperament and environment. When this misfit is not recognized and confronted as such, it may lead to a diagnosis of ADHD and a consequent indication for medication. The clinical example of Sally well illustrates this situation. The second modality refers to attributing a pathological meaning to the normal variations of a child's temperament, as in Steve's case.

One thing that must always be taken into consideration when defining certain behaviour as normal or pathological is the variation that results from comparing different environments and cultures. A comparative study carried out between a French centre for child and adolescent psychopathology and an Italian one, demonstrated that children who were diagnosed as normal in Italy, were considered to be hyperactive (and in some cases suspected as ADHD) by the French. Vice versa, children considered as normal in France were easily considered to be too dull, too rigid, and complaisant—if not obsessive—by Italian child neuropsychiatrists. In this case the cultures are very close to each other, but we can imagine what 'diagnostic' differences could be reached if the cultures were further apart.

Carey also emphasizes that one element that complicates diagnosis is the presence of 'co-morbid' mental health conditions. In fact, a good part of genetic research deals precisely with this condition, as I mentioned earlier, relative to the association of DRD4 in children with co-morbid conduct problems. The combination of a co-morbid mental health condition and an active or less attentive temperament could lead to a mistaken diagnosis of ADHD. The same considerations could apply to bipolar disorder or to Social Anxiety Disorder, as the author mentions.

Carey's suggestions for improving the situation take into consideration various aspects of the problem: promoting an improved understanding of a normal temperament and of the role of the environment; improving and modifying diagnostic criteria; improving education; and, last but not least, confronting the scandal of the frequent and unhealthy partnership between drug companies and physicians. The dimensions of this scandal can be illustrated by the relatively recent regulation that, in scientific congresses, there must be an explanation of the type of relationship that scientists have with the drug companies when experimenting or studying one of their products. I am in agreement with all of these suggestions, and I think they can contribute to reducing the damage caused by an indiscriminate and unreasonable use of medication based on inaccurate, if not incorrect, diagnoses.

Carey is correct when he emphasizes that this 'pharmacological' policy leads people 'to expect a "quick fix"—a pill … that will quickly make life beautiful again'. I think that psychoanalysts are fully aware of how deceptive this expectation is.

It only remains for me to thank the author for the work he has presented to us so well.

CHAPTER FOUR

Motion and meaning: Psychoanalytic inquiry of so-called ADHD children

Heidi Staufenberg

Introduction

In the title of my paper, with the word 'meaning' I am citing a central concept in the history and theory of psychoanalysis. The object of our word is to uncover meaning. Allow me to refer here to Freud who once said that, 'Interpreting means finding a hidden meaning.' And we all know that 'finding' is meant quite ambiguously here: finding something hidden, something that of course exists, but also finding in the sense of inventing, of something after the fact. I can not, and do not, wish to enter into the debate on the construction and reconstruction of meaning here, but I believe it is important to be aware of this set of issues. After all, in our work with children we encounter a danger inherent in psychoanalytical interpretation in an especially acute manner. By which I mean the danger of not addressing the subject, and with our interpretation imposing an outside meaning on the subject, namely the 'patient'. In other words, in psychoanalytical practice the focus must always also be on enduring the fact that there are things we do not know. Bion's (1963) famous statement that 'no memory, no desire' is reminiscent of the stance I call for here, namely inner openness toward the patient, that is, be cautious of 'knowing' and understanding in that 'understanding' is all too easily only an ostensible matter and can lead to conclusions that go straight past the subject. This admonishment to be cautious should really be taken to heart when working with children as the child does not speak to us with the same level of intellectual abstraction and self-reflection.

Which brings us to meaning and interpretation. And to motor skills. It would perhaps be more appropriate to talk of 'movement', as 'motor skills' connotes a mechanical view of things, that is, it assumes that movement is a purely physical matter, and construes it as being completely separate from 'meaning'. I am talking about an approach which centres on the complete opposite, namely the function of motor skills as psychological discharge and psychological defence, with the idea being to access the psychological properties that are defended. The psychoanalytical literature on hyperactivity on the one hand emphasizes the protective factor that the growing child retains from earlier days, as it were. By movement in space, by making a noise, the child endeavours to work off inner excitation and tension. The adult who curbs the movement easily slips into the role of an aggressor whom the child then feels it has to respond to by fleeing or counter-attacking. The child seeks in what it lives through to avoid a threatening situation and/or to gain control. Bodily movement understood in this way amounts to compensation for insufficient psychological self-protection. Beyond any pathology, we need to remember that movement is an elementary, vital expression: 'Starting from the fetus' first movements through to the child's or the adult's perfection of motor skills, we can understand processes of movements as a living expression of self- and object-related aspirations and psychological states' (Berger, 1993: 145).

Recent research on infants by Beebe, Lachmann, and Jaffe (1997), Stern (1985) and others underscores how important it is for the mother to find a way of attuning to the infant. When 'attunement' succeeds, the mother recognizes the way that the infant expresses itself and seeks to establish a relationship, and she responds accordingly. The result is the responsive interchange in the course of which the child finds itself reflected, such that it can adopt the 'gleam in its mother's eye' for its own image of itself. Repeated experience of this containment by the mother, which responds to the infant's initiative (or, as Winnicott [1971] puts it, the infant's 'spontaneous gesture') is imperative if the child is to develop the ability to regulate itself.

In the case I wish to present here the focus is on accessing the concealed, denied, and ostensibly threatening meaning contained in the boy's motor skills, and to render them acceptable to the boy, thus enabling him to develop more maturely. In this context, I have in mind Winnicott's (1971) 'holding function' and Bion's (1963) concept of 'containment', to which I shall primarily refer: containment as an elementary intra- and inter-subjective occurrence that constitutes the basis for an evolving psychological process and for the psychological structuring of the new-born infant; containment such as the mother accomplishes vis-à-vis the child by absorbing, empathizing, and working through the child's affects and feelings which it cannot yet itself tolerate and integrate. The child must project these affects, which it cannot endure as its own, and must treat them as not belonging to it if it is to liberate itself from them. By absorbing these affects, enacted violently in the form of yelling and fierce motor movement, and thus as a proxy containing and processing them, the mother can then give these intolerable affects back to the child in a changed form, as more tolerable feelings. In this way, she helps the child to develop its own ability to achieve psychological integration and provides the means by which the child can digest and itself work through what was previously intolerable. In other words, in this sense containment is closely linked, conceptually speaking, with the concepts of *interiorization, internalization, integration, symbolization,* and *mentalization.* The other side of the coin are the concepts of *externalization, projection, rejection, dissociation,* and *denial.* In our context, we discern above all such primitive defence mechanisms at work.

Research findings in the neuro-sciences have in recent years substantially expanded our knowledge of how the mature brain functions and the conditions under which it develops. We can describe with increasing precision the interaction of 'genetically conditioned' factors and influences from the social environment. Research by Panksepp (2007), Hüther (2006) and others shows that the genes do not set some automatic, determined programme in motion. Genetic expression is also shaped by psychosocial factors. The neuro-sciences are working to identify how environmental factors influence the pre- and post-natal maturation process. Allow me to quote neurobiologist Panksepp (2007: 67): 'The better a child's emotional needs are anticipated and the better they are addressed, the richer the positive knowledge matrix and the positive feeling of intersubjectivity are that then emerge in the child's cognitive apparatus.' Given these findings by 'hard' science, it is all the more astonishing that precisely in discussions on ADHD often far too little use is made of the insights offered. Instead, biologistically reductive notions of 'genetically conditioned' structures are encountered, references to 'functional metabolic disorders of the brain', as if all that were involved were organic material that can only be influenced chemically, that is, by medicines.

The case

The case I wish to present to you involves Alex, a boy who at the time that the treatment commenced was six and a half years of age. The treatment ran for 210 hours twice a week and lasted for almost three years.

Alex's treatment took place in the second half of the 1990s, and thus at a time when 'ADHD' was attracting greater attention in discussions. The patient's parents had, at the recommendation of the kindergarten care worker, opted to have their son examined by a psychiatrist. The diagnosis was ADHD and Ritalin® was prescribed. However, the father specifically and strictly rejected any medication. He was warned: 'It will be difficult for the child in school, so consider carefully whether Ritalin® is not administered, that would help your child.' The parents took this caution seriously and sought out psychotherapeutic assistance.

Some important anamnestic information on the parents and on the patient's prior history

The parents lead orderly lives. They both completed schooling and vocational training, the one in commerce the other in a crafts trade. The patient is their first child and they wanted the child. Their second child, and again the child was wanted, is a girl, and six years younger than the patient. They have regular, but not especially intensive, contact, to their respective families. Both sets of grandparents were divorced when the patient's parents had reached puberty.

The mother reports that initially the pregnancy put her on a high, she was full of zest and activity, until in the seventh month complications arose. There was the danger of a premature birth and she received tocolytics. During those last few weeks she felt that she had been abandoned, as her husband was on the road a lot for his job and actually only really at home at the weekends. No complications were encountered during the birth itself.

The infant, a screamer

Breast-feeding: frustrating for both mother and child, one hour at the breast, then an hour of sleep; the baby was weaned after six weeks.

The patient's early infancy involved many illnesses and complications:

In its first year: 'inexplicable diarrhoea'.

What followed were: 'fungal complaints, vomiting, stomach aches, excess weight and difficulties going to sleep and sleeping disorders during the first three years'.

At the age of three, the boy contracted neurodermitis, which eased after two years and several attempts at treating it. The child reacted defiantly to this.

After a difficult but complete toilet training, at the age of five, slight encopresis occurred whenever the boy did not wish to stop playing.

The mother insists that from the very beginning her son 'fled the nest'. Between his third and sixth years, he incurred several injuries through daring actions. She was especially shocked when, at the age of about three, he deliberately caught his finger in a door because he did not want to believe that it would really hurt him.

The birth of his sister signified the first separation from his mother. After five days in hospital, the mother returned home to find her son 'recalcitrant and hard to reach'. The parents were worried by the fact that their efforts to prepare him for the birth of his sister did not prevent Alex's intensive and constant jealousy of his small sister.

The parents describe him as a boy who 'happily walks across tables and benches', does not know his own limits, swiftly rages, has temper tantrums, no friends, seeks only to order others around, swiftly hits others if he does not like something, and who attracts negative attention in any social group. *In other words, we have the classic description of the behaviour of a hyperactive child who behaves in a way that stands out socially.*

On the other hand, the parents remember him as being talented from the very beginning, as having surprised them by his early independence, something they admired. *And I would like to point out here that when tracing his early motor skills, which made him appear autonomous, the parents were able easily to libidinously and narcissistically cathect their trying child.*

The mother describes herself as the calm pole at the heart of the family. In my experience she is a patient woman who is lovingly open to her children. She says she has the feeling that she always somehow owes Alex something, and that these guilt feelings never really dissipate and that she knows she gives in too easily, but simply always wants to make up for something. He had it so tough from the very beginning, she says. She reports, with reference to breastfeeding him: 'He was not able to find my nipple.' It is a formulation that to my mind encapsulates the lack of success, the 'mis-matching' in the early mother–child relationship. *The mother did not succeed in attuning well with her son. The infant, hardly ever to be calmed, did not enable the mother to experience herself as a 'good mother'. She herself experienced too little 'holding' that could have helped her with her regression with the infant. Neither her husband nor a helpful mother figure were sufficiently at hand for her.*

The father describes himself as the pole that is diametrically opposed to that of the mother. He himself, he says, is very fidgety and hectic. This description he gives of himself concurs with my own observations. He seems driven, restive, indeed 'fidgety'. The father defends himself for not having been able to better support his wife during pregnancy and in the period after the birth by citing the pressures of his job and his financial responsibility for the young family. He sheepishly confesses that he could not endure the infant's screams and that he fled to his local pub. The father mentions the worries both parents have that their son might rob himself of a possible future. Alex, he says, is already made the scapegoat for things.

In our conversations it becomes clear how much the parents endeavour to maintain their positive image of their active son and yet helpfully identify the problems of the boy, who stands out socially, without inwardly turning away from him in disappointment. This is a danger that threatens the parents–child triangle all the more, as now there is the second triangle with the sister, one that is not burdened down by feelings of guilt and failure. The mother says: 'She is a normal child. It's a quite normal mother–child relationship; she likes cuddling, and I can calm her. She enables me to be all the things as a mother that I could not do with my son.'

Allow me to state here unequivocally: The problems of holding emerge as early as the child's prenatal life, the issue of unclear limits/borders and the absent father, or lack of a father. The present anamnestic data is in keeping with a relatively typical picture as is often to be found in later diagnoses of ADHD. The countless aspects of early disturbances give rise to the question of what level of psychological structure the child or patient actually possesses.

Initial meeting with the child

In the initial session with Alex I meet a normally developed boy, six and a half years of age, slightly overweight like his father, whom he closely resembles. The impression he makes is of a child who is friendly, open, and sociable. Alex immediately seizes the initiative as I ask him in the waiting room if he would like to come with me, jumping off his chair and saying, 'But of course, I'll come on my own!' He rushes off into the corridor as if he knew his way about. In my consulting room he sits down at once and watches me wide-eyed and expectantly.

His eyes turn to a chestnut tree. He talks incoherently of chestnuts they had collected; there were so many that 'four men' had had to carry the sack to the car. And he had even got some chestnuts with him; he wanted to fetch them and would be back in a minute. It took a few minutes for him to return from the waiting room where his mother and little sister were sitting. —I feel that he needed to reinsure himself of his mother's presence like a small child, and his jealousy of his sister prevents him from feeling comfortable.

Even when he sits down there seems to be an aura of disturbance exuding from him. He appears to be under pressure. 'What are we doing now?' he asks, jumping up and rushing to the shelves of toys: 'Oh, Mikado!' We play the game according to his rules, picking up the sticks alternately. I comment on this strategy, and he says he always plays it like that with his mother. 'But then each of you has got the same number of sticks,' I say. His reaction is to look at me briefly in an irritated way and look for something new in the toy shelves—table football.

With this game it becomes apparent how critical and negative his self-image is. He comments on even the slightest mishap with 'Mind what you're doing!', 'I'm so stupid!', or 'I'm hopeless!'

Then he takes the doctor play case. He hits his knee hard with the reflex hammer. One of the plastic bits drops off and flies through the room. He is scared. Yet at once his fear is blotted out with a roar of laughter and a hysterical 'That's funny!' I say, 'That's how you get rid of the scared feeling.' His reaction is a brief and wide-awake glance that immediately disappears in his next splurge of activity.

He now turns to the dolls' house he had initially rejected as 'girls' stuff', and there commences a wild family scene of increasing violence. Grandfather, sister, grandmother, and mother all end up being pushed headfirst into the lavatory bowl. Alex comments on this anal sadistic scene in a tone of artificial friendliness. He identifies with a little black doll that is the perpetrator of all the cruel acts. I speak of his feelings of jealousy towards his sister and say how mean he thinks it is that she gets so much attention from his mother. I continue, saying that in spite of her smallness his sister might seem huge and powerful to him since she is getting so much attention from his mother. He agrees to this and continues in his wild scenario. He attacks her fiercely and rapidly, getting carried away in his shouts and movements. I cannot keep up with this pace and feel excluded. I have feelings of helplessness and tediousness and a readiness to leave him to his destructive drives.

In the second session it becomes obvious how difficult it is for him to accept limits. He wants to go onto the balcony and collect chestnuts. He has opened the window and climbs onto the window sill. I move up directly behind him in case he loses his balance on account of his restlessness. I repeat what he is planning to do and how difficult it is for him to renounce anything. It is not until I say, 'You'd better come back down now,' that he is prepared to leave his position at the open window. He slides down from the window sill hanging on to me like a little child. I have the feeling that he has taken a brief opportunity to come closer into direct contact with his child's needs for closeness, and yet feel a slight irritation that there is some quality to this touching which is inappropriate and somehow sexualized.

But Alex also expresses his explicit desire for limits that can hold him; he folds a paper plane out of the newspaper in the dolls' house and asks if he is permitted to do this. 'I see how hard it is for you to say "Alex, stop it!" to yourself.' It is almost ardent when he replies, 'You say it for me!'—'That's what you want. Then it's easier for you.'

Alex acts on impulse. His restlessness and excitement drive him to keep moving or require urethral anal rebuff. After a peaceful phase of painting or play activity he touches himself between his legs and says, 'I want to pee.' On the way back he runs ahead and before I can stop him opens the door to the other therapy room; shocked, he closes it again very rapidly and enters the next one, our room with the open door. 'Why are you looking so cross?' he asks me. I reply, 'You were afraid I would tell you off. But I'm thinking about it; you opened the other door and disturbed the therapy session. But you were scared. You didn't mean to disturb anybody.' He confirms this. I say, 'You do everything so fast that that sort of thing often goes wrong. People sometimes don't know if you did something deliberately or if it was an accident.' He nods once more. I say, 'And perhaps even you yourself don't know what's what.' He answers, 'Yes,' and he packs away the toys and games and takes out the doctor play case again.

I have the impression that he is revealing his fear about what will happen to him here. After this interpretation he gives himself an injection and explains that it's against the pain, just like at the doctor's. I say, 'So it's quite different from the game we played before about Granddad. He got speared up on Granny's knitting needle. That would make anybody scared.' He nods gravely. While we then both tidy up together, he asks me what is wrong with the other boy. 'You'd like to know why the other children come here. You've already seen one boy in the waiting room. Perhaps you were even looking for him when you opened the door. I could understand you doing that.' He listens quietly and attentively.

I have portrayed the initial sessions at length since all significant themes, conflicts, transfer, and counter-transfer phenomena become apparent that are to be the decisive factors in treatment and which also contain the typical elements for the psychodynamics of so-called ADHD children:

- need for closeness and containment that has never found good enough satisfaction;
- resultant problems of impulse control/restlessness in any instances of increasing aggressive or libidinous excitement;

- labile narcissistic balance, easily threatened;
- motor activity to release tension, self-regulation, and regulation of closeness and distance to object; tendency to sexualization as an attempt to reduce tension → he jumps off the table, runs out of the room;
- wish and search for limits for holding through objects → I should express orders;
- protest against orders;
- grasping towards infantile grandiosity as a defence mechanism against fear and for the regulation of self-esteem → reflex hammer from the doctor play set;
- *strict archaic devastating super ego* → 'I'm stupid!', 'I'm hopeless!' at table football;
- anal sadistic fear and wishes of destruction → in the dolls' house;
- fixation of pre-oedipal structures of defective indifference and defective separation avoidance of phallic-oedipal structured rivalry → Mikado game;
- *greed* → chestnuts;
- jealousy of sister;
- simultaneous object 'hunger' and object fear;
- difficulty in considering the object;
- concentration and peacefulness in harmonious/symbiotic non-threatening dyadic situations; and
- *reaction of the child therapist* → feelings of helplessness, tediousness, annoyance, and inner withdrawal, that is, my aversion of the question of the significance of his activity.

Treatment

I would like to show the course of treatment by describing central scenes. The themes revealed in the initial sessions will be picked up and will show the development in a dramatic way.

To the first phase of the therapy I have given the title 'Battles on the Setting and First Settlements' since Alex enacted his problems and demands on being granted a free hand with no holds barred extremely rapidly. He runs out of the consulting room, shouts in the corridor, and disturbs other colleagues working next door. Totally unexpectedly, he interrupts a quiet game, and runs out. Thus there develop the well-documented situations of helpless therapists with hyperactive child patients. On the other hand, I also regularly experience that I can reach Alex with my interpretations if they touch the central core for him. I say, 'You find it difficult to stay in the same room with me. You want to get out fast. This is often the case. There is something in you that makes you restless and makes you run up and down.' He calms down and wants to continue playing.

An impressive example of his reachability showing his ability for symbolization in a desperate scene, is when, in a tantrum, Alex accidentally damages a toy telephone, and then continues to destroy the toy phone on purpose. My spontaneous reaction is, 'Now it is totally wrecked. Maybe it shows how you sometimes feel inside.' He opens his eyes as wide as he can, stops, and calmly responds, 'Come on, let's play something.'

His running in and out culminates in a first escalation. He ran out of the room and climbed onto the balcony through the corridor window while I ran up after him, talking to him, trying to reach and hold him. The object he desires is the chestnut tree mentioned in the initial meetings that has now cast off all chestnuts. With conquering the balcony he makes it clear that verbal acceptance and comprehension of his wish are no longer adequate. He is not able to accept the insight that renunciation is a necessity. He is thus on the fourth floor on a narrow balcony that goes around the entire building without a firm railing and held merely by two steel ropes through which a child might easily fall and Alex wants me to catch him: 'Come on! Come on!' In my fear and tension I say, 'Alex, you can't go on like that. Stop, you have to move very carefully. I'm afraid you might fall down. Look at the railing. It's dangerous.' He now looks a little scared himself and, moving close to the wall with utmost caution up to the window of the consulting room, he lets me help him climb back in. I can feel his fear. But at once this moment of fear is transformed into a triumph and he shouts, 'I've got my chestnuts and you can't stop me!'

With this balcony scene we have a demonstration of the pedagogical and sociological aspects currently discussed in discourse on causes of ADHD; the loss of the inherent authority of the adult world that a child would automatically acknowledge and find hold in. *The philosopher and psychoanalyst Benasayag and the psychiatrist and psychoanalyst Schmit have evocatively entitled this problem in their original*

French text, 'Les Passions Tristes' *('Sad Passions') (2007) in which they give a lucid analysis of the difference between 'authority' and 'authoritarian' on which they insist.*

Alex likes to come to me but is unable to comply with 'my' rule that the sessions must take place in the consulting room. He runs in and out, discovering the library as a safe place for involving me in his game. Alex loves to put me in the situation of the stupid and inferior person under his total control. I am in danger of becoming the suspicious and persecuting object that wants to control every single step he takes and render myself untrustworthy. On an inner level I keep in touch with him by translating my helplessness and anger as a reflection of his inner situation towards the object and his oppressive affects.

Patient and therapist are at pains to find a mutual route. This presupposes that Alex feels accepted, and this fits in the process leading from 'my' to 'our' rules. Alex had indeed accepted that he was not to walk onto the balcony. But as later becomes apparent only in the sense of prohibition—that still retains the appeal of defying the limits.

He does in fact once more climb onto the balcony and there is a repetition of the scene: my serious worry, his nervous scare, his return with my help, and his triumph. I am obliged to realize that he has the power to destroy the therapy. I tell him, 'I cannot work with you like this and if you want to keep on coming we shall have to find a solution for the two of us.' His top half is lying on the table, his face hidden in his arms. He looks up and says in a quiet and clear voice, 'Ok. Agreed. No balcony, no more shouting in the corridor.' At once he jumps up, turns around, grabs into the cash desk of the toy shop where there are many toy banknotes, flings them up into the air so that the toy money falls like a rainfall, and says, 'But throwing money is not forbidden. We didn't agree on that.' At these words he smiles roguishly in a seductive way, but still shows he means it seriously.

With this behaviour he shows that he would genuinely like to find a mutual route with me. But he also shows that such a route is only tolerable for him if his feeling of autonomy is not hurt. It is as if there was some existential threat for his psychological survival if he is touched by the object, as if he were threatened of being devoured whenever he surrenders his control over others. That is why he must remain unpredictable. With his acting out he can deny his deep fears and use his aggressions. Above all with his acting out he makes it clear how much at threat he would feel if he did not protect himself with this externalizing behaviour. In a way Alex is testing his object to see if it remains when their own narcissism has been hurt by him. For Alex it was important that his object set limits but never in an aggressive or embarrassing way.

With this step towards 'these are our rules now because they make it possible for us to stay together', Alex has renounced his claim to be almighty and unpredictable and acknowledged that he assumes responsibility for his behaviour stemming from interest in his own object and whose protection he must take into consideration. Alex has also been confronted with my limits that I too am not allowed to do everything, but am constricted by the set-up of the institution.

Remarks on questions of technique

In the further course of treatment there were frequent repercussions on the subject of 'the rules'. On reflection it seems to me that some aspects both for me and for the patient could have been alleviated had I been able to react to him more rapidly and alter my position from the interpretative to the pedagogical therapist with greater flexibility and more systematically. Alex's words in the first interview—'Say it for me'—had already pointed in this direction. Through the following scene I finally understood how indispensable this concrete, unambiguous message from the object holding him was for Alex. He needed an object that accepted responsibility. By showing no fear of his protest it helps him to give up his protestation. At the beginning of the 60th session he goes straight away into the corridor and in the kitchen saying, 'Today I have to break a rule,' and, imitating the growling of wild animals, he rolls under the shutter of the kitchen that is a taboo zone for him. Instead of interpreting what he possibly wants to express to me, I merely say, 'Don't act as if you were a wild animal. You are not. You know that and you know that I know.' This intervention is not enough. He continues. I say in a sober and unimpressed tone of voice, 'I do not know why you behave like this. This is not the place to behave like that.' He glimpses briefly from under the shutter, gets up, and follows me into the consulting room. When working with children like Alex I am repeatedly impressed as to how much imagination, humour, and talent they reveal when they feel safe enough in a relationship. The competence they have is also tangible in the breaking of rules and provocation which had been consciously enacted and controlled.

At this stage I would like to add a few thoughts: on the basis of his concept of 'fundamental emotional systems' (*'grundlegende Gefühlsysteme'*) Panksepp (2007: 81) suggests that so-called ADHD children be considered as children whose natural and developmental play activity has been excessively restricted and who therefore tend towards forms of play that are socially unacceptable. Regarded from this aspect, the countless struggles for power between Alex and me could *also* be regarded as misunderstandings. The child has *its* play behaviour and fights desperately not to have to surrender to the rules of the adults. And the adult, who is blinded by the inappropriate rule breakings, can no longer meet the authentic wish of the child.

Peaceful and concentrated togetherness

In scientific texts we are regularly confronted with the finding that so-called ADHD children are capable of concentrating when they are in a dyadic situation in which they experience the undivided attention of another person. Parents sometimes fear that the therapist may not recognize the child's problem since they are well aware that their child can be sunny in a face-to-face relationship. In this case, they tend to oversee that even this harmony demands parental compliancy to the child's wishes. It is not the face-to-face situation per se, but rather the wish fulfilment and surrender to which parents are prone in order to avoid provoking the temperament of a difficult child. The interests of both parties appear the same ('indifference') and the conflict is thus suspended. This was also true for Alex and became apparent in the following scene: Alex had insisted on taking his mother into the consulting room. She had come without her baby and Alex was making the most of this infrequent situation of having his mother to himself. Mother and son are painting in harmony, each one their own picture; it is to be a tree, which was the task agreed on. It culminates in a catastrophe. Alex's tree is a typical child's picture: the tree is round, full, and green. But he had wanted a picture like his mother's, with the detail of branches and twigs.

He is not successful and throws the crayons across the room. The mother hesitates to show compliancy in my presence and refuses to fulfil his wish for her to draw 'her tree' for him. His screams and raging—'I want a tree like my Mummy's!'—are resumed when he gets home and he induces his mother to show him how to draw such trees.

He comes with pride to the next session and says, 'Now I can draw a tree like my mother.' From this statement there follows a development: He draws two trees, then paints a little bird in each tree, and says, 'That one's the Daddy bird and the other one's a Mummy bird.' The Daddy bird has got a long tail. The Mummy bird has got fluffier, brighter-coloured feathers. Alex says, 'I like the Mummy bird better.' And I respond, 'Yes the Mummy bird's nice and soft for cuddling,' to which he responds, 'But the Daddy bird's got a big tail and that's also something great.' I continue, 'Daddies and Mummies are a bit different in human beings too.' He promptly replies, 'I know what you're talking about, you're talking about making babies. I know how to do it.' With pride he explains how babies are created and concludes, 'When I'm grown up, when I'm grown up, I'm going to make a baby too.' As he says this he draws many tiny birds in the pictures.

These calm phases of concentration provide a basis for his inner psychological structuring. In these moments he can experience himself as subject able to hold conflicting emotions within himself and project himself into the future. He also shows his ability to tolerate a certain tension between his current existence as child and ideal vision of the adult male of the future; he also shows a stable masculine identity and fundamental identification with his father. In spite of all his difficulties Alex has clearly reached a level of oedipal structure. The goal of treatment will essentially be to retain and stabilize this self-image.

Alex varies the topics of his self-assertion and is in the throes of a process of integration; this cannot be straightforward but proceeds veering from progression to regression, from change to resistance. He makes good use of me as transference object and can sort out various aspects of his primary relationships in his interaction with me. For a long time I am unable to foresee when an interpretation can hold and structure him and when he takes the acknowledgement of his wish as permission to perform the wish. Not until the final third of treatment do we reach a somewhat more stable situation. In a humorous way Alex is able to express how familiar he has become with my demand for analytical abstinence. He is still sometimes furious, he still loses control, and still tends to seek his triumph—yet all of these reactions are milder, more mature, and in a 'held' manner. He enacts in games what he once acted out in a wild way. He threatens, for instance, to flood the toilet, turns the water tap on so that the noise of running water makes me scared, and then says with a smile, 'I once used to do things like that. Did you think I'd do it again?'

Playing Mikado shows his development and how he is able to handle the challenges of reality and rivalry. He wanted to know the proper rules of the game and put aside the 'motherly' world which suggested equality. Mikado became a symbolized confrontation with the rules of 'Father's' world and paternal law.

Before I turn to the significance of the father in my final point I should like to sum up what Alex has reached in the course of therapy: We were able to avoid the imminent relegation from normal school. In this critical phase I saw him for three sessions a week. In the new school his behaviour became more consistent. After moving house he came to a school whose headmaster was confident of finding a way to contact this 'wild boy'. He could handle his jealousy of his sister by resorting to the existing identification with the role of the protective big brother who views his oedipal child in the younger one. His relationship to his mother remained *the* reliable base for him in spite of earlier problems. His mother partly succeeded in being less lenient towards him. To her surprise she discovered that he did not mind her clear 'no'. The relationship towards his father remained the most difficult part. There were only phases where the father was able to participate and he then expected that everything would function perfectly. There were long phases in the therapy in which Alex used therapy to work through his disappointment and anger towards his father. He remained an impulsive and emotional child. But he was more able to control his impulses and no longer rendered helpless by them, but able to use his intelligence, humour, and imagination to express them in a symbolized way.

'The father and unfulfilled hunger for a father'

Self-doubts and feelings of personal worthlessness cause Alex to cling in desperation to his almighty pretensions. This is doomed to failure and he is re-exposed to self-condemnation and an undermining of his rigid, archaic super-ego. To halt this vicious circle a long therapeutic process with interweaving stages of working through is necessary. By working through various topics, conflicts, fantasies and stories Alex became able to moderate his pretence being omnipotent. They lead him to his story with his father where he unfolds his inner struggle. Alex admires him and wants him to be proud of him, yet gets only annoyance, anger, and disappointment. He is aware that his father himself has problems with controlling his affects. In play, Alex shows a cruel father image full of deprecation towards the object and unbridled anger. This father cannot serve as a triangulating object for him in a sufficient way; he is more the aggressor for him with whom Alex then identifies. He is thus bound in a malignant vicious circle of persecution and punishment that binds him to externalizing mechanisms.

In my paper I have emphasized the confrontation with rules since in my opinion these most clearly show the transference position in which for Alex I represented the father's world to which he was seeking entry and with totally unsuitable means of a grandiose encroachment with which he could not succeed. The image of 'wild boy' presented a positive masculine model in the eyes of both parents, available to the boy, yet giving him no structuring lifeline to achieve 'masculine' demarcation with which he can identify and model himself. Phases of rapprochement between father and son with mutual trips, exclusively 'masculine' undertakings such as fishing and repairing bicycles, put fresh impetus into Alex. He then shows an impressive structural competence after his hunger for a father has been satisfied and must no longer rely on the mother alone, who remains the archaic mother that he needs release from.

Like all patients who are referred to me with the diagnosis of ADHD Alex did suffer from an insufficiently available father. The movement of the children in the room—and I refer almost without exception to boys—appears to me as if they are actually seeking their father who can tell them to stop, who accepts them and introduces them into his world. From this aspect the apparent lack of purpose in this restlessness may also have significant meaning: as if the boys are constantly on the move to seek their father and their masculinity, yet, in never reaching the target, compensate in their restless movement. By alloying their inner restlessness with their fantasies of what is masculine, they can confirm to themselves that they are 'great guys' and can defend against the shame of being only 'wild boys'. Driven by need they idealize impulsivity to ascertain their masculinity. Their developing manhood—as is confirmed by a large number of authors—is under concrete threat in various ways. The child environment is dominated by the female and offers scant similarity to their object and no comprehension for specific needs of gender identity to try out the boy role (cf. Dammasch and Metzger, 2006). It is no mere coincidence that Alex's situation became more relaxed after changing school. Alex's wild behaviour and destructive activity in lessons at the old school had been addressed at his father: His father should pay attention and take time off to be with him.

In psychoanalytical literature the father's role as triangulating third party, offering the child the perspective from a third dimension, has been discussed from various aspects. Fonagy and Target (2002) emphasize the father's significance above all as the one opening the child's eyes to reflect the relationship experience. With this ability the child is able to see himself in his relationship to others, initially of course to the mother, and thus widen his space for thinking and transcend the 'perception of his psychological self' (*'Wahrnehmung seines psychischen Selbsts')* (p. 301). He can, as it were, enter the world. Alex had a problem with restricted ability to relate to others and move as equals (*'par inter pares'*). He could deny and reject his sorrow about his outsider status at school. But he was sad and desperate about not finding any friends and felt deep down inside that friends would open up a new world for him and help him towards genuine autonomy. That this had changed was the most important thing he wrote in his farewell letter: '... and I am happy that the other kids like me now.'

Bibliography

Beebe, B., Lachmann F. and Jaffe J. (1997). Mother-Infant Interaction: Structures and presymbolic self- and object representations. *Psychoanalytic Dialogues*, 7: 133–82.

Benasayag, M. and Schmit, G. (2007/2003). *Die verweigerte Zukunft.* München: Kunstmann.

Berger, M. (1993). 'Und die Mutter blickte stumm auf dem ganzen Tisch herum'. *Kinderanalyse, 1. Jg.*, 2: 131–49.

Bion, W.R. (1992[1963]). *Elemente der Psychoanalyse.* Frankfurt a.M.: Suhrkamp.

Bovensiepen, G., Hopf, H. and Molitor, G. (Hrsg.) (2002). *Unruhige und unaufmerksame Kinder: Psychoanalyse des hyperkinetischen Syndroms.* Frankfurt am Main: Brandes & Apsel.

Dammasch, F. (2002). 'Er weiß nicht, wo er anfängt und wo er aufhört!' In: Bovensiepen et al. *Unruhige und unaufmerksame Kinder: Psychoanalyse des hyperkinetischen Syndroms.* Frankfurt am Main: Brandes & Apsel. pp. 257–311.

Dammasch, F. and Metzger, H.-G. (Hrsg.) (2006). *Die Bedeutung des Vaters: Psychoanalytische Perspektiven.* Frankfurt am Main: Brandes & Apsel.

Diller, L.H. (2002). *ADHD: Real Disease or American Myth.* Rom, 10. October. Available from: http://www.docdiller.com

Fonagy, P. and Target, M. (2002). 'Zum Verständnis von Gewalt: über die Verwendung des Körpers und die Rolle des Vaters'. In: *Kinderanalyse,* 10. Jg., 3: 281–307.

Gilmore, K. (2000). 'A Psychoanalytic Perspective on Attention Deficit/ Hyperactivity Disorder'. *J. Am. Psychoanal. Ass.* 48 (4): 1,259–93.

Heinemann, E. and Hopf, H. (2006). *AD(H)S. Symptome—Psychodynamik—Fallbeispiele—Psychoanalytische Theorie und Therapie.* Stuttgart: Kohlhammer.

Hüther, G. (2006): Die nutzungsabhängige Herausbildung hirnorganischer Veränderungen bei Hyperaktivität und Aurmerksamkeitsstörungen. Einfluss präventiver Maßnahmen und therapeutischer Internventionen. In: Leuzinger-Bohleber, M., Brandl, Y., Hüther, G. (Hg.). *ADHS—Frühprävention statt Medikalisierung. Theorie, Forschung, Kontroversen.* Göttingen: Vandenhoeck & Ruprecht. pp. 222–37.

Lacan, J. (2001). "The Mirror Stage as Formative of the Function of the I", in Écrits: A selection, London, Routledge Classics, 2001, p. 5

Panksepp, J. (2007). 'Die psychobiologischen Langzeitfolgen der emotionalen Umwelten von Kleinkindern für das spätere Gefühlsleben—Forschungsperspektiven für das 21: Jahrhundert'. In: Streeck-Fischer, A. (ed.) pp. 45–104.

Pozzi, M.E. (2001): Ritalin für wen? Wie können wir das Bedürfnis nach Ritalin in der Psychodynamischen Beratung von Familien verstehen?' In: *Analytische Kinder- und Jugendlichen Psychotherapie* (AKJP) 112: 519–42, Frankfurt am Main: Brandes & Apsel.

Stern, D. (1922[1985]). *Die Lebenserfahrung des Säuglings.* Stuttgart: Klett-Cotta.

Streeck-Fischer, A. (Hrsg.) (2007). *Adoleszenz—Bindung—Destruktivität.* Stuttgart: Klett-Cotta.

Streeck-Fischer, A. (2006). '"Neglekt" bei der Aufmerksamkeitsdefizit—und Hyperaktivitätsstörung'. *Psychotherapeut,* 2: 80–90.

Winnicott, D.W. (1973[1971]). *Vom Spiel zur Kreativität.* Stuttgart: Klett.

DISCUSSION OF HEIDI STAUFENBERG'S PAPER

ADHD from the empirical and clinical perspectives

Annette Streeck-Fischer

Can psychoanalysis, with its approaches to explanation, hold out against biomedical models of ADHD?

In child psychiatry and psychotherapy, not only different ideologies regarding the healing and application of different therapeutic measures in relation to the syndrome ADHD have grown stronger, but also unexpectedly militant discussions, which can be explained, on the one hand, by different theories of illness and ideologies regarding disorders and, on the other, through reflecting occupational, political, and economic interests but, however, rarely placing the well-being of the child at the forefront of considerations. At the centre of the discussion is frequently the question of what primarily determines this disorder, the constitution or the conditions necessary for its development: the genes or the environment (Rutter, 2002).

And so, from time to time, the question is sometimes raised of whether the disorder is one that can only be explained outside the framework of psychoanalytic thought. A critical inspection of the biomedical models, however, highlights the significance attributed to gene expression and consequently the psychodynamic development perspective. Even indications of a high rate of inheritance of 90% (in behavioural genetics, monozygotic twins show a high concordance of 0.5–0.9) [Levi *et al.*, 1997]) does not mean that environmental conditions do not have a high influence on development (Rutter, 2002). Such behavioural genetic studies, which were carried out on three-year-olds, can likewise be viewed relatively, just like the dopamine-deficit hypothesis and with that the associated poorly developed receptor or transporter genes (for example, Taylor, 1995; Sandberg, 1996; Döpfner *et al.*, 2000). Findings obtained from animal experiments show, above all, that dopamine concentration in the brain is also dependent on social ranking (Spitzer, 2002). With a higher position in the hierarchy within a group of monkeys, a higher concentration of dopamine was also found and vice versa. As children with ADHD, as a rule, occupy a low position or have the role of an outsider, a lower dopamine level is to be expected in the brain. Also, indications of a disorder of neuronal development in ADHD does not mean that this has a primary genetic origin—as we know. Studies carried out by DeBellis *et al.* (1999), Kishiama *et al.* (2008), and Teicher *et al.* (2002), amongst others, highlight the negative effects of unfavourable environmental factors on the development of the brain. Finally, the deficits in self-regulation in working memory and executive functions, which are proclaimed to be genetically determined, have been made relative as a result of investigations of early mother–child interactions.

The question of which conditions result in the genetic expression of ADHD has, up until now, been insufficiently examined. From empirical research, it is clear that perinatal complications play an important role. The fact that a mother smokes has not been demonstrated as always being of importance for the development of ADHD (Ben Amor *et al.*, 2006). However, it has been shown that sensory motor disturbances, which are time and again stated as being constitutionally determined, can be the consequence of early disorders of regulation which are frequently to be found in ADHD (Desantis *et al.*, 2004). In addition, specific attitudes on the part of care providers towards children who develop ADHD have been established. This type of attitude is characterized by intrusive, over-caring, and/or negative patterns of relations that lead to disturbances in self-regulation and in the area of executive functions (Olson *et al.*, 2002; Silverman and Ragusa, 1992). Moreover, it has been possible to demonstrate specific family interactions, such as hostile attitudes and/or diffuse or rigid boundaries between members of a family (Jacobvitz *et al.*, 2004).

Is it meaningful to adopt the psychiatric diagnosis of ADHD in psychoanalytic terminology?

ADHD is recorded in a dimensional fashion in psychiatric diagnosis (Döpfner and Lehmkuhl, 1997). The disorder comprises three characteristic behavioural features, a disorder of attention, hyperactivity, and impulsiveness. However, these symptoms can be found with different manifestations in very many syndromes, such as borderline disorders, anxiety disorders, depression, narcissistic disorders, and traumatic stress disorders. In this context, it would be interesting to examine whether there are different rankings of the three symptom clusters in each of the different syndromes.

The diagnosis of ADHD from the psychodynamic perspective therefore includes, as a matter of course, a wide range of disorders which are manifest both as conflict dynamics as well as the result of deficient 'Ego' structure development. In the fist case, ADHD serves, with the triad of symptoms, as defensive and protective behaviour in the event of stressful and threatening dangers from inside or outside (for example, in order to avoid unbearable feelings of anxiety or sadness). In the second case, aspects of disorders of development are at the forefront, such as, for example, inadequate tolerance of tension or a disturbed control of impulse.

We therefore can say that it is a syndrome of disturbances which are associated with an ADHD symptomatic. Nonetheless, there are conspicuous features which are specific to ADHD which can be identified, which are imminent to the triad of symptoms, such as a lack of an ability to perceive and regulate affect, a lack of an ability to tolerate conflict and tension, mentalization disorders, and disorders of relationships (cf. guideline ADHD).

On the basis of the first proposals of child psychotherapists which were sent to experts from the statutory and private health insurance companies and which were used by child psychiatrists, paediatricians, and general practitioners for the diagnosis of ADHD, an evaluation was made of which diagnoses were made by children and adolescent psychotherapists. Of 30 cases, there were 10x a diagnosis of a narcissistic disorder, of which 5 were a narcissistic-depressive disorder, 8x depressions, 10x anxiety disorders, 4x borderline disorders, 1 asocial development, 2 disturbances of adjustment, 2 post-traumatic stress disorder, and 2 early disorders (Streeck-Fischer, 2005). The diagnosis of a narcissistic disorder was the most frequently named one. But, we did not find such a one in the ICD-10. One could, however, ask whether ADHD is congruent, to a large extent, with a narcissistic problem—a narcissistic disorder in this context is understood to be a problem which can occur at all stages of development.

The family situation, as well, shows specific attributes. Of the 30 cases referred to, in 18 the father was absent as a consequence of death, earlier, or later separation; 4 were frequently absent; 3 in a difficult position; one was chronically ill; and 4 fathers were not referred to. Of the mothers, 10 were intrusive; 7 were over-caring in a monopolizing sense; 7 set inappropriate boundaries; 2 were incestuously sexualizing; 2 were disciplinary and restrictive; 4 were rejecting; 3 depreciative; and 5 neglecting. This means that, in the event of the development of ADHD, the father is more likely to be absent and neglecting whereas the mother, for her part, is over-caring, intrusive, does not respect the boundaries of the child, going as far as sexualizing and being incestuous, and/or, on the other hand, ignores, rejects, is depreciative, and neglecting. Therefore, there is no uniform type of mother. However, disorders of self-regulation can arise both as a result of over-caring attitudes, as well as also as a result of neglect. Both attitudes can prevent the development of a corresponding competence.

When the dialogue fails …

Frau Stauffenberg has presented an impressive case of the 7-year-old Alex who was treated successfully, which is very interesting from a number of viewpoints. Here, it will only be possible to go into a few noteworthy aspects.

Unfortunately, there is much regarding the parents that remains unclear, as their anonymity must be guaranteed, but the question is raised of which transmissions of unconquered conflicts are present in them. In this context, it is not infrequent to find conflicts with the male sex on the part of the mother which are fought against or which remain unconscious.

In ADHD, the family frequently shows a specific constellation. The father is mostly absent, the mother shows intrusive, over-caring behaviour with tendencies infringing on incest. The lack of setting boundaries on the part of the mother induces anxiety in the young boy and this has exceptionally unfavourable consequences for the development of autonomy and competence (Dammasch, 2002). The child's own experience of being able to cause an effect, which results in mastery, are hindered.

In addition, as in the case of Alex, there are early stressful conditions, especially long-lasting chronic stress, which have unfavourable consequences for self-regulation, the executive functions, and the ability to control impulses and behaviour. Barkley (1997) has proposed an interesting model of how we can understand the development of ADHD. Although or precisely because he is a representative of the biomedical viewpoint and has well documented the structural problem of these children, this will only be gone into in brief here. He drew attention to particular correlations in development. The development of an inadequate ability to control behaviour through to goal-directed behaviour is based—according to Barkley (1997)—equally on four different pillars of development. First amongst these is self-regulation, the regulation of emotions, motivation, and arousal. This is linked to the ability to put off or delay and control needs and wishes, and the ability to adopt a perspective. From the psychoanalytic perspective, one could also add that, with this, the ability for negative capability (Bion, 1962) could also be meant, which means the ability to bear a moment of uncertainty, to be able to pause. Working memory as the second pillar determines the ability to anticipate, to have a time perspective, and to call up memories in the present situation as a treasure of experience. One could supplement this, at this point, by mentioning the ability to utilize anxiety as signal anxiety. The internalization of language represents the third column, with the ability to use language and to draw on this in carrying out an action, to reflect, and to mentalize with other words. The ability of reconstitution as the fourth pillar enables a kind of synthesis. From the psychoanalytic perspective, this will be attained with the synthetic integrative 'Ego' functions (Nunberg, 1959). The inadequate 'Ego' capacity in the case of ADHD children has been draw to our attention by Gilmore (2000) in his Rorschach investigations (cf. Streeck-Fischer, 2006).

In Alex's early development, there were a whole range of unfavourable factors. The baby could not find the mother's breast, an indication which allows one to suspect that the early sensitive tuning between mother and child caused problems from the very start and which then developed into marked disturbances. He was a howling baby; there were disturbances of eating; he had long-lasting diarrhoea. He frequently vomited. These are all circumstances that confront the mother with her own insufficiencies and deficiencies. Moreover, he reacted with neurodermitis, that is changes to the skin which result most frequently in aversive, painful experiences when contact is made with the skin. It can be assumed that the early interaction between the mother and the child was frequently stressful, a situation which was not compensated for by the presence of a third person. Alex was apparently confronted by conditions of pain, disorganization, and unregulated stress, which may have resulted in over-excitement and hyperactivity instead of peace and contentment. In comparison, a mother appears—probably as a result of feelings of anxiety and helplessness—to have tried unsuccessfully with inappropriate actions, which the infant may have experienced as being intrusive and overwhelming, to create bearable conditions. It can also be assumed that she was increasingly exhausted, brought to her limits, and that she possibly also reacted with annoyance or anger. Motherly functions of providing early care, like mirroring, neuropsychobiological regulation, and sensitivity, were not conspicuous, so that the ability of mentalization (Fonagy *et al.*, 2004) was adversely affected. In this way, there was an absence of the prerequisites for secure attachment. Securely attached children learn to make use of their feelings and their thoughts, and to determine their reactions based on these. They can express their feelings and are cognizant of their inner states. Instead of this, there were marked disturbances of encoding and decoding childish behaviour on the part of the mother. The alien gestures of the mother heightened the mismatch, whose consequences were intrusive and instrumental actions. confusion and helplessness, and probably also speechlessness, broadened.

In the case of disruptions to the early affect-motor sphere, hyperactivity and disorders of attention can be viewed as being part of a surfacing, but not yet experienced or reflected emotion. The multiple disorders in executive functions and self-regulation can be explained by the unfavourable conditions of care.

When the play becomes real and runs out of control

The child's play, which takes place in a room designed for the purpose, is constituted by the space of the As-If in which the child can think, speak, act, and develop. The play is real and, at the same time, not real. The play develops into real action when the space in which the play takes place is not (safely) anchored (Solnit, 1987). In such cases, the restoration of dangerous, exciting, overwhelming, and forbidden real scenes may arise. Under such circumstances, transitional space, in which therapy, communication, and development are made possible, break down (Streeck-Fischer, 1997). The play goes out of control and becomes a real event. Overwhelming and forbidden scenes are restored, in which the therapist is so helpless, so paralyzed, and shocked, or behaves in a rigid manner which the child experienced with the earlier care providers. The boundary between 'I' and 'you' and the oedipal law then ceases to exist. The therapist is then just as glued to the child as it was to the earlier care providers and is, without boundaries between self and object, good, allowed, and bad, forbidden, outside of time and space.

Alex creates such scenes again and again, and completely unexpectedly. Initially, the therapist is not able to contain her anxiety and confusion, as the situation is truly dangerous, forbidden, and seductive, and she herself becomes truly overwhelmed—and then she is initially so petrified or intimidated, or reacts threateningly, like Alex's internalized early object. The therapist is, however, successful in the course of the therapy in creating such a space in which therapy can take place. She sets limits and makes mutual agreements with him, which the child is more and more able to comply with.

The therapist mentioned the fact that she needed pedagogical interventions instead of interpretations. Here the question is raised of whether it really needed pedagogical action. In development therapy, as is needed in this case, we discover the sense of the unconscious not in the concealed, but in concrete actions. The framework which is represented by the ecological milieu, as Treurniet (1995) says, formulated differently, a basic mild and positive transference relationship, is destroyed or damaged by attacks, for which one needs to be prepared. In this case, active work on the framework and a stable relationship is necessary. The structure of the self provided by the framework (Green, 1975) is a prerequisite for the ability to symbolize and to mentalize (Fonagy *et al.*, 2004).

Alex creates direct, real threatening situations—on the balcony without grounds, for instance, guided by his need for immediate satisfaction (getting chestnuts). At this point, the therapist can only react in reality in the same way—stop—stop—watch out—combined with affective reactions, such as *I do not want you to be endangered, that makes me afraid.* And then—*I cannot work or play with you when you do such things.* We need agreements. Such authentic reactions set the boundaries which he could not experience before, because it refers to a mother absent in one way or another, perhaps paralyzed or traumatized. Such an answer is not pedagogical, but points to the original sense. An affective reaction is offered that draws boundaries from a new development object which, in its supporting and orientation-giving function, has not existed up until now (cf. Hurry, 2002). Inasmuch, the work on framework and boundary setting is a basic offer promoting development. Only then, when there is correspondence here, will it be possible to reflect, to use words, to contain, and so forth.

Outlook

With regard to the clinical picture of ADHD, there are challenges presented to psychoanalysis, which in a certain way are similar to those which have been emphasized by Argelander (1972) with reference to the narcissistic neuroses, that it is, namely, important to concern oneself with the modality of the specific psychic processing. These considerations moved Argelander at that time to describe on the flier a character disorder which is associated with superficial and passing object relationships and less subjective involvement of feelings. With regard to ADHD, there are similar challenges. Inasmuch, it is exceptionally important and helpful to precisely observe the case histories and treatments of children with the diagnosis of ADHD.

The neglecting of the sphere of emotions or, formulated in a different way, the loss of the meaning of emotionality, which is inherent in this clinical picture, is still forced by therapeutic approaches which do not view the child as a whole.

Children with ADHD are—according to Balzer (2001)—the mar ginalized avant garde of an increasingly sensory coded culture with poor attachment security and deficient symbolizing and mentalizing. Thinking and reflection can veil within themselves a threat to land in a deep state of confusion and a state of being abandoned, which are prevented by the formation of autistic-contiguous defences. The formation of autistic-contiguous defences is, according to Ogden (1989) the attempt to replace missing (physical) cohesion, for example, by rhythmic muscular activities. The motor hyperactivity appears, in this way, to create a sensory surface which serves the purpose of preventing the anxiety of falling into a deep hole of being alone and confused, observed and seen by no-one.

Alex gained something else in his therapy and for him a new experience—he was seen.

Bibliography

Argelander, H. (1972). *Der Flieger.* Suhrkamp Frankfurt/Main.

Balzer, W. (2001). Lust am Nichtdenken? Zum Verhältnis von Erregung und Bedeutung in beschleunigten und entgrenzten Lebenswelten.

Barkley, R.A. (1997). 'Behavioral Inhibition, Sustained Attention, and Executive Functions: Constructing a Unifying Theory of ADHS'. *Psychological Bulletin,* 121: 65–94.

Ben Amor, L., Grizenko, N. and Schwartz, G. *et al.* (2005). 'Perinatal Complications in Children with Attention-Defizit Hyperactivity Disorder and their unaffected Siblings'. *Rev. Psychiat. Neurosci,* 30 (2): 120–26.

Bion, W.R. (1962). *Learning from Experience.* London: Heinemann.

Dammasch, F. (2002). 'Er weiß nicht, wo er anfängt und wo er aufhört!' In: Bovensiepen, G., Hopf, H. and Molitor, G. (eds) *Unruhige und unaufmerksame Kinder.* Frankfurt: Brandes & Apsel.

DeBellis, M.D., Keshavan, M.S., Clark, D.B., Giedd J.N., Boring A.M., Frustaci, K. and Ryan, N.D. (1999b). 'Developmental traumatology Part II: brain development'. *Biological Psychiatry,* 43: 1,271–84.

Desantis, A., Coster, W., Bigsby, R. and Lester, B. (2004). 'Colic and Fussing in Infancy, and Sensory Processing at 3 to 8 Years of Age'. *Infant Mental Health J.,* 25 (6): 522–39.

Döpfner, M. and Lehmkuhl, G. (1997). 'Von der kategorialen zur dimensionalen Diagnostrik. Prax Kinderpsychol'. *Kinderpsychiat.* 46: 519–47.

Fonagy, P., Gergeley, G., Jurist, E.J. and Target, M. (2004). *Affektregulierung, Mentalisierung und die Entwicklung des Selbst.* Stuttgart: Klett-Cotta.

Gilmore, K. (2000). 'A Psychoanalytic Perspective on Attention-Deficit/Hyperactivity Disorder'. *J Am Psychoanal Assoc.,* 48: 1,259–293.

Green, F. (1975). 'Analytiker, Symbolisierung und Abwesenheit im Rahmen der psychoanalytischen Situation'. *Psyche*, 29: 503–40.

Hurry, A. (2002). 'Psychoanalyse und Entwicklungstherapie'. In: Hurry, A. (Hrsg). *Psychoanalyse und Entwicklungsförderung von Kindern*. Frankfurt: Brandes & Apsel. pp. 43–89.

Jacobvitz, D., Hazen, N., Curran, M. and Hitchens, K. (2004). 'Observations of Early Triadic Family Interactions: Boundary Disturbance in the Family Predict Symptoms of Depression, Anxiety, and Attention-Deficit/Hyperactivity Disorder in Middle Childhood'. *Development and Psychopathology*, 16: 577–92.

Kishiyama, M.M., Boyce, W.T., Jimenez, A.M., Perry, L.M. and Knight, R.T. (2008). 'Socioeconomic Disparities Affect Prefrontal Function'. *Children J Cogn Neurosci.*

Levy, F., Hay, D.A., McStephen, M., Wood, C. and Waldman, I. (1997). 'Leitlinie ADHS aus psychodynamischer Perspektive (noch unveröffentlicht)'. *J. Am. Acad. Child Adolesc. Psychiat.*, 36 (6): 737–44.

Nunberg, H. (1959). *Allgemeine Neurosenlehre.* Huber Stuttgart.

Ogden, T.H. (1989). 'On the Concept of an Autistic-Contiguous Position'. *Int J. PsychoAnal.*, 70: 127–40.

Rutter, M. (2002). 'Nature, Nurture, and Development: From Evangelism through Science toward Policy and Practice'. *Child Development*, 70 (1): 1–21.

Sandberg, S. (1996). 'Hyperkinetic or Attention Deficit Disorder'. *Brit. J. Psychiat.* 169: 10–17.

Solnit, A.J. (1987). 'A Psychoanalytic View of Play'. *Psychoanal Stud Child.* 42: 205–19.

Spitzer, M. (2002) 'Editorial: Dopamin in der Wohngemeinschaft'. *Nervenheilkunde*, 4: 166–68.

Streeck-Fischer, A. (1997). 'Verschiedene Formen des Spiels in der analytischen Psychotherapie'. *Forum Psychoanal.* 13: 19–37.

Streeck-Fischer, A. (2006). '"Neglekt" bei der Aufmerksamkeitsdefizit—und Hyperaktivitätsstörung'. *Psychotherapeut*, 51: 80–90.

Streeck-Fischer, A. and Fricke, B. (2007). 'Lieber unruhig sein, als in einem tiefen, dunklen Loch eingesperrt'. *Prax. Kinderpsychol. Kinderpsychiat.* 56: 277–302.

Taylor, E. (1995). 'Syndromes of Attention-Deficit and Overactivity'. In: Rutter, M Taylor, E. and Hersov, L. (eds) *Child and Adolescent Psychiatry.* Oxford: Blackwell Sciences. pp. 283–307.

Teicher, M.H., Andersen, S.L., Polcari, A., Anderso, C.M. and Navalta, C.M. (2002). 'Developmental neurobioloy of childhood stress and trauma'. *Psychiatric Clinic of North America*, 25: 397–426.

Treurniet, M. (1995). 'Was ist Psychoanalyse heute'. *Psyche*, 49: 111–40.

CHAPTER FIVE

Further comments on Sophia's mimetic autism, with special reference to Bion's theory of thinking

Jorge L. Ahumada and Luisa C. Busch de Ahumada

Sophia's clinical narrative has had an eventful journey, meeting different psychoanalytic outlooks and cultures. What follows is our attempt at a second look at some topics raised by our paper 'From Mimesis to Agency: Steps in the Development of Psychic Two-ness' (Busch de Ahumada and Ahumada, 2005), depicting the first eighteen months of treatment of a case of mimetic autism. Of the many valuable suggestions received we shall take special heed of Antonino's Ferro's comments to its Spanish version, putting forward a dialogue with a Bionian, and partly Meltzerian, conceptual frame. Given the current upsurge of autistic spectrum psychopathologies, our argument concerns the conceptual and technical tensions between the autism-derived Tustinian conceptual frame we put to work and the Kleinian and Bionian ones which in goodly part we share; but before going into such issues some historical notes seem necessary.

On the evolution of the concept 'autism'

Autism is a term Eugen Bleuler coined in 1911 as part of the symptomatic triad diagnostic for schizophrenia. It was brought to child psychiatry by Leo Kanner (1943) in his classic paper 'Autistic

Disturbances of Affective Contact'. There, and in a later paper written in 1951 after examining a hundred patients, he described what he considered a child psychosis starting before age two. He astutely noticed that the autistic child does not differentiate between himself/herself and others, between an 'I' and a 'you', highlighting the extreme autistic loneliness, an obsessive concern about preservation of the same in their routines, milieu, and relationships, echolalia, and a neat deficit in spontaneous activity; he also noted an able handling of objects, a phenomenal memory for unconnected data, and as concerns language, either mutism or a type of language that was not put at the service of interpersonal communication. Such children resist education (lived as dire intrusion). The title of the 1951 paper, 'The Conception of Wholes and Parts in Early Infantile Autism', relates centrally with our present interests: as he puts it, for the autistic child the whole must be preserved in its entirety, the totality of the experience coming to the child from the outside must be reiterated, and the slightest change of arrangement, even those which are hardly perceived by others, may evoke a violent outburst of rage; the behaviour of the autistic child differs from ordinary obsessive ritualism in that they force the people in their world to behave even more obsessively than they do themselves. Independently, in 1944 Hans Asperger described a similar syndrome, which differs in that language is preserved and people with the syndrome often show surprising abilities. To this date the official US psychiatric classification, the DSM-IV, admits both clinical pictures and adds two others, the Attention Deficit Disorder (ADD) and the Attention Deficit Hyperactivity Disorder (ADHD), which taken together come now to be known as the 'autistic spectrum'.

Within the psychoanalytic literature the term came to the forefront with Margaret Mahler's classic paper 'Autism and Symbiosis: Two Extreme Disturbances of Identity' in 1958. However, its Budapest roots are obvious enough, and it fell upon another Hungarian analyst migrated to the US, Therese Benedek, to firstly speak of the mother–child 'primary unit'. Interestingly, although Melanie Klein had trained for years in Budapest, she made no space for the Ferenczian idea of an initial psychic fusion of the child with its mother, and gave no place to autism in her painstaking enquiry of childhood disturbances: thus the concepts of 'autism' and 'symbiosis' are not part of the Kleinian conceptual framework. Although post-Kleinian authors such as Donald Metzler explored autism at length, this did not change such basic Kleinian conceptual bearings.

It fell upon an analysand of Wilfred Bion, Frances Tustin, to clearly distinguish the dynamics of childhood autism from those of childhood psychoses. After some three decades of research on autism, in her 1986 paper 'Thoughts on Psychogenic Autism with Special Reference to a Paper by Melanie Klein' Tustin revised at more than a half-century distance Melanie Klein's classic 'The Importance of Symbol Formation in the Development of the Ego', which had been published in 1930, this is, a dozen years before Kanner's description of early infantile autism. Tustin points out that Klein registers substantial differences between her patient Dick and the schizophrenic children she had analysed, noting that such cases are often classified as mental deficiency, that Dick was largely devoid of affects and only rarely displayed anxiety and then only in an abnormally small degree, and that 'against the diagnosis of dementia precox is the fact that the essential feature of Dick's case was an *inhibition* in development and not a *regression*' (quoted by Tustin 1986: 50; emphasis in original). She also registers substantial differences from Klein's usual technique: Klein acknowledges that she does not interpret the material until it has found expression in various representations but in this case, where the capacity to represent was almost entirely lacking, she was obliged to interpret on the basis of her general knowledge (Tustin, 1986: 52–53). Tustin highlights that in the schizophrenic child the processes of projective identification are quite active and we find a contact with the awareness of an inside and an outside, jointly with an acknowledgement of objects distinct from himself/herself, while the autistic child connects with sensations rather than with objects as such, feeling continuous with the world rather than separate from it. Living as he or she does in a state of imitative fusion with objects in the outside world, Tustin (1986: 55) insists that a primal sense of 'me-ness' has to be well-established before long-standing awareness of the 'not-me' can be tolerated. The result is an extreme vulnerability, where behind the apparent imperviousness the child's energies focus on generating a protective covering of 'me' sensations in order to keep off the threatening 'not-me'.

Her clinical research brought Tustin to partly revise the Kleinian conceptual frame she had used up to that time, taking support in the work of Ferenczi's heir at Budapest Imre Hermann in what concerns the emotional turbulence coming up in the 'crisis-of-two-ness' which takes place when the child comes to contact the terrifying 'not-me'. The ensuing changes in conceptual understanding were in no way restricted to children or even to autism proper. The title of Tustin's final books, *Autistic Barriers in Neurotic Patients* (1986), and *The Protective Shell in Children and Adults* (1990), are witness to the current widening in the understanding of autistic dynamics to neurotic patients and in the case of Gaddini (1984) of the expansion of autistic-mimetic dynamics to the understanding of social processes. Having posited twenty years ago the presence of an autistic level of the personality (Ahumada, 1986) our effort strives to enlarge the Kleinian conceptual frame taking as a point of departure the Budapest notion of an initial 'me'–'not-me' indifferentiation, as has been done by Tustin, Gaddini, and Sydney Klein, and in the steps of Margaret Mahler by José Bleger. Of course in case one does take the Freudian notion of 'primary identification' as meaning a 'primary identicity' between the child and their mother then the differences between the Freudian and the Ferenczian frames iron out; such a view can be borne out by Freud's 'Leonardo' paper (1910) as well as by his later assertion in 'The Ego and the Id', to the effect of that 'At the very beginning, in the individual's primitive oral phase, object-cathexis and identification are no doubt indistinguishable from each other' (1923: 29).

Anyhow, Melanie Klein's path-breaking research on the infantile psychoses and neuroses assumed an initial distinctiveness between ego and object, projective identification becoming the central link between the child's mind and their objects. However, such a model does not seem to make enough place for the issues of attaining tolerance for self-object differentiation—in Tustin's terms, of attaining psychic two-ness—which play such a huge role in the autistic spectrum disorders and which our clinical material on Sophia purports to illustrate in detail. Following Ferenczian lines, to Tustin the baby's body flows into its mother's, and perception of discontinuity can usher in psychic catastrophe. Therefore, as Renata Gaddini (1995) beautifully puts it, the baby confronts two paradoxically opposite tendencies: it tends to continue being at-one with the mother in a state of fusion, while at the very same time it exists as a separate person, outside or even against her. From the 1970s on, Eugenio and Renata Gaddini have studied the *precursor object*, the thumb or pacifier or any nipple-like object, which being felt as *'me'*, or as the 'breast'; 'me' and 'breast' being at this early stage the same thing for the baby re-establishes continuity and cohesion. Imitation belongs at such a level, and failures involve the agonies of loss of self.

Our work with Sophia attempts to expand Tustin's work on the working through of primary loss and emotional and intellectual differentiation, and the attainment of psychic two-ness as an essential component of psychic growth and development. It centrally purports to expand the concept of the precursor object: instead of limiting it to the 'contact' issues of the thumb and the pacifier in the initial stages where bodily union of mouth and nipple abolishes separation, our clinical material will highlight fusional contact with the maternal object at the level of the dynamics of the gaze, a dynamics which extends in time well beyond the earliest stages vehicling in a rather obvious fashion the agonies of loss of self and the ensuing paralysis of the processes of symbol formation and then of psychic growth.

Before passing on to consider the clinical narrative, it must be signalled that the present understanding of autistic and mimetic dynamics goes quite beyond Kanner's description of early infantile autism. In our view such dynamics form a conceptual tripod with neurotic and psychotic dynamics, on an even keel with them. This idea was put forward already a decade ago by André Green in a cover note of a memorial book in tribute to Frances Tustin, edited by Theodore and Judith Mitrani (1997), stating that 'Tustin influenced not only those interested in the specific problems of autistic states but also those who shared an intuition that autism could play the role of a new paradigm for the study of the mind.' Such a perspective is propelled by the current changes in psychopathology, given that paediatricians and psychiatrists are startled by the increase in the incidence of autistic pathologies. While Kanner (2004) estimated the incidence of early infantile autism at 1 in 10,000, presently Christakis *et al.* (2004) consider on the basis of the current bibliography that between 4 and 12% of children in the US are affected by ADHD, which has become nowadays the foremost affection in infancy, being found more frequently than child neuroses and of course more often than child psychoses.

Highlights in Sophia's clinical narrative

For motives of space and pertinence we shall introduce the case and then bring up some steps in the clinical process which are relevant to the conceptual issues examined.

Sophia came into treatment at age 3 years 10 months at the prompting of the grandmother; up to then she had been rather tenderly accepted by the family as a 'dummy', being unable to solve problems designed for 18-month babies. Her history was unremarkable except that it evinced no trace of a transitional object. She did not recognize colours, was unable to count, took no initiatives on her own, and did not choose between proposals, responding, 'I don't know,' as a cliché. An older brother was her translator and interpreter of the world, grasping what was meant behind her speech and her wishes much better than the parents. At the kindergarten she followed another girl in all activities; although to her teacher she was 'a lovely', never a bother, it was soon noticed that she did not act on her own or achieve basic goals. That maternal mind-blindness was an issue comes up neatly in her stating that she did not sing or talk to Sophia when she was a baby 'because, anyhow, babies do not understand'. Her vocabulary was restricted to some 20–25 words, most of them mispronounced except for 'mum', 'dad', 'water', and some few others.

In the initial interviews play was poor and stereotyped, with no distinction of individualities, no attribution of names or roles, no agenda, and no process. She would, for instance, haphazardly align dolls or animals, serially feed them *'opa'* (soup), clean their mouths with a napkin equally serially, or undress them all and make them serially pee. At times her face brightened up, her gaze seeking the analyst's (LBA), expecting her to take initiatives. A twice-weekly treatment was agreed upon; after the first vacation a third session was added.

The initial sessions often went on without a word on her side. In the first months repetitive games and drawings went on and on with few variants: her drawings of human figures were sometimes more or less organized, at other times just a haphazard collection of dissembled parts, in the manner of mechanically 'copied' remnants coming out of nowhere. Once she came accompanied by her elder brother; she asked for him to stay in session, which she had never asked for her mother to do. This led to a totally synchronized scene where her brother talked and she adoringly repeated in eco the last syllables; samely whenever Sophia talked the brother went into simultaneous translation.

Her clinging to the analyst's gaze became more evident after the third month, constantly seeking the analyst's eyes for approval. She become vital or she crumbled down depending on whether or not I sustained her gaze. In this frame came her first fit of rage in session: after several interchanges with her puppets saying of some, such as a tiger, that they were friendly, that they all looked at her, she threw an old man/witch to the ground saying that it did not look at her, picked it up and threw it again with all her might, repeating that it did not look at her and that it was bad. Such a display of fury rescued her from crumbling down; later, when the analyst examined the old man/witch puppet she realized that its eyes were in fact almost closed.

A session in the fifth month of treatment dramatically illustrates the place of the dynamics of the gaze in helping to eventually attain a tolerance for the 'me'–'not-me' distinction. She came into session in a happy mood, the analyst greeted her and asked her how she was, and for the first time she responded '*Bem*' (well). Sitting in their identical small chairs in front of each other she looked expectantly at the analyst's eyes. The analyst realized that Sophia's posture exactly mirrored hers, noting that she copied her own posture; she decided to wait. When the analyst moved slightly Sophia seemed to lose her support, her gaze veiled, and she started collapsing; she looked at the floor and then again at the analyst, this time with dull eyes. The analyst vividly felt that Sophia was her marionette, held by strings to her eyes, depending for her very existence on being held alive by her gaze, and then felt it necessary to modulate the tension, asking, 'But what are we doing?' Sophia's eyes brightened, seemingly waiting for a proposal by the analyst; as this was not forwarded, again her gaze roamed the floor. Again the analyst waited, feeling that this would be the only way for Sophia to take initiatives on her own; tension was in the air. After three or four minutes Sophia looked at the analyst, who smiled but did not speak: her gaze went slowly over the analyst's face and then her hands. At that point the analyst said that it seemed to her that Sophia cannot think of what to do because she gets afraid to do so and thus has to wait for the analyst to tell her. Sophia stood up, her face glowing, and went to her case saying that she was going to take the puppet out; this she did, and she approached smiling, saying, 'Hello.' Addressing the puppet, the analyst said, 'Hello, how are you doing?' and Sophia answered, 'I don't know.' The analyst asked the puppet for her name and Sophia responded, 'Lola', for the first time giving a proper name

(Lola is the name of the girl at the kindergarten that she followed everywhere). Asked what she was going to do, she said—still talking as if she were the puppet—that she was going to draw.

Sitting the puppet on the table, and now apparently speaking for herself rather than on behalf of the puppet, she said that she was going to draw Lola, the head, the hand, the foot, the nose; the analyst mentioned that Lola had decided to draw and now Sophia is drawing also. She seemed to reflect on this, drew some hair around a head, and said, 'It's mum,'; then she said, 'It's Iago' (her younger brother), drawing his hair more and more forcibly and then scratching his face so strongly that she broke the pencil's point. The analyst told her that after drawing Mum and Santiago she had grown angry with Santiago, perhaps wanting to be mother's little baby. Nodding in agreement she ripped the sheet to pieces, and thereafter drew in each little piece a small Santiago, which she then cut to pieces. The analyst told her that she might be afraid that Mum might have more babies. Sophia put the bits together and threw them into the wastebasket, taking care to pick up each small piece from the floor and then looked triumphantly at the analyst. Emphasizing the term 'drawn', the analyst told her that now she feels that she can throw the little drawn Santiagos into the bin.

A few minutes later she recapitulated at a tactile body level the 'not-me'–'me' discrimination that shortly before had taken place at the level of the gaze. She drew Santiago again and asked the analyst to draw her mother, which she did; she again drew a very small Santiago, took a small piece of adhesive tape, and asked the analyst, 'How does it go?', meaning on which side the glue was. The analyst responded that she didn't know as she was not touching it; she looked at the analyst fixedly, bewildered by the lack of a response. The analyst responded that she seemed to be afraid at finding out for herself. Amid strong tension, and still looking fixedly at the analyst's eyes, seeking support, she touched the tape with her fingers without looking at it. Finally she looked at the piece of tape, unstuck it from her fingers, turned it around and stuck it over the small drawing of Santiago while saying softly, '*Así va*' (thus it goes). She slowly and deliberately cut another little piece, touched it on both sides, and looked at the analyst; this sequence was repeated several times at an increasingly faster pace, and then she laughed. The analyst told her that she was glad at her realizing by herself how it goes. This drawing of Santiago 'immobilized' by the Scotch tape was not cut to pieces; instead she kept it in her folder.

By the seventh month in treatment devitalization and crumbling had lessened, it was possible to engage in dialogue with her, and her vocabulary had expanded hugely. Notably, she had started confronting and fighting her elder brother. On coming into one session in a good mood she constructed a house, putting some pillows against the desk legs, got into it, said that we must sleep, and asked the analyst to lie down in front of the 'house's door': which the analyst did, saying that in such a way Sophia felt safe, like a baby in the mother's belly. They then rested in silence for some time in what Tustin (1986: 210) calls a 'womblike communal situation'. Sophia then got out saying that she was going to draw the analyst, wrote the analyst's 'name' at the top of the sheet and 'hers' on a side, and thereafter in what seems to be a new episode of 'me'–'not-me' discrimination, she copied many times the outline of her hand and the analyst's hand; then she made a line with the green marker, said, 'It's Iago,' started sticking the marker on it—'Go off, go off, I don't want Iago'—and angrily threw the sheet to the floor. She painted a finger green, and then painted all her fingers, until she ran out of paint; only when the paint became dried and cracked did she go to the lavatory to wash. Soon after she openly came to acknowledge that her cliché 'I don't know,' was due to the fact that she didn't want to think, suggesting that instead of thinking they played a game where the analyst was the mother and she was her two-year-old daughter. In the next session, however, she reverted the roles: she played the mum who taught the analyst how to put together a puzzle.

A clinical fragment at the 14th month of treatment illustrates the emotional storms that can arise as a result of the differentiations entailed by symbol-formation. Sophia came in happy, as was already usual by this time, and engaged in a game where she was a doctor having a daughter called Caroline, while the analyst's daughter had hurt her hand and had to be cured. Somehow she was not a doctor anymore, just the mother of Caroline; as the game seemed to be ending she saw the blackboard, lit up, chose the 'best' chalk and said that she was going to write 'Caroline'. Up to now on announcing that she would write she only made some scrawl, but she knew the letters of her name, which in session she would use haphazardly. She asked the analyst to tell her how 'Caroline' was written, then copied laboriously the letters and asked whether it did say 'Caroline'. When told 'yes' she was happy and asked the analyst to write something. The analyst wrote 'Sophia'. Sophia looked at it and exclaimed, 'I do not know how to read.' Suddenly she lit up again and said in a surprised tone 'Sophia!' The analyst told her 'yes' and then she wrote herself 'So-phi-a'; she was quite happy and showed the analyst the numbers in a chart recognizing them correctly from zero to nine. After doing this something both intense and startling took place. She had been happy and loose until she realized all that she had done by herself: she then became anguished, her gaze turned opaque, and she went into a full-blown crisis of two-ness in the manner of a temper tantrum. She violently turned around whatever was in her toy box, then got on all fours and went around the office barking. The analyst asked what had happened, and said that it seems that when she realizes that she knows how to do things then she gets afraid. Sophia sat on the floor, looked at the analyst very seriously and possibly sadly, and with a small voice asked, 'Can we play that I am a small baby and you are my mum?' The analyst told her that it seemed that she got scared of being independent and so had to come back, even if only playing, to be a baby having a mother who cares for her, and who takes charge of everything. She listened, looked around, and insisted, 'Come, play.' At this time was heard the voice of her small brother in the waiting room, coming with the mother to fetch her: Sophia said, 'Mum has come,' and took off. On arriving there the analyst found her sitting on her small brother's pram, looking at her triumphantly—perhaps also mockingly—as if to say, 'Look where I am.'

We closed our clinical narrative at this point, Sophia having attained a delightful spontaneity. Indeed, the family commented on how lively she had become.

About our conceptual comments

On Sophia's broad diagnosis suffice it to say that she amply complies with the requirements established by the DSM-IV for the diagnosis of 'autistic disorder'. Of the diagnostic categories Tustin described, Sophia is not a shell-type, encapsulated autist, nor an entangled, schizophrenic-like one: she is, as her family put it, a convivial, attractive, submissive, 'dummy'. Mahler's notion that symbiotic psychoses may go into a secondary autism (Mahler *et al.*, 1975) does not fit either, because no psychosis can be said to be present: here we find, as Tustin (1988: 103–104) finds in autism, 'very little mind', a void of fantasies, and an obstructed transference. As we see it, the mimetic/symbiotic component is the healthier part of her psyche opening the way to analytic progress. Also, here deficit and conflict are to our mind intertwined and, importantly, it is in the access to conflict immediately following an emotionally holding link—the 'context of togetherness'—that progress is made. Much, if not most, of such holding initially happens within a mimetic transference mirroring with the maternal object, this being why we describe her case as a 'mimetic autism'. In our understanding, overtly autistic phenomena and mimesis correspond to polar moments of the structure.

Some degree of pathological symbiosis may likely have been enacted with the mother; what is observable, however, is the mimetic entente with her elder brother as her overall world interpreter, then that with her friend Lola as her leader and interpreter at the kindergarten, and finally with her analyst in the transference. In fact, it was mind-blindness as a parasitic component of the pathological symbiosis that, after an initial period of rather absent-minded rambling and perseverations in session, came firstly to the forefront in Sophia's enacting on her dolls the mind-blind, mechanical mother—her identification with the stronger victorious opponent, to use Ferenczi's (1932) term. Thereafter and increasingly, a mimetic transference relational frame came to be established, mainly at the level of the gaze and eye-to-eye contact with the analyst, with Sophia continuing in such a frame to handle the dolls and animals serially, with no individual distinctions. Moments of a 'context of togetherness' (Tustin, 1986: 303) started to evolve.

We mentioned before Eugenio and Renata Gaddini's (1995) concept of the precursor object, this is, the object of primary identification sustaining the baby's imageless illusion that he/she is mother and the mother is baby, with no differentiation of inner and outer: at this stage failure precipitates the agonies of self-loss; also, our extension of the concept to the dynamics of the gaze. Upon what we can clinically discern, a significant step occurred after about three months of therapy, whereby she constantly sought the analyst's gaze for her approval and depended on her recognition for liveliness or dejection; additionally she started greeting the analyst in a friendly manner by way of the tiger puppet. Coincidentally, there emerges a split of two psychic universes, those of her friendly good objects—those looking at her granting recognition—and persecutory bad ones, the man/ witch that withholds recognition by not looking at her.

A further step in the evolution of the gaze as precursor object in the transference towards transitionality by the way of the crisis-of-twoness comes up in the scene at five months of treatment. By this time the link to the analyst has become more resilient, and Sophia responds 'well' to her greeting. The effort at visual fusion mirroring herself on the analyst posture is obvious, as are her taking the analyst as the source of all initiatives and an agonizing tension when guidance is not provided. Mention of her fears of her own thinking and her dependence on the analyst's initiatives help Sophia act on her own, including attributing to her puppet for the first time a proper name, 'Lola', the name of her mimetic partner at the kindergarten. Then she draws her mother and immediately her younger brother; she attacks her brother's image first with the pencil, and thereafter by tearing the sheets to pieces and carefully throwing the pieces into the wastebasket. (As we can see in several scenes, side by side with differentiation from the analyst/ mother, her baby brother Santiago comes up as a main persecutory object whom she attacks.) A new drawing of the mother and a very small Santiago follow, which is continued by the far-reaching scene with the bit of Scotch tape, with the—to Sophia—stunning finding that the analyst cannot know which side of the tape the glue is on given that she does not touch it. Sophia thereby starts to differentiate her own actions from the analyst's initiatives, and presumably her own body from the analyst/mother's, in what amounts to a definite eureka process of discovery, which she studiously repeats several times.

Additional steps in discerning herself from the primary identification enacted with the analyst, marking the step-by-step, resistance-plagued, and laborious passage from use of the analyst as precursor object to her being used transitionally on the way to separateness comes up at six months of treatment, just after the summer holidays. There she ascribes the analyst a name which she 'writes' in her copy-cat manner. Painting her own fingers and hands as a way of differentiating her own body and actions from the mother's unspontaneity seemed to be part of her process of self-discovery. Contact with spontaneity and bodily separateness brings in a tirade of stunts while brandishing her cliché slogan 'I don't know.' However, her voicing 'I don't know, you say it, I don't want to think,' shows that she can now think further about her cliché. Thereafter she transparently dramatizes the motive for her anti-thought stance, asking that the analyst be the mother and she her two-year-old daughter, and openly asking for milk.

Leaping forward now to the session in the fourteenth month of therapy, we find it retraces at a higher level of self-discrimination and symbol formation the processes and huge resistances observed at the fifth month of treatment. In the 'doctor' game, as the mother of her daughter Caroline, she suddenly spotted the blackboard, lit up, asked the analyst how the name 'Caroline' was written and carefully copied its letters. In this emotional context, when the analyst then wrote 'Sophia', she came for the first time to really read her name, and then to write it. Emotional turmoil and enacted regression again followed on the eureka discovery, including massive muscular discharge, her going on all fours, and her acting the barking dog. She soon, however, was able to regain containment at the level of play, asking the analyst to 'come, play'.

The shift towards transitionality of phenomena in the analytic space and expansion in Sophia's personal space coincided with a lessening of persecutory anxieties. As Christmas neared, the once intensely persecutory old man/witch, which she had thrown to the floor in a fit of fury because he did not look at her, came to be included in the play/celebration, metamorphosed into a Santa Claus.

To end this clinical presentation we must emphasize that its focus resides on the transference installation of the analyst as precursor object and the evolution of the analytic link towards the predominance of mimetic and then transitional phenomena in the road to two-ness and, in Alvarez's (1995: 242) terms, to agency over one's mind: on what might be called the 'work of two-ness'. Discovery of separateness and spontaneity, the accomplishment of symbol-formation and the access to agency over one's mind, ushers in emotional turbulence, because progress in the work of two-ness involves renouncement of unity at the level of the mimetic link.

On the need to expand Bion's theory of thinking to account for autistic-mimetic dynamics

Of the various comments to our earlier paper (Busch de Ahumada and Ahumada, 2005), we shall single out for its relevance Antonino

Ferro's (2007) commentary to its Spanish translation. Generously, he deems the paper important on several accounts:

1. because it puts to the fore the issue of the psychoanalytic approach to autism at a time when it is being widely contested;
2. because it shows an analyst that does not evade the profoundest level of psychic suffering, managing to conduct Sophia towards a level of psychic normalcy in a relatively brief time span; and
3. because it engages in an exquisitely psychoanalytic manner the deepest level of psychic life: autism and stupidity as a defence, whereby its value reaches beyond child analysis into the deep functioning of adult analyses.

At a more conceptual level, Ferro offers considering, on the side of the author's model which he finds coherent, agreeable, and rich in results, another model or perhaps another language, inspired by Bion's ideas.

The state of indistinct sensoriality includes proto-emotive states which need to find the *reverie* of a receptive mind so that, passing from reception to transformation, it allows progressive alpha-betization of sensoriality. By this process, *beta-elements* (sensoriality—proto-emotions) are transformed into *alpha-elements*, this is, into emotive pictograms giving place to the development of wakeful dream-thoughts which is at the base of a capacity for thinking, feeling, and dreaming. In the absence of such a process, or due to a negative or reversed *reverie*, the most diverse defences come up, the most extreme of which being autism, which empties itself not only of alpha-elements but also of the apparatus to produce them; this is, it empties itself of the *alpha-function* with bi-dimensionalization of the mind. Stupidity and flattening are extreme defences erected to avoid everything being destroyed by the tsunami of beta-elements.

In bi-dimensionality, he says, we find a sort of undifferentiated fog where everything turns indistinguishable and there is no emotional thickness, a kind of dyslexia of the emotions, if not an alexia, which does not allow them to be perceived nor discriminated consequent of a lack of the transforming reception of the maternal *alpha-function*.

If things go well, we are on the road from the clouds of sensoriality to the emotive pictograms. We find then that it is possible to discern the different emotional states, and thereby to give a name to and to contain the emotions, this is, to gain access to consciousness (Sophia) which in the first place is being conscious of oneself and our internal world. In the absence of such a road we will find '-Sophia' (-K) leading to an unknowing of oneself and to any possibility of deciphering the internal world (impoverished by emptying or evacuation), and the external world (invaded by projective identifications). Through her analyst, argues Ferro, Sophia meets for the first time a capacity for positive reverie, someone that can psychically perceive her, that can be on the same wavelength (*at-one*), that is able to receive her communicational fragments and complete them (alpha-betization processes); but, specially, someone who is not afraid of proto-emotive states: her analyst can accept to be dirtied by emotive stains because she is aware of having a way for removing such stains (this is, to receive, contain, and transform proto-emotive states). Dirtiness (the mass of *beta-elements* that do not scare the analyst) samely as the tiger, the furies, can be accepted because the analyst has the instruments to accept and transform them. Also, the analyst is sensitive to the emotional voltage that Sophia is able to tolerate (the personified game, Lola), so that such personifications allow for the transit from emotional indifferentiation to a capacity to individualize the diverse emotional states. We assist, holds Ferro, to the feminine development through the analyst's ability to be receptive and let herself be penetrated by the girl's emotions: the analyst knows that she has to attain *alpha-function* (lavabo function) so that trust can be established. At the end of the alphabetization process the child can read her name as well as the numbers from 1 to 10. Also, the child now has a separate identity. The analyst is unafraid of emotional violences, knowing their importance for psychic evolution, and is able to contain and transform them: which allows her to vehicle to the child the method to contain and 'cook' her emotions with no need to fall into terror or camouflage herself in indifferentiation or stupidity.

We have quoted at length from Dr. Ferro's exquisitely thoughtful comment in order to build the background for our response. We must now thank him for providing the stimulus for an examination of Bion's theory of thinking made from the standpoint of Sophia's clinical narrative: in other words, for a comparison between the conceptual model Bion built upon his clinical work with adult schizophrenic patients, and what emerges from the clinical process of childhood mimetic autism. We coincide in that stupidity and emotional flattening attempt to hold off what is felt to be an emotional tsunami and that in the terrain of 'two-dimensionality' (to use Metzler's [1975] terms) we find, as Ferro (2007: 850) puts it, 'a sort of undifferentiated fog where everything turns indistinguishable and lacks emotional thickness'. The lack of emotional thickness results in our view from what Ferenczi (1924) called *autotomy*, the emotional dematerialization as a consequence of cumulative trauma.

We will take as a point of departure for our discussion the Bionian term 'alpha-betization' that Ferro uses, which to us covers some issues—but only some—of what takes place in this psychoanalytic process. In our view, our communicational tool is not in the beginnings, nor perhaps fundamentally, verbal language; as Freud (1913: 161) puts it, quoting Goethe's *Faust*, 'in the beginning was the Deed', and given that emotionally relevant deeds take place within a relationship, this may be alternatively put as: 'in the beginning is the relationship'. In Ferenczian terms it might be stated that achieving a verbal language that is valid for communication with others is possible for the autistic child only inasmuch as the emotions that had been dematerialized by a lack of adequate responses along his development (in Ferro's terms, by negative reverie) can come to be 're-materialized' in the session. And we coincide also in that the road towards 'alpha-betization' often involves traversing strong emotional turbulence which in the clinical material presented tends to take the form of the crisis-of-two-ness.

Let's attempt to pinpoint an aspect of the task that in our opinion does not adequately fit into the Bionian idea of reverie. These patients, as Kanner noted in the early fifties, do not distinguish between a 'me' and a 'not-me', and thereby between an 'I' and a 'you': to attain such a distinction is an essential part of the psychoanalytic task. We must achieve on the one hand a function of *contact* and *holding* (the dimension of reverie, the *at-one*), and, on the other hand, we must achieve also a function of *delimitation*, it being indispensable for arriving at a tolerance of the discrimination of the analyst as part of the 'not-me'. It does not suffice to bear the paradox, as Winnicott (1971) assumed, because in case me–you discrimination is not achieved the analyst would continue to be indiscriminately co-opted as internal to what the child deems to be 'me'. It happens, however, that as we approach discrimination of the analyst as part of a 'not-me', we unavoidably also approach the violences of the crisis-of-two-ness.

Accesing delimitation requires a measure of confrontational slant of the analyst's actions and/or verbalizations whenever the issues of me–you distinction come to the fore, which becomes notorious in the dramatic scene at the fifth month of treatment, in which the girl mirrors in a strictly mimetic manner the analyst's posture, and the analyst decides to keep such a posture. As a result, the girl manages to make conscious contact with the corporeal mimesis with which she was sustaining herself emotionally, which in turn leads such mimesis towards fracture. We are then witness to a transformational cycle in the passage from *mimetic mirroring* to the emergence of *a self-interpretive space* as concerns a relationship, which is initially mute: following her collapse and after three or four minutes the girl looks at the analyst, the analyst smiles at her but does not speak, the girl's gaze examines the analyst's face and hands, the analyst points out that thinking by herself seems to scare her, and then, in front of a question that the analyst poses, after seeking a puppet and speaking 'from' the puppet, the child for the first time poses a proper name, 'Lola'. Some measure of tolerance to a discrimination of the 'me' and the 'not-me', this is, of the self and object as two distinct terms in the relationship, comes up in this sequence as a requisite first step in the way to an acknowledgement of individuals and their nomination, namely for 'alpha-betization'.

What seems to be the most difficult clinical point to investigate and conceptualize is the relation between the functions of contact and holding in the *at-one*, and the functions of delimitation and insight, which depend on each other inasmuch as that only in the context of the *at-one* can a tolerance for psychic pain and for the emotional turbulence accompanying the 'me'–'not-me' discrimination be built up. Dependence on *at-one* togetherness of the 'me'–'not-me' delimitation and the resultant opening up to genuine symbol-formation seems to happen not only in the sequence just described but in other sequences also, such as, and perhaps foremostly, in the scene of intra-uterine communion after the first vacation, which is followed by a crucial progress inasmuch as Sophia arrives to realize, and to verbally express, that she does not want to think. We consider this dependence on the communion of the *at-one* as being due to the issue that fusional 'wholes' are teared apart by the processes of thought. In any case, the clinical material presented shows that moments of ego integration and symbol-formation in turn lead to emotional turbulence, as is most notably present in the session at 14 months of treatment, after realizing that for the first time she has written 'So-phi-a'.

A comment on the term 'sensoriality', which Bion takes as the socle of his theory of thinking. The term comes from philosophy: Descartes ontically opposed psychism as what is properly human, this is the reasoning mind (*cogitatio*) and conscious will, to a purely mechanical sensoriality belonging, samely as affects, to what is merely animal in man, and thereby mechanical in the strong sense of this term. The impact of Descartes was widely felt on both sides of the Channel: as a foremost Cartesian scholar, John Cottingham (1986: xxxvii) reminds us that not only the philosophers on the Continent but also Locke, Berkeley, and Hume in the British islands 'bear the unmistakable imprint of Descartes' thought concerning the structure of human knowledge, the nature of the mind and the relationship between mind and matter'. In the philosophy of consciousness sensoriality is opposite to the properly psychic. But, how can 'sensoriality' be clinically distinguished from the primordial psyche, from what Bion himself calls the proto-emotive and the proto-mental? In our clinical material we have been witness to Sophia's self-differentiation from the analyst as it evolves in the very same fifth-month session through different sensorial modalities: at the level of the gaze and soon after at at a tactile level with the piece of Scotch tape. But what matters there is not the 'sensoriality' as such but the psychic evolutions transcurring thereby. So it might be preferable for our domain to leave the term 'sensoriality' aside as a mere philosophical—and if one so wishes, psycho-physiological—abstraction. The situation is different, given that they can be pinpointed clinically well enough, in the case of concepts such as 'auto-sensuality' (Tustin, 1986: 59) or 'mimetic identicity' with an other not acknowledgeable as such, which are both at the service of obviating contact with the 'not-me'.

In our view the terms 'relationship' and 'indifferentiation' do not oppose each other at the level of primordial psychic stages. This can again be exemplified by the scene at the fifth month of treatment where the girl's mimetic mirroring sustained itself by her 'hanging' from the analyst's gaze; this shows that mimetic identicity and relationship go well hand-in-hand. Also, that we hold that the capacity for a 'me'–'not-me' distinction is not found at the level of primordial psychism in no way goes against our considering the presence of an initial ego, given that from the start the baby undergoes affects and anxieties, and builds upon them in their experiences.

In our view the clinical material presented and, more amply, experience with the treatment of children in the autistic spectrum range, requires an extension of Bion's theory of thinking in order to make a distinct place for the daunting issues of self-primal object differentiation, with their attending pain and turbulence. This is to say, it needs to be extended to include the most primordial, pre-schizo-paranoid levels of mind where there is no distinction between baby and mother. Phenomena of self-primal object differentiation are we think particularly explicit in the clinical course of the unfolding of Sopha's mimetic autism, but we gather—and here again we agree with Ferro—that they apply in some manner or other to other clinical pictures and to adult patients. Such a two-level model of mind, at a time fusional *and* schizo-paranoid from a certain point in development on, would likely help throw additional light on such controversial concepts as 'primary envy': acknowledgement of the goodness of the object *as* goodness belonging *to* the object entails a surrender of fusional identicity, and thus entails the agonies and furies of self-loss.

Let us end with a hopeful note: three years after finishing her analysis Sophia is well advanced in elementary school, academically holding her place solidly in the middle of her class. Socially she is well regarded and has plenty of friends. This should tell something about the potency of the psychoanalytic approach to the autistic spectrum, when treatment begins early enough.

Bibliography

Ahumada, J.L. (1986). 'Trauma, identification, evolution'. In: *The Logics of the Mind. A Clinical View*. London: Karnac. pp. 115–24.

Alvarez, A. (1995). 'Verbal rituals in autism: the concept of autistic object and the countertransference'. In: Mitrani, T. and Mitrani, J.L. (eds) *Encounters with Autistic States*. Northvale NJ & London: Jason Aronson.

Busch de Ahumada, L.C. and Ahumada, J.L. (2005). 'From mimesis to agency: Clinical steps in the work of psychic two-ness'. *Int. J. Psychoanal.* 86: 721–36.

(2007). El autismo: ¿un nuevo paradigma? Respuesta a los Dres. Velleda Cecchi, Antonino Ferro y Virginia Ungar. *Revista de Psicoanálisis* 64: 863–72.

Christakis, D.A., Zimmerman, F.J., DiGiuseppe, D.L. and McCarthy, C.A. (2004). 'Early television exposure and subsequent attentional problems in children'. *Pediatrics*, 113: 708–13.

Cottingham, J. (1986). 'General introduction. The Meditations and Cartesian Philosophy'. In: Descartes, R. *Meditations on First Philosophy.* Ed. by J. Cottingham. Cambridge: Cambridge Univ. Press. pp. xviii–xxxviii.

Ferenczi, S. (1980[1924]). *Thalassa: A Theory of Genitality*. London: Karnac.

Ferenczi, S. (1955[1932])., Notes and fragments'. In *Final Contributions to the Problems and Methods of Psychoanalysis*. London: Hogarth.

Ferro, A. (2007). 'Comentario al trabajo "De la mimesis a la espontaneidad: Pasos en el trabajo de la separatidad psíquica"'. *Revista de Psicoanálisis*, 64: 849–51.

Freud, S. (1910). 'Leonardo de Vinci and a memory of his childhood'. *S.E.*, 11.

Freud, S. (1913). 'Totem and taboo'. *S.E.*, 13.

Freud, S. (1923). 'The ego and the id'. *S.E.*, 19.

Gaddini, E. (1984). 'Changes in psychoanalytic patients up to the present day'. In: Wallersten, R. S. (ed.) *Changes in Analysts and their Training.* IPA Monograph No. 4.

Gaddini, R. (1995). 'From fear of change to mourning'. In: Mitrani, T. and Mitrani, J.L. (eds) *Encounters with Autistic States.* Northvale NJ & London: Jason Aronson.

Kanner, L. (1943). 'Autistic disturbances of affective contact'. *Nervous Child*, 2: 217–50.

Kanner, L. (1951). 'The conception of wholes and parts in early infantile autism'. *Am. J. Psychiat.*, 113: 23–26.

Mahler, M. (1958). 'Autism and symbiosis, two extreme disturbances of identity'. *Int. J. Psychoanal.*, 39: 77–83.

Mahler, M., Pine, F. and Bergmann, A. (1975). *The Psychological Birth of the Human Infant: Symbiosis and Individuation.* New York: Basic Books.

Meltzer D. (1975). 'Dimensionality as a parameter of mental functioning'. In: Meltzer D. *et al. Explorations in Autism: A Psycho-Analytical Study.* Pertshire, Clunie Press. pp. 223–38.

Mitrani, T. and Mitrani, J. (eds) (1997). *Encounters with Autistic States: A Memorial Tribute to Frances Tustin.* Northvale: N.J., Aronson.

Tustin, F. (1986). 'Thoughts on psychogenic autism with special reference to a paper by Melanie Klein'. In *Autistic Barriers in Neurotic Patients.* New Haven CT & London: Yale Univ. Press. pp. 48–66.

Tustin, F. (1988). 'Psychotherapy with Children who Cannot Play'. *Int. Rev. Psychoanal.* 15: 93–105.

Tustin, F. (1990). *The Protective Shell in Children and Adults.* London: Karnac.

Winnicott, D.W. (1994[1971]). *Playing and Reality.* London: Karnac.

DISCUSSION OF JORGE L. AHUMADA AND LUISA C. BUSCH DE AHUMADA'S PAPER

Angela Joyce

This paper by Jorge L. Ahumada and Luisa C. Busch de Ahumada is implicitly motivated by the challenge from clinical practice in child psychiatry that has seen a hitherto unexplained explosion, frequently noted in the professional literature and popular press, in the numbers of children who are diagnosed with so-called autistic spectrum disorders (ASD). Psychoanalytically based treatments tend not to be considered in a culture where organic explanations predominate. Justification for this is hard to find as there is meagre understanding of why this explosion is taking place. Explanations in the aetiology and inter- and intra-psychic dynamics of these conditions perhaps can best be demonstrated by detailed reports of cases that do or do not respond to treatments, and accounts of psychoanalytic treatment seems to be best placed to provide this. One might assume that those that respond well, including development of function and recovery, indicate that the organic explanation (genetic, inherent brain structure, bio-chemistry, and so on) is not sufficient. It requires a wider and deeper elaboration including an understanding of complex psychic functioning in the developmental environment.

The authors are interested in teasing out both at a conceptual and technical level, psychoanalytic understanding of the treatment of one kind of ASD, that of psychogenic autism, the case that forms the heart of this paper. My discussion will be clinically focused, and I will then turn to the psychoanalytic conceptual and technical matters that are raised by the clinical material.

The clinical case

We are told that the nearly four-year-old Sophia is regarded by her family as a rather sweet natured dummy, whose mother herself had an IQ of 70 when she was a child, perhaps indicative of an inheritable organic cause for her daughter's condition. However the grandmother brings Sophia for treatment to a psychoanalyst suggesting a question in her mind as to the origin of these features of the females in the succeeding generations. Could the 'dummy' be caused by factors other than inherent limitations to intelligence? The assessment indicates autism possibly of a psychological origin, which is described as 'mimetic'. Sophia echoes the words spoken to her, her own language being almost non-existent and she is lacking in initiative. Her clichéd response, 'I don't know,' to most questions invites us to wonder what cannot be known, indeed what may be forbidden from being known. We are also told that her mother did not talk or sing to Sophia as a baby 'because anyhow, babies do not understand'. It seems that her other children, older and younger boys, if they had received the same treatment (we are not told), had not turned out the same way. This might make us wonder why? Was there something in having a daughter that brought out the mother's 'mind-blindness', silent and mechanical, an expression of a way of relating or being related to, encoded in her procedural memory of herself as a girl baby, now re-presented with her own daughter? Her low IQ as a child may well indicate her own infantile inability to understand what could not be understood in the relational environment. Perhaps her mother, the grandmother, recognized something of the past, now re-enacted by her daughter with her granddaughter, and sought to repair it by the referral for psychoanalytic treatment. We are not told if there is any concurrent parent work, although one would expect that this would be a *sine qua non* with the individual treatment of a young child.

As the treatment gets going Sophia re-presents with her analyst her silent early life. Her only existence is as an echo; devoid of a self and the spontaneity that would indicate its existence, she functions in an imitative way, mechanically repeating behaviours of 'care' with the doll figures. This seems to be the limit of psychic representation: the play lacks imaginative elaboration and seems to be simply a repetition of events to which she has been subjected. There is no aggression. We have the sense that the analyst allows this to unfold, not pre-empting or forcing premature understanding.

As the analytic setting is established where the analyst is receptive to Sophia's psycho-somatic states, particularly her 'constantly seeking the analyst's eyes for approval', Sophia can risk 'her first fit of rage' against the puppet (old man/witch) who does not look at her. Not seen by her 'subjective object' (Winnicott, 1962a: 57) Sophia's archaic self is imbued with the affective sense of non-existence, just as her object also does not exist, which is the stuff of the autistic mimetic bubble that she inhabits. This play suggests that Sophia is already beginning to move from the imitative form, indicative of Ogden's (1992: 30) 'autistic contiguous position', where sensory-based experience not yet psychically represented predominates, towards a space where the transitional object as a primitive symbol is 'both a memorial to the lost unity with the object and an attempt to re-instate it *in effigia*' (Wright, 1991: 104).

This play gives material for re-construction in our formulation: the almost closed eyes of the puppet suggest a 'witch mother' whose non-availability ruptured Sophia's 'going on being' (Winnicott, 1956: 303) prematurely, with her resulting mind less ness. The powerful affect suggests that Sophia suffered a profound de-cathexis from her primary object, now represented in the displacement of play. The analytic space provides her with an experience of congruency where her analyst is attentive and adapts to her unique presentation, not disrupting the establishment of her being in this context. Sophia's rage, held by the analyst's mind-full presence, promotes ego integration rather than fragmentation: she does not 'crumble down'.

The session in the fifth month condenses the predicament of the child with her analyst. The mimicry of posture concretely expresses the false self that Sophia has defensively constructed to deal with the falling forever/annihilation feelings that have been intimated previously. But how is she to relinquish this false self if the consequences are so horrific? No wonder the analyst in her counter-transference felt that she held Sophia's very existence in her gaze! Intuitively, however, the analyst senses that Sophia is ready for something more; she is not 'mind-blind' but is confident that her young patient is beginning to understand. Her judicious interpretation of Sophia's fear of thinking is predicated upon this recognition. Its effects reflect Sophia's sense that the analyst recognizes that she, Sophia, has a mind now that can work, already different within this new analytic relationship. Sophia goes to the puppet (the locus of the earlier transformative enactment) and for the first time she could personalize it, giving it a name; not her own but that of 'Lola' with whom she is identified. Sophia, seemingly working out of her sense of self, speaks for herself, separating out from the imitated object 'Lola' whom she then 'objectifies' by drawing. The figure is transformed into 'Mum' and then 'Iago' (the name she gives Santiago, her younger brother) and subjected to a violent attack. Sophia's immense jealousy is thus enacted in the play and articulated by her analyst as anger and her wish to be her mother's little baby (implicitly in the place of Iago). We might hypothesize that this is the re-presentation of the compounding trauma in Sophia's young life: her mother's pregnancy and the arrival of her younger brother. The analytic work allows this, taking place at the level of the body and enacted in play. Increasingly we can see its elaboration in psychical representation. The analyst's de-adaptation or 'disillusion' (Winnicott, 1963: 87) is contingent with Sophia's growing ability to find her own agency; Sophia is now on the road to relinquishing her false self and finding her own psychical elaboration of experience, her representational world, with the help of her analyst.

Throughout the clinical presentation the gradual emergence of Sophia's aggression reflects her growing vitality, and her propensity to collapse recedes as her ego coheres and integrates. She plays in a significantly different way than before, engaging her analyst as an other who can be relied upon to be interested; the play becomes more complex involving both the expression of her regression to dependence in the play of the baby in the belly which can be risked now (Winnicott, 1954), and progressively in her reading and writing her name on the blackboard. However this is all understood, this clinical account gives a convincing description of the successful psychoanalytic treatment of a child that is rarely available currently outside the consulting rooms of private practitioners.

Conceptual discussion

The central conceptual question raised by the authors is an aetiological one concerning the nature of early mental life and the impact of its psychopathology on on-going development. This necessarily includes a question about the early relational environment, the essential context of earliest development. Despite there having been a long history within psychoanalytic developmental theory of a split between those that proposed a primary unity of infant and mother and those that took an albeit primitive separateness as present from the beginning of life, and the compounding differences accorded the relational environment, there seems a greater contemporary consensus on these matters. Partly as a result of shifts within psychoanalysis (certainly Bion [1962] but also Bowlby 1940 and Winnicott 1945) and the influence of findings from developmental psychology (Stern, 1985; Trevarthan, 1979) which prompted such analytic thinkers as Margaret Mahler and Frances Tustin to alter their own theorizing (Tustin, 1991), the multi-layered complexity of the inter-psychic and intra-psychic contributions to development and its disturbance seems more appreciated today. However this raises the question about how these different conceptual frameworks relate to each other. Sometimes it can seem that different words are being used for essentially the same concept, so that, for instance, Bion's 'container-contained' theory (Bion 1962) and Winnicott's (1960: 41) theory of 'holding' are often used interchangeably. However they are predicated upon quite different theories about early mental life and the primary link between infant and mother in just the realm that the Ahumadas are writing: is there a primary separateness or not at the beginning of life?

In my reading of this clinical case I have used a primarily Winnicottian frame which espouses a subtle view of early mental life where merger and separateness are paradoxically both present. In the state of what he calls 'the illusion of omnipotence' (Winnicott, 1945: 154) the mother's almost complete adaptation to the baby's needs at the beginning means that 'omnipotence is nearly a fact of experience' (Winnicott, 1951: 238). Thus the baby starts off with the sense that all that happens comes from the command of his own need: the mother's existence is recognized in this way but only as congruent with the baby's need. The sense of mother, a 'subjective object' (Winnicott, 1962a: 57), resides in the infant's experience of the emotion felt 'within the subject–object compound', where 'relating really means "being in a given emotional state"' with the object (Scarfone, 2005: 40). This is prior to true separateness and with it the availability of the defences of projection and introjection, as in Bion's explanation (1962). This central paradox where the alive and present mother is 'created out of need' and only later 'found' to have a separate existence, is held over time by her holding adaptation and graduated failure to adapt such that the baby gradually comes to experience 'me' as different from 'not me' and to benefit from, 'use' what the m/other provides (Winnicott, 1968: 101).

In Winnicott's account if the mother is unable to sustain the baby's experience of illusion initially before facilitating the necessary 'disillusion' the resulting impingements expose the baby to extreme anxiety, described as 'falling forever' and 'annihilation'. The baby is forced into premature states of awareness that can lead to the development of a false self or a schizoid retreat. In 'Providing for the Child in Health and in Illness' (1962b: 66) Winnicott describes how 'environmental failure' at the stage of extreme dependence (that is, in the first months of life) leads to 'mental defect, non organic [and] childhood schizophrenia'.

We see that in the case of Sophia these concepts can contribute greatly to understanding both her condition and also the psychoanalytic process described. In the context of an intergenerational dynamic this girl's early experience of her primary 'subjective object' was one where the predominant feeling was of mutual mind-less-ness: they could be said to be both 'dummies'. The mother's lack of imaginative elaboration of her baby's primitive somatic being rendered Sophia devoid of the opportunity for the integration of her psycho-somatic integrity and establishment of her self, 'unit status'. It seems that her elder brother afforded a relationship where a false self, a caretaker self, based on imitation, could be established (Winnicott, 1960). All this seems to have been compounded by Sophia relinquishing her primary aggression that alternatively could have been harnessed in the service of the integration of her ego and the 'destruction of the object' in omnipotent fantasy, allowing her to find this object then as a separate external entity (Winnicott, 1968: 105). For this to have been possible Sophia needed an available maternal object who could 'survive' this destruction, that is to be there to be found. But even if her mother had begun to see her daughter as more of a mind-full person as she approached toddlerhood (which is sometimes the case in my clinical experience of mothers who do not talk to their babies because they 'do not understand'), the pregnancy and arrival of the younger brother as I have suggested above seems to have compounded the earlier trauma and reinforced Sophia's sense of her self and object world as non-existent.

In the clinical process we see the antithesis of this; Sophia has a 'new developmental object' experience in her analyst that enables her frozen development to begin again (Winnicott, 1954: 281; Hurry, 1998: 32–73). During the early months the analyst facilitates Sophia's being to emerge, without premature interpretation, which would have represented further impingement. Sophia very soon demonstrates her use of the setting as she moves to a more transitional way of relating, as the puppet play suggests a re-enactment of the early trauma. This time, however, Sophia's affects are fully engaged, as her rage indicates. The analyst holds the setting, allowing Sophia over time to integrate these accruing experiences.

The significance of the gaze is linked to the gradual move towards separateness both in its somatic nature (a gaze is held across a distance between two bodies) but also in its expressive potentiality. Wright (1991: 107) suggests that the face and the gaze, particularly the recognition of facial expressions, are crucial elements in the process of symbol formation, itself inextricably linked with the development of separateness: 'The expression that shines through the face is the prototype of emergent meaning occurring before language begins to draw the child into a cultural world of symbols.' The analyst holds Sophia's gaze, seeing in it meaning about Sophia's need of her; her approval is sought indicating that she matters to Sophia. Indeed we see just how sensitive and receptive the analyst is to Sophia's states, and particularly to Sophia's use of play as the arena for the emergence of her re-presented history. The difference now is that the object (analyst) is available to her young patient, mindfully elaborating meaning with her. The analyst's timely de-adaption where Sophia's imitation of her posture so eerily tests whether this autistic world of non-existent objects is to prevail, succeeds because it coincides with Sophia's readiness to relinquish her distorted infantile omnipotence and instead find both her self, and the separateness of the other in her analyst.

Throughout, the role of aggression is central. It is indicative of life (or its absence) and indeed if one takes a Winnicottian view, it is the very stuff out of which self, otherness, and separateness is established. Sophia's psychoanalytic treatment provides a setting in which her life-giving aggression could be harnessed and given meaning, thus bringing her out of the autistic bubble in which she was imprisoned. The clinical description ends with Sophia triumphantly conveying to her analyst her newly acquired sense of self: 'Look where I AM', something that had been impossible so very recently.

Bibliography

Bion, W.R. (1962) 'The Psychoanalytic Study of Thinking', *International Journal of Psychoanalysis*, 43: 306–10. (And in Bion, W. [1962]. *Learning from Experience*. New York: Basic Books.)

Bowlby, J. (1940) 'The Influence of the Early Environment in the Development of Neurosis and Neurotic Character', *International Journal of Psychoanalysis*, 21: 154–78.

Bowlby, J. (1958). 'The Nature of the Child's tie to his Mother'. *International Journal of Psychoanalysis*, 39: 350–73.

Hurry, A. (1998). 'Psychoanalysis and Developmental Therapy'. In: Hurry, A. (ed.) *Psychoanalysis and Developmental Therapy*. London: Karnac.

Ogden, T.H. (1992). *The Primitive Edge of Experience*. London: Karnac.

Scarfone, D. (2005). 'Laplanche and Winnicott meet … and Survive'. In: Caldwell, L. (ed.) *Sex and Sexuality: Winnicottian Perspectives*. London: Karnac.

Stern, D. (1985). *The Interpersonal World of the Infant*. New York: Basic Books.

Trevarthan, C. (1979). 'Communication and cooperation in early infancy: a description of primary intersubjectivity'. In: Bullowa, M.M. (ed.) *Before Speech: The Beginning of Interpersonal Communication*. New York: Cambridge University Press.

Tustin, F. (1991). 'Revised Understandings of Psychogenic Autism'. *International Journal of. Psycho-Analysis*, 72: 585–91.

Winnicott, D.W. (1982[1945]). 'Primitive Emotional Development'. In: *Collected Papers: Through Paediatrics to Psychoanalysis.* London: The Hogarth Press. pp. 145–56.

Winnicott, D.W. (1982[1951]). 'Transitional Objects and Transitional Phenomena'. In *Collected Papers: Through Paediatrics to Psychoanalysis.* London: The Hogarth Press. pp. 229–42.

Winnicott, D.W. (1982[1954]). 'Metapsychological and Clinical aspects of Regression within the Psychoanalytic Set-up'. In: *Collected Papers: Through Paediatrics to Psychoanalysis.* London: The Hogarth Press. pp. 278–96. 1982.

Winnicott, D.W. (1982[1956]). 'Primary Maternal Pre-Occupation'. In: *Collected Papers: Through Paediatrics to Psychoanalysis.* London: The Hogarth Press. pp. 300–15.

Winnicott, D.W. (1972[1962a]). 'Ego integration in child development'. In: *The Maturational Processes and the Facilitating Environment.* London: Hogarth Press. pp. 56–63.

Winnicott, D.W. (1972[1962b]). 'Providing for the child in health and in illness'. In: *The Maturational Processes and the Facilitating Environment.* London: Hogarth Press. pp. 64–72.

Winnicott, D.W. (1972[1963]). 'From Dependence towards Independence in the Development of the Individual'. In: *The Maturational Processes and the Facilitating Environment.* London: Hogarth Press. pp. 83–92. London: Hogarth Press.

Winnicott, D.W. (1972[1965]). 'Ego Distortion in Terms of True and False Self'. In: *The Maturational Processes and the Facilitating Environment.* London: Hogarth Press. pp. 140–152.

Winnicott, D.W. (1974[1968]). 'The Use of an Object and Relating Through Identifications'. In: *Playing and Reality.* London: Pengiun Books. pp. 101–11.

Wright, K. (1991). *Vision and Separation.* London: Free Association Books.

CHAPTER SIX

Early affect regulations and its disturbances: Approaching ADHD in a psychoanalysis with a child and an adult

Marianne Leuzinger-Bohleber

1 *Approaching affect regulation and its disorders through psychoanalysis in times of theoretical pluralism*

For all of the theoretical and conceptual differences, most psychoanalytic authors agree that disturbances in early affect regulation are one of the main factors in the genesis of ADHD and other developmental pathologies. In times of theoretical pluralism in psychoanalysis, however, there are differences in the approaches used to explain the source and effects of an early disturbance in affect regulation. This rich diversity in contemporary psychoanalytic theory allows us, on the one hand, as if looking through a kaleidoscope, to perceive ever new information patterns in the complex clinical material and make use of them for the joint process of acquiring knowledge with our patients, as I would like to illustrate with examples from two cases. On the other hand, epistemologically and methodologically, as Charles Hanly will elaborate for us in his paper, the pluralism in psychoanalysis today puts us before demanding problems which, however, I cannot discuss in this context (cf. Leuzinger-Bohleber and Bürgin, 2003; Leuzinger-Bohleber, in press). To stay with the metaphor: the view through the kaleidoscope may very well give us access to the abundance and multiplicity of clinical observation, but, as Hanly explains, this does not relieve us of the need to recognize irreconcilable contradictions in the theoretical explanations of clinical phenomena and make them the subject of an intrapsychoanalytic, interdisciplinary, dialogue devoted to research and unification of the psychoanalytic base knowledge. In this process, as I see it, a form of psychoanalytic conceptual research has a central role to play, which stays close to the clinical research in psychoanalysis while taking the results of empirical and interdisciplinary research into account in its critical reflections on psychoanalytic concepts. Therefore, in my paper I'd like to try to make use of the view through the plural kaleidoscope to search for common features as well as contradictions in explaining the genesis of ADHD, and—together with clinical observations—integrate them into a current understanding of this syndrome.

Ego-psychology authors emphasize that the primary object in a characteristic 'ADHD family' has hardly made it possible for the child to develop enough good, stable ego functions. The child is existentially dependent upon receiving reliable and continuous support from the primary objects to regulate its behaviour, which is to say, its physiological, sensory, motoric, and affective processes. If the parents are not able to provide the child with this kind of support, it will hardly be able to develop adequate primary regulation of its drive impulses and affects: hyperactivity may be one of the consequences! Moreover, drive impulses that have not been sufficiently integrated psychically will flood the ego, especially in situations favouring this, and thus will inhibit or impede altogether the development of secondary-process symbolic thinking—in other words, the ability to focus attention on a particular situation, to verbalize affects, needs, and fantasies, as well as the ability to concentrate.

Be that as it may, according to Spezzano (1993), it was above all William R.D. Fairbairn who, in the 1940s, initiated the explicit discussion of affect regulation. He can be regarded as the *pioneer of psychoanalytic object relations theory*. He became known above all for noting that the libido is not primarily pleasure-seeking but object-seeking. Affects offer the means of distinguishing between 'good' and 'bad' objects and/or experiences and the related ego states, which is of great significance for the psyche because the unbearable negative internalized objects, parts of the ego, and relational experiences are repressed into the unconscious. This is why authors close to *psychoanalytic object relations theory* focus on internalizations of important relationships in earliest childhood when they are looking for plausible explanations for the emergence of ADHD symptoms. They regard internalization processes as central to the formation of psychic structures, but also of drive needs and personality traits. More recent—clinical and empirical—studies have shown that it is important to distinguish between two states of affect in infants: states with relatively low affect activation and states with strong, intensive affect, so-called 'peak affects' (cf. Kernberg, 2001; Laplanche, 1996). In the first, 'mild' affective state, 'normal' internalizations of our experiences can take place through contact with other persons, which lead to the development of normal ego functions. The experiences are tied to pleasant body feelings that are adequate to reality, which—as discussed by Leuzinger-Bohleber and Pfeifer (2002)—leave an impression on the child's 'embodied' memory as sensomotoric-affective coordinations. In later situations with analogous information that we take up over the various sensory channels (auditive, visual, haptic, and so forth), these sensomotoric-affective coordinations help us to produce 'memory'. In other words, based on earlier experiences as orientation in reality, we can develop expectations in terms of what we consider 'normal' behaviour on the part of our interaction partners and 'adequately' interpret them. In the course of development they are connected to images and language. This differs from the experience with so-called 'peak affects', that is, intensive positive and negative affects that exceed the infant's ability to process stimuli. Such extreme affective states, of joy, euphoria, happiness of being together with another person, or of anxiety, fright, rage, or pain, give rise to psychically problematic, but extremely viable, 'embodied" memories: images of idealized relationships that are oriented to the happy moments of the child on the breast and leave their impression on the psyche as wishes for fusion with the love object, of union, and absolute devotion. The extremely negative affects—analogously—produce extreme self-images of a hating being that is at the mercy of intensive aggressions, helplessly exposed to attacks from the outside. The more intensive the frustrations and the experiences of pain—in traumatic experiences, for example—the more intensive will be the aggressive impulses that have been triggered by them, which the child's ego cannot psychically bear or attribute to its own self: this is why it projects these aggressive impulses immediately onto others and consequently feels threatened and persecuted from the outside as well. As a result, a memory of relational experiences that were negative and dangerous—for the self and the object—become engrained as 'psychic truths'. Consequently, at times when peak affect is discharged, or in traumatic situations, there is a psychic tendency to categorize events and experiences as absolutely good or absolutely bad: relationships are split up into an idealized part and a persecuting part.

Under normal, non-traumatic, or as Winnicott calls them, 'good enough' conditions, an increasing tolerance develops vis-à-vis such extreme situations, so that the archaic-primitive experience, splitting between 'good' and 'bad', can finally be psychically integrated (cf. Melanie Klein's distinction between the 'paranoid-schizoid position' and the 'depressive position'). Psychoanalytic object relations theory has emphasized that the external object has to help—through empathy with the helpless infant's condition—to enable the peak affects to be relieved repeatedly, 'reliably' and predictably. Therefore, it conveys a primal trust in a good object. In parallel to this, the 'emerging self' feels itself psychically capable of making its own contribution towards helping to rid itself of extreme frustrations, of anger and hate. Therefore, it defines itself as a fundamentally active, potent self that is not just passively at the mercy of another. In the process, the self can—in the terminology of psychoanalytic self-psychology—eventually do without archaic primitive defence mechanisms, such as the fantasy of the grandiose self or the omnipotent parental imago, and develop a supportive, secure, and coherent core sense of self (cf. Parens, 2010, among others).

In recent years, it has been above all the *empirical findings of affect and infant research* that have roused the interest of psychoanalysts in affect regulation. Numerous studies have shown that the most important reinforcement system in early childhood is the affectivity of the social partner (Krause, 1998, 2005). This is true not only in the first months of life but later as well, when the child as a one-year old, for example, with the increasing mobility and related cognitive, speech, and emotional changes, has to depend more on a social, security-providing assurance of its 'home base' by its primary reference person. A number of impressive studies have been forthcoming on so-called 'Social Referencing'. The most well-known experiment is probably a modification of the crawling over a 'visual cliff', which was originally used to test the child's perception and age-adequate anxiety reactions. New analyses of the video tapes have now shown that crawling children seek eye contact with their mothers as soon as they perceive a (presumed) danger. It provides impressive evidence that it is not the purely cognitive or verbal feedbacks that alleviate the children's fear: it is above all the resonating, emotional reaction of the reference person that can give the child a feeling of security. This example also shows us the relevance of empathic guidance in the early stages of development for the formation of emotional, cognitive, and social skills. If the capacities for 'attunement', containing, and holding, as well as (later) for social referencing are lacking, the child will not be able to identify with these capacities through identification with the 'good enough' object and successively develop its own inner impulse and affect regulation.

Daniel Stern (1985), to name just one example, impressively showed in microanalyses of video-recorded interactions how infants react to their depressive mothers. He distinguished various types of such reactions. Infants of one type seem to try, with all they've got, to bring their 'dead mother' back to life: an observable hyperactive behaviour is the result. Moreover, these babies do not seem to have enough internal and external space for them to experience their own impulses and feelings as indicators of an 'emerging self'. They are too little able to have the recurring experience of a 'self-effect', 'self-coherence', and 'self-affectivity', which gives them the basic feeling of having their own self-history, a feeling which, as we know in the meantime, is one of the prerequisites for the development of a stable core feeling of self. This may be one of the reasons why the development of a 'false self' is often observed in ADHD children in psychoanalytic psychotherapy.

Important contributions to affect regulation have also been forthcoming in empirical attachment research (cf. Döll-Hentkscher, 2008, among others). In this tradition, Peter Fonagy, György Gergely, Elliot L. Jurist, and Mary Target (2002/2004) recently presented an original understanding of affect regulation, which I'd like to mention only briefly here, since Peter Fonagy and Mary Target have elaborated on their concepts in their own papers in this volume. They take up many of the above-mentioned psychoanalytic explanatory models, but formulate the claim to explain the development of affect regulation and its disturbances, as well as the closely related development of mentalization capacity, on the causal basis of a social biofeedback model for the first time. 'Coordinated interactions with the mother' (Jaffe, Beebe, Feldstein, Crown, and Jasnow, 2001; Stern, 1985) often go hand in hand with affect mirroring, which is to say that the mother represents to the child, through her facial and vocal expression, the feelings that she thinks it is having, in order to calm and alleviate the baby's emotions. In our opinion, affect mirroring supports the capacity for affect regulation by giving the child an opportunity to build up secondary representations of its constitutional states of affect. The internalized image of the reference person who reflects what is going on inside the infant becomes the organizer of the child's emotional experience. So, the self is not merely accessible to environmental influence, but is to some extent constituted by its interactions with the social environment' (Fonagy *et al.*, 2002/2004: 15). Consequently, for these authors the concept of 'affect regulation' plays a central role in the constitution of self-development and the development of mentalization capacity.

For the developmental disorders that are the focus here, such as ADHD, it is especially relevant that problematic early relationships, maltreatment, or other traumatizations hamper the development of mentalization and reflection, for, as Fonagy and Target have pointed out, mentalization and secure attachment are primarily the results of good containment experience, in the sense of early affect regulation as just described, in early socialization. Insecure attachment can be understood as the child's identification with the mother's defensive behaviour. These mothers are, for example, not able to mirror the child's negative affects and stress, because they themselves feel threatened by them. When such negative affects are perceived, they probably revive memories of their own unbearable experiences, which then have to be warded off. Consequently, these children can only maintain the closeness to their mother if they sacrifice their ability to reflect at the same time. In the case of so-called 'entangled mothers', on the other hand, negative affects in the child are mirrored in an exaggerated way or are confused with their own experiences, which then seems strange or alarming to the child. In both forms of insecure attachment, the children will internalize the reference person's attitude. The lack of synchronicity between the child's own state of affect and that of its mother then becomes the content of the child's experience of self.

Early severe traumatizations have an even more dramatic effect on the development or, as the case may be, lack of development, in mentalization capacity. In a recent paper, Fonagy (2007) reports on severely traumatized children and adolescents whom he interviewed and/or treated in therapy in prison. One of the main contributing factors behind their acts of violence was that they had developed little if any capacity for mentalization, and consequently were not able, for example, to put themselves in their victims' place, mentally. He speaks of 'violent attachment' and/or of attachment trauma. These adolescents could be most aptly described with the diagnosis of 'borderline disorder'.

Although many of the ADHD children in the Frankfurt Prevention Study (FP) and the therapeutic efficacy study currently underway have also experienced early traumatizations (and exhibit insecure attachment types), most of them could not be characterized as borderline children. The following two case examples are intended to show that they often suffer from serious disorders in affect and drive regulation nonetheless, albeit in a different way.

At this point I would like to raise the question of whether the subgroup of ADHD children, to which the following two patients belong, involves a specific deviant of the early affect mirroring that is related to the depressive illness of the primary object, which proved to be a traumatogenic factor for their children. Depressive mothers, as Daniel Stern's studies also show, will mirror above all the negative peak affects of their babies in a specific *'incongruently, categorically distorted'* (Fonagy *et al.*, 2004: 201, italics, M.L-B) way, and will therefore hardly be able to help their babies develop adequate affect regulation in this regard.

Therefore, from a psychoanalytic point of view, and as one will see from the case examples, it is absolutely necessary to uncover the idiosyncratic trauma history of an ADHD child or adult together with the patient, in order to recognize the specific causes behind the affect and impulse regulation disorder (cf. Bohleber, 2007; Grubrich-Simitis, 2007, among others). In contrast to a form of medication-based treatment, for example, exploratory therapeutic work of this kind offers an opportunity to forego the unconscious roots of the failures in the inner regulation processes which may lead to the ADHD symptoms and instead make an active effort to tackle the weakness in affect and impulse regulation. In the transference to the analyst, the 'embodied memories' of the traumatogenic object relations and related fantasies become recognizable, as well as the yearning for alternative experiences that are used in effective treatments in the sense of the above-mentioned internalization processes, for the development of stable affect regulation.

2 Psychoanalytic treatment as an opportunity to understand the specific causes behind the disorders in affect and drive regulation, and treat them with lasting effect in the therapeutic relationship: Two cases

Because I can only present fragments of clinical material in this framework, I am drawing on two treatment cases that I have published in greater length elsewhere (Leuzinger-Bohleber, 1984, 2000).

2.1 Early disturbance in affect regulation—one of the main determining factors in AD/HS. Insights from the analysis with a child based on a catamnestic follow-up 31 years after the termination of treatment

Nora was referred to me as a ten-year old for psychological evaluation, because her parents, both Ethnology Professors, felt they had 'come to the end of their rope' with her. They had already tried a number of different therapies and advancement programmes with Nora: all of them without success. Now Nora was to be put in a special education programme for children with low IQs because of her chronic failure in school. Nora suffered from an extremely short attention span, low concentration, adipositas, serious sleep disturbances, skin rashes, an almost complete social withdrawal, and forms of self-destructive behaviour (occasionally she cut herself with a knife), as well as sudden aggressive outbursts towards her younger brother.

In the Kramer Intelligence Test Nora had an IQ of 132. The projective tests revealed her absolutely rich, albeit very threatening, inner fantasy world. The Göttinger Form Reproduction Test that was in widespread application at the time revealed signs of an MCD (Minimal Cerebral Dysfunction).

In the four-year child psychoanalysis (three sessions per week), we pieced together the following picture of Nora's trauma history like a puzzle:

> Two days after Nora's birth with many complications, her mother's father died, a serious loss for Nora's mother. She suffered from severe bouts of depression for months and took antidepressants. When Nora was six months of age, she fell out of her father's arm through the open second-storey window. 'Maybe that's the reason for her MCD,' her father said during the evaluation, full of guilt feelings. Nora was laid up in hospital for several weeks and developed severe sleeping and eating problems. When she was one and a half years of age, her brother was born: she reacted with massive jealousy and frequent obstinate 'temper tantrums'. When she was three years old, her parents took on a research project in Africa. Her parents both described the next three years as 'the family's happiest'. Her mother in particular enjoyed her interesting career activity and having her children taken care of by warm-hearted 'surrogate mothers in a loving village community'. In order to give Nora a good education, the family moved back to Germany when it was time to enrol her in school. Nora's mother commented, 'That's when the problems started. Nora had been driven out of her children's paradise—she hated the German school, German children, and became the chronic rebel …' Nora finally became depressive, pseudoasthenic, and psychosomatically ill. Nor did moving to a place near her paternal grandparents in a rural area of Switzerland have much influence on Nora's dire mental and psychosocial condition.

Fortunately, Nora allowed me to open a window to the state of her psyche. She had a gift for drawing and conveyed her frightening unconscious fantasies to me in them, the burden of guilt about her mother's depression as well as her deep-seated feelings of insufficiency, that she had not been able as a 'sunshine baby' and toddler to lift her mother's mood—through her (hyperactive) behaviour. She was also unconsciously convinced that she wanted to kill her brother out of unbearable feelings of jealousy, and that her father's serious physical ailment when she was four was her fault. We eventually understood her psychosomatic symptoms as well as her short attention span and the related pseudo mental subnormality as products of her tendencies to punish herself due to archaic feelings of guilt, fantasies of revenge, and a deep-seated hatred for her primary objects. In the analytic work it became clear that Nora had developed little if any fundamental, supporting feeling of self or enough good regulation mechanisms in dealing with her affects and drive wishes. When her problem with aggression came to the fore in the transference, Nora did not speak a word with me in the sessions for three months. I ultimately felt desperate, helpless, and powerless and was often convinced that Nora would break off the treatment. Over and over and over again, I tried to verbalize the desperation that I perceived in Nora and link it to possible fantasies and anxieties—but without being able to have my impressions actually confirmed by a verbal reaction from Nora. I had to rely on my associations to the drawings for this, for example. We finally achieved a breakthrough in one session when Nora completely painted over garish luminous colours in neo-colour chalk with black and then timidly attempted to scratch coloured figures from out of the black. 'You know, this picture seems to me like our work in all of those sessions that have been so difficult for us the last few weeks. A despairing blackness is spreading out between us and covering up everything that is alive and colourful. You have literally lost your tongue here—maybe because unconsciously you want to let us know that this blackness, this heaviness, in your soul also comes from a time when you couldn't talk yet and your mother was in a "black, depressive" mood, which you felt but didn't understand. It's entirely possible that your body and your soul remember it without you noticing it, and are now trying to make themselves understood in your silence. You are probably yearning for us here to succeed in scratching up something colourful again, something unbearable, that is underneath all that black ... and rediscover the life inside you ...' Nora began weeping profusely ... the dam seemed to have broken. In the following sessions we were able to talk about how much she still felt responsible for her mother's depressions and attributed them to her own murderous impulses.

For Nora, it seemed decisive that I (as a 'good object'), but also the analytic treatment, had survived her desperate, aggressive silence as well as her fantasized destructive attacks.

I will never forget how changed Nora was when she came to the first session after the summer break following the months just described: beaming, self-confident—bubbling over with vitality and a love of life. She told me that she had had her first menstruation during the break and was able for the first time to open her mouth at the dentist's so that he could treat her aching tooth.

In the months to come, her performance at school improved tremendously. She was able to concentrate better and was able to sit still in her seat and follow what was being taught in class. We understood how much psychic energy she had had to keep investing in dealing with her depressive moods and fantasies up to then. 'My heart was usually never in school anyway …', was her comment once. It was clear that she was now verbalizing her fantasies in a form of 'black humour' and had become very sharp-witted, getting lots of laughs out of her pubescent classmates when, for example, the class had arguments with their teachers. This was one of the reasons why she was now able to overcome the social isolation, and find a place for herself in the class and a few good friends. Three years later, she expressed the wish to terminate her psychoanalytic treatment.

Last year, 31 years after completing the treatment, Nora wrote me an e-mail (she had found out my address by chance). In a long phone conversation she told me that she had found her way, professionally and personally. She could not remember any of the details of the therapy, just how important it had been for her in order 'to leave the darkness of my childhood behind …'. She mentioned that she had taken care of her father until he died and was able to talk with him about a lot of things in her childhood again—her mother's depressions, the accident during the first year of her life, the temper tantrums after her brother was born, her desperate reaction after returning to Europe, her poor performance at school, and her numerous fruitless attempts at therapy

It seems interesting to me for our subject here to note that Nora told me that although she still had to deal with depressive moods, especially if she was disappointed in love relationships, she had overcome her severe problems with concentration and attention span: her work had taken on compensatory functions for her—also in times of depressive moods.

In my full-length case report (Leuzinger, 1984), I had limited myself primarily to the description of the analytic process, with a focus on the work that was done on the unconscious conflict and fantasy world in the transference. It was not until the subject of ADHD became an issue in recent years that I began wondering whether the mentioned phase of the extreme negative transference, for example, which—as I perceived it—had proved to be a breakthrough for Nora's process of change—could also be understood in connection with the problem of affect and impulse regulation. During those months, as mentioned, Nora brought me into the position of a depressive, helpless mother who is incapable of understanding the discomfort and desperation of her speechless little baby and leading it out of an unbearable inner state. In this sense—in the sense of 'embodied memories'—she seemed to be repeating central experiences with her depressive primary object in the transference. In addition, Nora's extreme aggressive-destructive impulses as well as her fantasy of destroying her object became very real. The strong affective reaction to my reconstructive interpretation was apparently a 'turning point' (and/or a 'Now Moment', see Daniel Stern) in the treatment. As I see it now, however, it is likely that the changes were not attributable to just this interpretation alone. Presumably my continuous efforts in the previous months to keep verbalizing these fantasies and impulses as well as the state of extreme desperation and loneliness, contributed to a symbolization and/or mentalization capacity in Nora, so that the aggressive-destructive impulses, for example, could be understood and ultimately verbalized by her and no longer had to be mentally split off, acted out, or somatized in an extreme way, as they had been before.

In my presence, with me as an emotionally supportive and containing object, Nora was willing to try to face the threatening world of extreme (destructive) affects and impulses. In contrast to her depressive primary object, I was in a better position to perceive these affects, let myself be emotionally infected by them in the sense of a resonant attunement, and mirror them back to Nora in a more mature, more bearable form in my verbalizations. Nora was gradually able to identify with this way of dealing with affects—and/or to internalize my analytic, affect-regulating posture.

Just as an example of what I mean: together with her brother, she would take off in her father's Mercedes late at night and drive it up and down the winding curves of an Alpine road—at breakneck speed. This seemed to me like an enactment of her conviction that her primary objects don't even take note of the mortal dangers to which their children are exposed. At first I was horrified and panic-stricken by what she was telling me. In terms of clinical technique, I didn't quite know how to deal with these 'confessions', being new to the profession at the time. After a supervision with Jaques Berna, an experienced child analyst, I finally said, 'You must sense how scared I am that something bad might happen to you and your brother on these risky undertakings. At the same time you seem to be testing me to see whether I will stick to our agreement and keep everything you tell me to myself and not tell your parents about it. But if I just sit here on my hands and don't do anything about it, this could also be an affirmation for an unconscious truth inside you that we know from many other scenes here, namely, that your counterpart, which also means me, in other words, basically doesn't care whether you live or die ...' Fortunately, Nora seemed to understand this interpretation. That night she 'happened' to let the garage door fall shut with such a loud sound that her parents woke up and saw what was going on. I found it noteworthy that her father didn't take it the wrong way or punish her harshly for it, but reacted above all with a great deal of concern, recognized and was sensitive to Nora's suicidal intentions, and therefore wanted to know why Nora was putting herself and her brother in such extreme jeopardy. Nora experienced his interest in her and her motives as an existential proof of his love for her. In the analysis sessions that followed, as I read in my notes, our work focused on regulating her extreme aggressive-destructive impulses towards herself and her parents. (In retrospect, this seems to have been an important phase in the struggle for enhanced affect regulation, both in the transference relationship with me and in the outside world—precisely, for example, in the relationship to her parents.)

I'd now like to present in brief a similar reinterpretation of the clinical material from the psychoanalysis of a young man with extreme concentration and attention problems and extreme hyperactivity.

The struggle for affect regulation in an adult analysis

The 28-year old Mr A, a well-built young man, who was apparently of Arab cultural origin, was unemployed and socially completely isolated when he sought therapeutic help. As he described it, being close to other people was a big problem for him. 'Whenever someone gets close to me, at work on the occasional jobs I get, for example, or a woman, I panic—I feel an internal compulsion to go to the nearest airport, book a "last-minute flight" and, if at all possible, fly to another continent ...' We also related these anxieties to a possible therapeutic relationship: '... There are a lot of things I can do, of course, to try and relieve these anxieties,' I said, in a spontaneous association, 'but I can't pick up my couch and get on the next plane with you ...' We were both able to smile to ourselves about this fantasy which did not seem to hurt anyone's feelings or put a distance between us, an indication to me that a form of unconscious communication could develop between us.

I learned next to nothing about his life-history in the two initial interviews, except that Mr A was the product of an intercultural marriage between an Iranian refugee, an engineer, and a German secretary, a relationship that he described as being chronically unhappy. Both of them had a problem with alcohol. His father was now very sick with a physical ailment and still worked from time to time in a snack bar. His mother ran a carpet-cleaning company, which was at risk of folding. He had three siblings—two brothers, both older than him, and a younger sister. Both brothers had drug problems, were repeatedly involved in acts of violence, and had been unemployed for years. His sister was still in school and was adipose. He suffered from occasional 'eating binges' himself, he said, which were followed by severe stomach cramps and insomnia.

After his training as an auto mechanic, Mr A went back to get his A level qualification through adult education programmes, in spite of having big problems with attention span and concentration, and then finished a bachelor's degree programme in the USA in two years. He returned to Germany to save his mother's business, but without success. 'I've been unemployed myself for over a year now and only earn a little money every once in awhile as a tour guide ...'

As in Nora's case, there was a phase of strong negative transference in Mr A's psychoanalysis and a massive crisis in the treatment, which had to be worked through and then also proved to be the turning point of the treatment. This is why I'm excerpting this sequence of the treatment here:

> During the second year of the psychoanalysis, Mr A eventually stopped saying anything at all on the couch. I was less and less able to reach him emotionally and felt at a loss myself as to what to do, desperate, and very depressed. Mr A wouldn't

> say anything for weeks. Helplessly I tried to verbalize what I thought I was picking up without any visible reaction from Mr A. I was extremely concerned, above all because Mr A often came to the sessions as much as half an hour late. Often I was afraid that something catastrophic had happened and wondered whether I should actively seek the patient. At the same time, I felt terrorized by his behaviour and sensed the analysand's destructive aggressive impulses towards me and the analysis. After waiting over 30 minutes for him again one time, I was plagued once again by fears that Mr A had killed himself; I was feeling helpless and powerless. Then, all of a sudden, my affects changed—I felt a mixture of anger, obstinacy, and rebellion and thought to myself: 'Well, after all, I'm not Holy Mary—if he doesn't want to, then that's just the way it is ...' Obstinately, I left my practice and went to the mailbox—at this very moment, Mr A came around the corner ... I felt caught off guard and started the session by saying: 'For some reason, you seem to have reached a point with me where I don't expect you to come to the sessions anymore and am starting to give up. I don't know what you're trying to tell us by remaining silent in all of those sessions and by coming too late. I think I'm picking up a mixture of desperation and helplessness, but also aggression and anger towards me. I'm wondering whether unconsciously you feel that you have to enact that I, too, am losing interest in you and don't care whether you come to the sessions or not—is that it?' Mr A then broke his silence and told me that he had just had the association of finding his mother in bed in a dark room when he came home from school as a seven-year old. 'She wasn't able to cook a warm meal for years—I had to do that myself already in second grade and take care of my siblings ...' 'Could it be that you are now pressing me, too, into the role of a depressive, helpless mother and/or are convinced that I'm not taking care of you anyway and don't care whether you come to the session or not, since you don't get anything nutritious to eat here anyway, nothing that you need to stay alive?'

Mr A then described how he had practically withdrawn altogether from the real world the last few weeks, had been spending all day at home alone, often lying in bed for hours, frequently masturbating compulsively or 'feeding his face' in order to alleviate the inner feelings of emptiness at least a little bit. Often he dragged himself to the analysis sessions with only the greatest of effort. He confirmed my suspicion that he was extremely suicidal and told me, for example, that he could hardly drive by high-rises without feeling an internal compulsion to go up to the highest floor of the building and jump off. His silence during the sessions was, as in Nora's case, also an enactment of an unconscious truth, that the primary object is incapable of putting itself in his desperate and existentially threatening state and getting him out of this mental horror. Being close to a love object evidently reactivated such an archaic yearning to be loved and understood that he felt completely overwhelmed by it and had a panicky anxiety about losing his autonomy, his self. But this was also connected to his conviction that being near his love object would cause him to lose control over his own aggressive-destructive impulses and destroy the object, mentally or in reality, fantasies and impulses which, as I am about to mention, had presumably been overly stimulated by the severe emotional neglect from his mother, traumatic separation experiences, as well as his father's suicide attempt when the patient was 11 years old. This is why he experienced being close to a love object—in reality, but also in the analytic relationship with me—as life-threatening, both for the self and for the object.

As in the psychoanalysis with Nora, the scene just described opened a door to the history of Mr A's trauma, which gradually unfolded in the course of the intensive four-year psychoanalysis. I can only summarize it briefly here and hope that it will still become clear that the fear of losing control runs like a thread through his biography.

After his birth, his mother suffered from severe post-partum depression and was treated with anti-depressants for months. When he was two, A was separated from her for six weeks because of a stay in hospital. He was already a problem in kindergarten due to his hyperactive, unconcentrated behaviour and often got entangled in aggressive conflicts with other children. At age four, he was in a children's home for almost half a year, because his mother was suffering from depressions again and felt that it was just all too much for her. During the whole time he was in elementary school, his mother also, as just mentioned, often stayed in bed for days at a time. He had to take care of his little sister himself. In the psychoanalysis we found that the intimate contact to the toddler got through to him in his great loneliness and therefore meant a lot to him. One time, before entering puberty, when he was age ten or so, he had an erection while the little girl was sitting on his lap, which alarmed him; he was presumably afraid of losing control over his sexual impulses. After that, he refused to babysit for his sister anymore and turned his attention to a group of boys that played soccer together. At age 11, he found his father after a suicide attempt with pills and saved his life by mobilizing the emergency rescue unit. After this dramatic event, he gave up all activities in the soccer club and tried to concentrate on school. When the German teacher he idealized made fun of him in front of the whole class by reading his paper aloud with belittling comments, this was a further catastrophe for him: He lost interest in school, was often truant, and came increasingly under the influence of a group of violent, right-wing radicals. In the psychoanalysis, the memory of a physical conflict with his father became a key scene: His father beat him up in front of his peer group in a pub. He remembered being afraid that he might hit back and kill his father, as one of his friends had done to their father: This adolescent had stood in front of his mother to protect her when his drunken father started beating up on her; he threw the father up against a radiator so hard that the man died of a severe head injury. After the scene in the pub, A's parents refused to let him go on living with them: He lived on the street for almost a year, was able to get by with petty crime, was involved in right-wing radical actions, took drugs, and was extremely suicidal. It seemed almost like a miracle to us that one day one of the few friends he had from grade school ran into him and took him home with him. They took him in there lovingly and he fell in love with his friend's sister. With the help of this 'adoptive' family, he was able to extricate himself from the violent youth group and ultimately started the training to become an auto mechanic.

As mentioned, I've summarized the analytic process elsewhere which brought Mr A out of his complete social isolation and unemployment and enabled him to have an intensive, stable love relationship. His psychosomatic symptoms also steadily improved. As in the report on Nora's case, I concentrated my summary of the treatment on the successive work on Mr A's archaic fantasy and conflict world as it was manifested to me in the transference. I did not notice until now, in conjunction with our subject matter here, that the analytic process 'could also be told' from the focus of struggling for an understanding of the factors behind the lack of affect and drive control and the 'deferred development' of this capacity. It is only now that I noticed how tremendously important it had been for Mr A that during his third analysis-year he started reflecting on his eating habits and went on a very strict diet to get it under control. He got up two hours early every morning and chewed on a hard, bone-dry bread roll for a whole hour as called for by the diet. In fact he visibly lost weight and systematically restructured his eating habits with the help of a dietician. He tried to do much the same thing in the sexual domain by finally giving up his excessive masturbation and compulsive visits to prostitutes (both, incidentally, had often created problems for him in his job). Instead he sought regular sexual gratification with his girlfriend. Finally, he devoted himself to a martial arts sport, which we understood as an attempt to deal constructively with his aggressive-destructive impulses. It was impressive for me to see that—in parallel with these efforts to gain control—he was able to overcome his extreme work and concentration disorder as well as his symptom of constantly having to walk back and forth in his work-room and/or alleviate his enormous inner tension by disappearing into the lavatory so often in order to masturbate. He had already lost two jobs because of it. Now he was able to experience the structure in a large-surface office as helpful and achieved stable good performance results in his job because of it, which ultimately led to a permanent position.

As in the psychoanalysis with Nora, it now seems to me that in the analytic process it was not only a matter of a containing and holding function, as I had described it in my report at the time, but also of a process of searching for the reasons behind the critical weakness with regard to affect and impulse regulation in the patient's life-history. Moreover, I was something like a well-meaning, affectively involved, and 'mirroring' companion in his diverse attempts to get a hold on his body and, in this fundamental sense, become the 'boss in his own house' again. It also seems to me that my role was also one of an affectively resonating guide, a 'good' and 'indestructible' object that could understand and verbalize panic, desperation, anger, and hatred—presumably experiences that he had only had in an inadequate way with his two depressive primary objects—which, in addition to the separation traumatizations mentioned, was most likely one of the main reasons for his weakness with regard to affect and impulse control.

Summary

The two cases have been presented as examples in the sense of a re-interpretation of the analytic process that had taken place to call our attention to the manifestation, understanding, and acquisition of sustainable affect and impulse control. In my view, psychoanalysis offers a unique instrument of knowledge with which to probe the idiosyncratic, complex set of factors involved in a concentration and hyperactivity disorder, and thus to provide the basis for overcoming these symptoms by getting a new hold on the body through a 'deferred' process of developing the control over one's own impulses and affects. The opportunity to make use of a therapeutic relationship for such processes of change and insight seems to be spoilt by a medication-based treatment.

At the same time, I hope that the two case descriptions also showed that there is more involved in the psychopathology of the focus group of ADHD children than that of the severely traumatized borderline cases described by Peter Fonagy. One of the main differences, it seems to me, is clear from the scene where the adolescent A is afraid that he could lose control and become his father's murderer. Although the lack of affect and impulse control, as outlined, ran like a thread through his life-history, in this scene he was able to perceive the inner conflict, draw on a rudimentary capacity for mentalization (the perception of his father's inner state was precise), and cope with the situation (on the outside) thanks to an extreme form of affect control (he talks about putting his affects 'on ice'). Fonagy's adolescents would presumably not have been capable of controlling their affects in this manner: Many of them had become murderers in similarly humiliating situations because their impulses overflowed and broke through. It seems to me that one biographical difference between the two diagnostic groups is that the primary objects of the ADHD children discussed here (and/or the subgroup represented by Nora and A) suffered from the consequences of traumatizing experiences in early childhood; and that their psychically absent, depressive primary objects had largely proved to be incapable of helping them develop adequate affect and impulse regulation with a reliable, resonant holding and containing function, especially in the case of negative peak affects. The primary objects of the juvenile murderers described by Fonagy were extremely violent physically, to some extent cold and calculating, and nowhere close to being capable of putting themselves in their victims' place, mentally. As mentioned, the result, due to an unconscious identification with the perpetrator and the 'embodied memories' of his boundless violence, was an extreme form of mentalization disorder, a virtual lack of anything like the capacity to know what another person feels like inside. In spite of such differences, however, I would say that the lines between the two diagnostic groups are fluid.

Finally, I have juxtaposed core scenes from an *analysis with a child* and an *analysis with an adult* with the implicit message that a psychoanalytic treatment of ADHD as early as possible could not only help to prevent enormous mental suffering for those who are affected by it, but also proves to be tremendously cost-saving in many respects. I chose to present the second case as an example to give at least some idea of the kind of social dimensions that therapeutic, psychosocial, and pedagogical early prevention has in children with affect and impulse regulation disorders because, in all probability, it will help to avoid violence and destructiveness in the future.

Bibliography

Beeghly, M. and Cicchetti, D. (1994). 'Child maltreatment, attachment, and the self system: Emergence of an internal state lexicon in toddlers at high social risk'. *Development and Psychopathology*, 6: 5–30.

Bion, W.R. (1963). *Elemente der Psychoanalyse.* Frankfurt a.M.: Suhrkamp.

Bohleber, W. (2007). 'Erinnerung, Trauma und kollektives Gedächtnis—Der Kampf um die Erinnerung in der Psychoanalyse'. *Psyche—Z Psychoanal*, 61: 293–332.

Brentano, F. (1997[1874]). *Psychology from an Empirical Standpoint.* London: Routledge.

Dennett, D.C. (1987). *The Intentional Stance.* Cambridge: MIT Press.

Döll-Hentschker, S. (2008). *Die Veränderung von Träumen in psychoanalytischen Behandlungen. Affekttheorie, Affektregulierung und Traumkodierung.* Frankfurt a.M.: Brandes & Apsel.

Fischer, G. and Riedesser, P. (1998). *Lehrbuch der Psychotraumatologie*. 2. Aufl. München: Reinhardt, 2009.

Fonagy, P. (2007). Violent attachment. Vortrag auf der Tagung "In Gewalt verstrickt—psychoanalytische, pädagogische und philosophische Erkundungen", Universität Kassel, 9./10.2.2007 (unpublished).

Fonagy, P. and Target, M. (2000). 'Neubewertung der Entwicklung der Affektregulation vor dem Hintergrund von Winnicotts Konzept des "falschen Selbst"'. *Psyche—Z Psychoanal.*, 56: 839–62.

Fonagy, P. and Target, M. (2006[2003]). *Psychoanalyse und die Psychopathologie der Entwicklung*. Stuttgart: Klett-Cotta.

Fonagy, P., Gergeley, G., Jurist, E.L. and Target, M. (2004[2002]). *Affektregulierung, Mentalisierung und die Entwicklung des Selbst*. Stuttgart: Klett-Cotta.

Grubrich-Simitis, I. (2007). 'Trauma oder Trieb—Trieb und Trauma: Wiederbetrachtet'. *Psyche—Z Psychoanal.*, 61: 637–656.

Hobson, J., Stickgold, R. and Pace-Schott, E. (1998). 'The neuropsychology of REM sleep dreaming'. *NeuroReport*, 9: R1–R14.

Jaffe, J., Beebe, B., Feldstein, S., Crown, C.L. and Jasnow, M.D. (2001). *Rhythms of dialogue in infancy: Coordinated timing in development*. Boston [u.a.]: Blackwell.

Kernberg, O.F. (2001). 'Object relations, affects, and drives'. *Psychoanalytic Inquiry*, 21: 604–19.

Krause, R. (1998). *Allgemeine Psychoanalytische Krankheitslehre*. Bd. 2.: Modelle. Stuttgart/Berlin/Köln: Kohlhammer.

Krause, R. (2005). 'Drive and affect in perverse actions'. In: Fonagy, P., Krause, R. and Leuzinger-Bohleber, M. (eds). *Identity, gender, and sexuality*. London: International Psychoanalytical Association. pp. 161–75.

Laplanche, J. (1996). 'Der sogenannte Todestrieb: ein sexueller Trieb'. *Zeitschrift für psychoanalytische Theorie und Praxis*, 11: 10–26.

Leuzinger-Bohleber, M. (1984). 'Nora. Die Analyse einer Zwölfjährigen'. *Arbeitshefte Kinderanalyse*, Nr. 4: 29–90.

Leuzinger-Bohleber, M. (2000). 'Wandering between the worlds: From an analysis of a late adolescent'. In: Klitzing, K.v. (ed.). *Psychoanalysis in childhood and adolescence*. Basel: [u.a.]: Karger. pp. 104–25.

Leuzinger-Bohleber, M. and Bürgin, D. (2003). 'Pluralism and unity in psychoanalyitc research: Some introductory remarks'. In: Leuzinger-Bohleber, M., Dreher, A.U. and Canestri, J. (eds) *Pluralism and unity? Methods of research in psychoanalysis*. London: International Psychoanalytical Association. pp. 1–25.

Leuzinger-Bohleber, M. and Pfeifer, R. (2002). 'Remembering a depressive primary object: Memory in the dialogue between psychoanalysis and cognitive science'. *International Journal of Psychoanalysis*, 83: 3–33.

Leuzinger-Bohleber, M. (in press): Psychoanalysis as a 'science of the unconscious' at the IPA centenary. Unpublished paper given at the IPA centenary celebration in London, March 2010.

Parens, H. and Rose-Itkoff, C. (1997). Parenting for Emotional Growth—Workshops on Aggression. Nicht veröffentlichtes Textbook.

Parens, H. (2010). Parenting for emotional growth: A textbook, workshops and curriculum for students in grades k thru 12. Philadelphia: Jefferson University, 1 CD.

Segal, H. (1957). 'Notes on symbol formation'. *International Journal of Psychoanalysis*, 38: 391–439.

Stern, D.N. (1992[1985]). *Die Lebenserfahrung des Säuglings*. Stuttgart: Klett-Cotta.

Spezzano, C. (1993). *Affect in psychoanalysis*. Hillsdale: London: The Analytic Press.

PART III

PSYCHOANALYTIC RESEARCH: HOPES, VIEWS, CONTROVERSIAL DISCUSSION

CHAPTER SEVEN

Logic, meaning, and truth in psychoanalytic research

Charles Hanly

On unity and verifiability in psychoanalytic theory

It has been hoped that psychoanalysis would evolve toward the unity of a mainstream, integrated theory based on amendments of, and additions to, the persisting elements of Freud's theory (Rangell, 1997; Hanly, 1997). In my opinion, there is little evidence of this tendency occurring spontaneously. For example, there is evidence of an abundance of pluralism, and a poverty of unification, in the last issue of *The Psychoanalytic Quarterly* devoted to theories of therapeutic action. The eight authors stated their own theories in more or less splendid isolation, leaving it to the commentators to identify any similarities or differences that there might be. It suggests that the flame of hope for a unified mainstream psychoanalytic theory is burning low.

In terms of the ideas of convergence and divergence, the theme of the Chicago Congress, it would appear that divergence in theory and practice is on the rise and that convergence is on the decline. I shall argue that there is also little likelihood of a direction towards greater integration developing unless analysts are prepared to make it happen because there have been, and still are, logical, conceptual, and methodological barriers in its way. We have known about these barriers, but have tended to rationalize doing nothing about them in the spirit of Wallerstein's (1988) unsustainable argument that only clinical theory, about which analysts agree, is descriptive while the rest of psychoanalytic theory is based on metaphors about which we can exercise the privilege of personal preference without damage to psychoanalysis. Not surprisingly, as it turns out, analysts do not agree all that much about clinical theory either on the evidence of the *Quarterly* issue cited above. The result is isolated division or passionate disagreement at the expense of dispassionate enquiry. Given these views, you can imagine how satisfying to me it is to find myself among colleagues who are passionate about enquiry; passionate enough about enquiry and psychoanalysis to enquire into the reliability of even one's most passionately held ideas.

A body of knowledge may lack integrity because its theories are unconnected, incomplete, or inconsistent. Darwin left evolutionary theory incomplete; it lacked an explanation of individual variation which the theory required and which Mendel's genetics was able to supply. It has sometimes been thought that physics is inconsistent because Newton's theory of gravity is at odds with Einstein's relativity theory. But, in fact, it is not. Newton's theory can be derived from relativity theory as a special case. I propose to look at inconsistencies in psychoanalytic theories that result in a lack of unity in psychoanalytic knowledge.

There are three reasons why we should be concerned about the unity of psychoanalytic knowledge. The first reason is scientific and logical. If nature abhors a vacuum, knowledge abhors a contradiction. When two psychoanalytic theories are contradictory, both cannot be true and if one is true the other is false. Contrary theories are no better, since they offer only the cold comfort that although both cannot be true, they may both be false. Any body of knowledge that harbors contradictory or contrary theories has a problem. The logical inconsistency of theories renders eclecticism untenable and sets a specific limit to pluralism—limits beyond which contemporary psychoanalytic pluralism has gone.

The second reason is didactic. Candidates legitimately complain that they are left confused scientifically and clinically by the inconsistent theories and divergent clinical techniques in psychoanalysis taught with conviction and, too often, without scepticism or testing by their adherents. Pity the conscientious candidates who try to find their way through the eight different theories of therapeutic action outlined in the *Quarterly* in search of a reliable clinical orientation with which to work in their beginning clinical practice.

The third reason is public enlightenment. We avoid the difficult tasks involved in unifying psychoanalysis at the risk of promoting the meaningless idea that psychoanalysis *is* what psychoanalysts *do*. Psychoanalysis is a clinical discipline. As such, and unlike philosophy which has toyed with this self-definition, it is not good enough for psychoanalysis to be a smorgasbord of alternative ways of interpreting human nature. The smorgasbord of available therapies is already heavily laden with alternative psychotherapies without psychoanalysis adding further varieties of its own.

The following question presents itself: Are we turning a blind eye to contradictions in contemporary psychoanalytic theory or is it just that there is some uncertainty and confusion resulting from a lively, beneficial pursuit of new and better ideas with the inevitable lag of their clinical trial by analysts who try them out and see how they work? I have listed several examples of contradictions to which, in my opinion, we have turned a blind eye.

1. Freud advanced two theories of aggression: one, implicit and undeveloped in his theorizing before 1920, the other, explicitly developed, formulated, and adopted—the death instinct. Freud's implicit theory required no suspension of the pleasure principle. It was consistent with the wish fulfilment dream hypothesis and the hypothesis that masochism is sadism turned against the self (Brenner, 1971; Hanly, 1978). The death instinct theory implied motives that are not subject to the pleasure principle, dreams that are not wish fulfilments and the primary masochistic organization of aggression. Freud's two theories of aggression are inconsistent. In particular, their implied dream theories are contradictory and their implied theories of the relation between masochism and sadism are contraries.

The inconsistency within Freud's theory has been built into post-Freudian theorizing by Freudians who adopted a modification of Freud's first theory of aggression and those who adopted Freud's second theory of aggression. The result has been a basic logical problem that remains scientifically unresolved within psychoanalytic pluralism.

Note that this problem cannot be solved by an appeal to coherence. Both of Freud's theories of aggression are coherent but they cannot both be true. So much logical analysis can show us. Moreover, logical analysis is, at best, only one step towards a mainstream theory that is as unified as possible. Further light can be shed on this problem by research currently in progress under the heading of conceptual research into the implicit theories of analysts. Perhaps shifts of conviction are taking place that are not reflected in publications. Perhaps there is a greater tendency toward unification of theory in the implicit theories of analysts as distinct from their explicit reporting, teaching, and publishing. Even so, we would still be left with the crucial task of finding a reliable method to determine which implicit conviction about the nature of aggression is most probably true. Otherwise, we risk getting caught in an *argumentum ad populum.*

1. The classical theory of the Oedipus complex holds that the complex is a developmental vicissitude of constitutionally endowed libidinal and aggressive drives. Identifications rooted in relations to parents are crucial to the resolution of the Oedipus complex but not to its genesis. Self-psychology holds, on the contrary, that it is not the vicissitudes of instinct life that causes the Oedipus complex; rather, it is caused by parental failure to satisfy the narcissistic need of their children during a phase of 'innocent' precocious sexual and aggressive flowering. Relational psychology, for its part, considers the Oedipus complex to be an artifact of the relation between analyst and patient. For relational psychology, interaction between the analyst and patient is a kind of Kantian *synthetic a priori*, a pure form of intuition like Kantian space and time, which determines what the analyst can know of the patient and what the patient can know of himself/herself. These theories are not exactly on all fours. The Freudian theory is psycho-biological; the Kohutian theory is psychological; the relational theory is epistemological. But, in addition to these differences, they are contradictories. If one of them is true, the others are false. In addition, the self-psychological and relational theories are incomplete in a respect in which the classical theory is not. The classical theory has an explanation of the formation, health,

and pathology of conscience; an explanation that is missing from the alternative theories.

2. The list could go on to a logical analysis of (a) Freud's drive/object relations/defence aetiological model as against the American Freudian drive/defence model and the relational psychology model that adopts the premise of the primacy of object relations; (b) the conflict model of pathogenesis versus the deficit model; (c) Freud's hypothesis of narcissism as a first organization of libido versus the self-psychology hypothesis of an independent line of narcissistic development such that sexual and aggressive drives are derivatives of parental empathic failures; (d) Freud's anaclitic theory and Bowlby's attachment theory (see Bowlby, 1973); and so forth.

The number of contradictions is a measure of the extent to which pluralism in contemporary psychoanalysis oversteps the limits of science and logic. Here I do no more than identify a problem. Work is needed to find solutions. Perhaps some of these contradictions are only apparent; perhaps others can be avoided by abandoning the universality of the conflicting theories. Moreover, logical analysis is, at best, only one step towards a viable as unitary as possible mainstream theory. In addition, and this is a crucial addition, we need to know which of two or more contradictory or contrary theories is true. As we have seen, the satisfaction of the coherence criterion is necessary but it is not sufficient to establish the truth of a theory. Independent evidence is required to decide the issue. The unification of psychoanalytic knowledge requires us to go beyond speculation and logic to fact.

For this purpose consistent interpretation, 'making sense of things', is not enough. Freudians and self-psychologists can make sense of manifestations of oedipal ambivalence in associations and transference. Kleinians and relational psychologists can make sense of symptoms of oral trauma. But their explanations (the sense made of them) are not consistent. Interpretability in psychoanalysis can easily give rise to a mistaken complacency when it is used to defend a theory against clinical observations that falsify it and to a, no less mistaken, subjectivism about the possibility of intersubjective observation in clinical psychoanalysis.

Fortunately, empirical research offers us an alternative route to intersubjective facts about psychic development and functioning.

In my opinion, we continue to need more empirical studies of all kinds but especially just now, we need outcome studies in order to better assess the efficacy of therapeutic psychoanalysis in its different theoretical and technical modalities. There are many difficult questions that I need not expand upon for this audience: what, if any, difference does frequency make to therapeutic outcome? And the fundamental question of whether difference of theoretical orientation and technique makes any difference at all to outcome? Empirical research is an indispensable methodological third in our pursuit of psychoanalytic knowledge.

Freud conducted the first, albeit informal, outcome study when he observed that the cures predicted by his seduction theory and its technique were not occurring as the theory predicted. This historical fact is of special interest for two reasons: first, Freud's outcome study led him to modify his aetiological theory to include infantile sexuality; it made a profound difference in his theorizing; second, Freud's capacity for self-criticism enabled him to function as a third in relation to his own work; his commitment to a theory which he had published with great pride had not blinded him to the observation of negative instances—negative facts that falsified the seduction theory as a universal aetiology of neurosis and the adequacy of the cathartic method.

Psychoanalysis needs thirds—methodological vantage points from which observations can be made that can test psychoanalytic theory and therapy. Empirical and conceptual research activities, despite necessary overlapping, provide distinctive thirds for the advancement of psychoanalytic knowledge. The brief exercise above was intended to explore the use of logical analysis as a third. It is an exercise in conceptual research but, of course, logical analysis is also useful in empirical research. As forms of conceptual research, the EPF (European Psychoanalytical Federation) working groups provide yet other strategies for seeking a measure of objectivity about clinical psychoanalysis and training.

But what about clinical research? Are we to despair of the observational value of clinical psychoanalysis? Is clinical observation necessarily irremediably vitiated by subjectivity despite the assertions and arguments of postmodern psychoanalysts? Is it never to reacquire the epistemological status claimed and exhibited by Freud on behalf of psychoanalysis?

It is my hope that psychoanalysts can bring about a revival of clinical research. Much needs to be done. I think that the epistemological debate will gradually cease with the demise of the postmodernist vogue leaving behind a useful reminder of the difficulties that stand in the way of clinical objectivity. Therefore, I want to conclude with a simple proposal that is at best a small beginning towards making clinical psychoanalysis empirically viable.

My suggestion owes something to philosophy in so far as it is based on a modification of the verification theory of meaning of the Vienna Circle. The verification theory posited that the meaning of any statement is to be found in its verification. Hence, any statement that is unverifiable is meaningless. Historically, the verification theory was used by skeptical philosophers as a weapon against the high flown, elational ideas of metaphysics and, in particular, of Hegelian idealism and its descendents. Obviously, false statements are meaningful. Verifiable in this definition means 'capable of being shown to be true or false'. I do not think that this definition is an adequate general definition of meaning (Hanly, 1970). However, in my opinion, it states a necessary condition for any meaningful scientific statement. If so, any psychoanalytic theory, if it is to be scientific, must be verifiable.

Thus, in order to qualify as scientific, a psychoanalytic descriptive or explanatory hypothesis must provide for inferences that would unambiguously specify the observations that would determine its truth or falsity. In particular, the hypothesis would need to inferentially and unambiguously specify negative instances, that is, observations that would falsify it. No idea that provides only for interpretative instantiation, without unambiguous descriptions of observations that would falsify it, could qualify as a potential addition to an evolving mainstream psychoanalytic theory.

At the present time, psychoanalysis has a plenitude of theories and a scarcity of significant clinical observations to test them as well as a lack of patients on which to make the observations. Is this conjunction accidental? I do not know, but, just in case it might not be accidental, I think that Conceptual Research should include clinical research with a mandate to explore, and hopefully to revive, the connection between psychoanalysis as a therapy and as a method of empirical observation.

In my opinion this connection is essential to psychoanalysis as therapy and as observational science. Nor does it, in my opinion, break the link between poetry and scientific objectivity in clinical work. The scientific task of clinical psychoanalysis is rooted in our humanistic therapeutic obligation not to make over patients according to either our own best wishes and hopes for the patient or according to our favoured theories but, rather to help patients against their own wishes and fears to find themselves as they are, as they were, and as they can be. If we can manage this much we have a fallible but sufficient field of observation for an observational science of psychic reality.

It is not just that the enlightened laity lacks a sufficient knowledge of psychoanalysis to discriminate between prejudiced and reasoned criticisms of it; they are often at a loss to know what benefits clinical psychoanalysis could have for them. The lack of coherent, simple, accurate knowledge of psychoanalysis deprives people of a sufficiently informed understanding and leaves too much to chance when they seek therapy.

The Ptolemaic belief that the sun orbits the earth coheres beautifully with, and makes sense of, our daily experience. The belief is consistent with using the sun for purposes of orientation in time and space which offers a kind of specious pragmatic test. It took mankind a long time to realize that immediate, unreflective, experience is made 'irreducibly subjective' by the fact that there is nothing in our immediate experience to indicate to us that it is we who are in motion and not the sun.

To adjudicate among theories we need impersonal facts of human psychic functioning. Logic informs us that it is not good enough to be able to give coherent interpretations of discernable clinical facts. For example, internally consistent interpretations of oedipal transferences can be constructed on contrary Freudian and Kohutian premises. Similarly, clinical evidence of oral trauma can be given a self-consistent Kleinian interpretation or an object relational Fairbairnian interpretation. Consistent interpretation, 'making sense of things', is not enough. We need to get beyond coherence criteria to reliable factual evidence and pragmatic criteria.

Above I have characterized empirical research as being second-order clinical research because methodologically it takes up a third position in relation to the analytic diad. Empirical research has been differentiated from conceptual research, although both need to be guided by the logic of theorizing discussed in a very limited way above. The epistemology of psychoanalysis is a topic for conceptual research. However, postmodernism has precipitated an epistemological controversy that will soon die down with the waning of the enthusiasm for the iconoclasm and the weight of its own contradictions. However, its vogue is a symptom of a failure of nerve among analysts concerning the scientific status of their knowledge and the worth of their therapy. In my opinion, we do not need a revival of enthusiasm for psychoanalysis; we need a revival of scientific work by psychoanalysts both extra-clinical and clinical. For this we need the leadership by example and instruction as well as the results of the work of our researchers.

Early in the last century, the Vienna Circle of Logical Positivists posited the verification theory of meaning from which it followed that any statement that could not be verified was literally meaningless. With this simple postulate, the logical positivists were able to repudiate all metaphysical and theological statements retaining only natural science and common sense. While metaphysics and theology are unverifiable their tenets are scarcely meaningless so the logical positivists overplayed their hand. But the verification theory does surely state an essential criterion of a scientific statement. In order to qualify as scientific a statement must provide for inferences that unambiguously specify the observations that would determine its truth or falsity. In particular, the statement would need to inferentially and unambiguously specify negative instances, that is, observations that would falsify it.

Too often interpreting is equated with testing. Candidates who interpret according to the premises of relational psychoanalysis are often enough deemed to be equally prepared for graduation with candidates who interpret according to the premises of classical theory or of self-psychology even though these premises cannot all be true. It does not improve the reliability of psychoanalytic knowledge when analysts espouse the idea that psychic life is intrinsically ambiguous.

There are more methodological issues to be considered if clinical observation is to be adequate to the task of testing psychoanalytic theories. New hypotheses are essential to the growth of psychoanalytic knowledge but a proliferation of theories without clarification of their logical relation to existing and alternative theories and without specific methods for clinical and non-clinical evaluation disqualifies psychoanalysis as a body of scientific knowledge.

Like evolutionary biology at the time of Darwin, psychoanalysis is an observational science. Darwin is said to have always carried in his pocket as a momento a tablet, inscribed with the simple but profound inductive injunction, 'Look for negative instances.' No maxim of better leavens enthusiasm for an idea with enquiry. Our clinical work cannot proceed without anticipatory ideas but it will be neither scientific nor therapeutic if we fail to appreciate that patients are not in analysis to instantiate our theories; they come to be understood as they were, are, and as they can be, and not as our ideas require them to be.

Bibliography

Bowlby, J. (1973). Attachment and Loss, Vol. 11. Separation: Anxiety and Anger. New York: Basic Books.

Brenner, C. (1971). 'The psychoanalytic concept of aggression'. *International Journal of Psycho-Analysis*, 52: 137–44.

Hanly, C. (1970). 'On being and dreaming'. In: Hanly, C. and Lazerowitz, M. (eds) *Psychoanalysis and Philosophy*. pp. 155–87.

Hanly, C. (1978). 'Instincts and hostile affects'. *International Journal of Psycho-Analysis*, 59: 149–56.

Hanly, C. (1997). 'Commentary'. *Journal of Clinical Psychoanalysis*, 6: 485–93.

Kohut, H. (1977). *The Restoration of the Self*. New York: International Universities Press.

Levin, D. (1969). 'The self: a contribution to its place in theory and technique'. *International Journal of Psycho-Analysis*, 50: 41–51.

Rangell, L. (1997). 'At century's end: a unitary theory of psychoanalysis'. *Journal of Clinical Psychoanalysis*, 6: 465–84.

Wallerstein, R. (1988). 'One psychoanalysis or many?' *International Journal of Psychoanalysis*, 65: 5–21.

CHAPTER EIGHT

Trauma or drive—drive and trauma: Revisited

Ilse Grubrich-Simitis

Preliminary note

The paper reproduced below was presented at the 44th Congress of the International Psychoanalytical Association in Rio de Janeiro on 29 July 2005. The Congress theme was 'Trauma: New Developments in Psychoanalysis' and my paper formed part of a Conceptual Research Committee Panel on 'What does Conceptual Research on Trauma Really Mean?', chaired by Marianne Leuzinger-Bohleber and including Ricardo Bernardi, Jorge Canestri, and Sverre Varvin.

I had not originally intended my paper for publication, as it is substantially based on my essay 'Trauma or drive—drive and Trauma', published in The Psychoanalytic Study of the Child *in 1988; some of the formulations of the new text take up those of the original contribution, and certain passages are even reproduced verbatim from it, because I could not today express many of the ideas in question better or differently after a lapse of some twenty years. My paper was well received in Rio and many members of the audience stated that they would like to be able to see it in print. There are other arguments in favour of publication too: on the one hand, a new generation of psychoanalysts has since grown up, and, on the other, the subject matter of the earlier essay has manifestly remained relevant today and is considered, in the last quarter of the present paper, in the light of modern psychoanalytic trauma research. Finally, for the purposes of the oral presentation I had summarized the thoroughly elaborated ideas put forward in the essay, making them easier to absorb in the time available.*

As stated at the beginning of the paper, it was Marianne Leuzinger-Bohleber, as Chair of the International Psychoanalytical Association's Conceptual Research Committee, who suggested that my essay—an expanded version of the Thirty-Seventh Freud Anniversary Lecture held at the New York Psychoanalytic Institute in 1987—should be brought back into the debate. Although the 1980s witnessed a number of individual efforts to clarify psychoanalytic concepts, in the form, for example, of vocabularies and dictionaries, conceptual research on a quasi-institutionalized basis did not then exist. It is no coincidence that it now does: it could be assigned a particular kind of supervisory function, not in the sense of verification, and certainly not of orthodox censorship, but in that of a patient process of remembering and comparing. Incorporation of the historical dimension into present-day conceptual research could once again highlight the intellectual wealth and human wisdom that once imbued psychoanalysis and were for decades the source of its fascination. This would not only contribute to ensuring that the conceptual work and theoretical reflections of previous generations of psychoanalysts were not forgotten; the resulting awareness of the history of specific concepts could also have a direct impact on present-day psychoanalysis.

'Present-day psychoanalysis' might sound like a positively illusory expression in the age of much-vaunted pluralism. Two trends have in recent years blurred the outlines of our discipline: first, the narcissism of small—or not so small—differences, often bound up with an omnipotent overestimation of the explanatory force of one's own concepts and a radical dismissal of those espoused by colleagues who hold other views; and, second, the understandable longing to be released, by ever new approaches that hold out the promise of simplification, from the hypercomplexity that confronts us in our daily clinical work. Both trends have led, and still lead, to various forms of reductionism. Entire areas of clinical experience are disregarded if it is asserted, for instance, that only the transference matters, that the here and now is the only relevant time plane, or that reconstructive work is of little therapeutic value—that is, a waste of time—because it concerns only explicit memory. In this situation, how likely is it that an analysand who, when free-associating, says something that falls outside such axiomatic reference systems, will be heard by an analyst who is scarcely in a position to

deploy evenly suspended attention if he always thinks he knows what is and what is not important?

Conceptual research that reminds us of our intellectual past could not only encourage openness of thinking and of clinical listening, but also sharpen our perception of what actually connects us—in theory, concepts, and, above all, our particular, highly specific method. In retrospect, I see Marianne Leuzinger-Bohleber's idea of returning to the subject matter of my essay of 1988 as a spur to engage in conceptual research of this kind. What in this case emerges is not only the stimulating mobility of Freud's theoretical reflections on trauma and drive, but also his perceptual acuity in relation to certain phenomena of trauma and traumatization. For example, his concept of the 'compulsion to repeat' seems to anticipate observations by present-day trauma researchers of traumatized subjects' disturbed experience of time.

Dear colleagues

It was Marianne Leuzinger-Bohleber's idea to begin our Panel with a summary of a paper entitled 'Trauma or drive—drive and Trauma' (Grubich-Simitis, 1988), which I published some twenty years ago. I must confess that my immediate response was sceptical. However, in view of the vast growth in the volume of psychoanalytic literature on trauma that has since taken place, it is, I believe, perfectly reasonable for the Conceptual Research Committee to set itself the task of recalling the complexity and variability of the trauma concept in certain works of Sigmund Freud. Such reconstruction of some of the historical lines of development seems particularly appropriate at this time, as there are those among us who evidently consider it progressive to regard the Freudian tradition as anachronistic. Another aspect of this work of recollection is to understand the reasons why, throughout his life, Freud spontaneously reacted with ambivalence to newly presented trauma theories of every kind. Since my contribution drew attention for the first time to some of the fundamental elements of this conflict-ridden issue, it appears to be still relevant today. Indeed, a French translation came out only recently (Grubich-Simitis, 2003).

This essay is, however, long and complex. Owing to limitations of time, I can therefore mention only a few selected points. The occasion for my investigation at that time was my chance discovery in 1983, among papers from the estate of Sándor Ferenczi, of the hitherto unknown manuscript of Freud's draft of the twelfth metapsychological paper of 1915, entitled 'Overview of the Transference Neuroses' (Freud, 1985a). The fact that I then read this text primarily as a re-assumption of the trauma model of the aetiology of the neuroses, which had seemingly been totally abandoned, no doubt had to do with my preoccupation, at this time, with the theme of extreme traumatization. This interest had developed in the context of my clinical work, commencing in the mid-1970s, with patients from the second generation of Shoah survivors (Grubich-Simitis, 1981, 1984). Unlike the present situation, in which trauma is apparently all the rage in psychoanalysis, in those days it was still anathema in our trade.

I

The draft, then, belongs in the context of the twelve metapsychological papers that Freud had originally wished to bring out in book form. As you know, only five of these important texts, including 'The Unconscious' (Freud, 1915e) and 'Mourning and Melancholia' (Freud, 1916–1917g), were then published in the *Internationale Zeitschrift für ärztliche Psychoanalyse*, some in 1915 and others in 1917. There is no trace of the other seven. It is assumed that Freud later destroyed the manuscripts. The sudden appearance of the draft of the last of the set, which Freud had sent to his friend Ferenczi for critical appraisal, was therefore all the more surprising. He emphasized in his accompanying letter of 28 July 1915 (see Falzeder and Brabant, 1996: 73) that the fair copy conformed sentence by sentence to the draft. As its title indicates, his intention with the twelfth paper was to provide an overview or synthesis. The text of the draft falls into two distinct parts. The first is noted down in the form of telegraphic jottings only, as the author was here on familiar ground. He examines the three transference neuroses—anxiety hysteria, conversion hysteria, and obsessional neurosis—in accordance with six factors, including repression, anticathexis, and the relation to the sexual function. From the sixth factor, *disposition*, he then launches, in fully written-out sentences, into the speculative flight of fancy of what he himself calls his 'phylogenetic fantasy' (in a letter to Ferenczi of 18 July 1915; ibid., p. 68). Moreover, he here also includes the 'narcissistic neuroses'—his term for the psychoses.

Let me briefly outline the basic idea of this innovative second part. In the context of a wide-ranging review of the aetiology of mental pathology, Freud reconstructs, or, as the case may be, constructs, the events and actions that might have had hereditary repercussions on constitution and disposition. He ultimately traces the hereditary disposition to the transference neuroses back to the radical environmental transformations that confronted our ancestors when they were overtaken by the climatic cataclysm of the Ice Age, which put an end to their former paradisiacal existence. In order to survive, they found themselves compelled to undertake far-reaching changes to their affective reactions, sexual customs, and ego capacities—characteristics that in Freud's view recur in modified form in the symptoms of the transference neuroses. As the phylogenetic substrate for the affective storms and ego alterations of the psychoses, he takes up theses from *Totem and Taboo* (Freud, 1912–1913a) and sketches out a chain of postulated violent acts in the human primal horde that had crystallized by the end of the Ice Age into an archaic form of social and communal existence: to assure himself of his mastery—that is, of his total power and right of disposal over women—the jealous primal father persecuted his sons and castrated at least the older ones. The sons took flight, organized themselves as a homosexual clan of brothers, and eventually murdered the primal father.

Many arguments could of course be adduced for dismissing Freud's construction as scientifically untenable and indeed abstruse. Let me mention just two. First, there is no incontrovertible evidence for a Lamarckian mode of transmission; the organism's environmental experiences cannot be incorporated directly into its genome, so that castration and patricide in the mists of prehistory could not have left a direct precipitate in the form of a hereditary disposition to psychosis. Second, forms of behaviour do not petrify and cannot therefore be discovered as fossils, so it is idle to rack our brains over whether actual castration and patricide in prehistory, of which nothing has been handed down to us on the level of symbols, were widespread modes of behaviour over a prolonged period of time.

Freud may be assumed to have been perfectly aware of these objections. After all, by the use of the term 'phylogenetic fantasy' he himself had drawn attention to the *fantasy* character of his reflection. Precisely in view of the current demand for a scientific approach to psychoanalytic work—the word 'scientific' being understood in the strictest, if possible empirical, sense—I should like to remind you at this point of the description of the 'mechanism' of scientific creativity which Freud gave, not coincidentally, at the time of gestation of the draft of the twelfth metapsychological paper: he characterized scientific creativity as 'the succession of daringly playful fantasy and relentlessly realistic criticism' (in a letter to Ferenczi of 8 April 1915; ibid., p. 55). When he subjected his daringly playful phylogenetic fantasy to the second step, that of relentlessly realistic criticism, he decisively rejected and never published it.

Here, however, we wish to concentrate precisely on the first step in the sequence, daringly playful fantasy, which is indispensable to creativity in psychoanalytic research. In setting down the draft, Freud had fantasized his way, along neo-Lamarckian lines, towards answering a question that plainly never ceased to exercise him. That question might have been: What is the ultimate origin of the pathogenic terror inherent in the fear of castration, the ardour of oedipal love wishes and death wishes, and the force of the associated guilt feelings? Perhaps Freud could not put an end to his surprise at the *reality quality* of the unconscious fantasy world that he had discovered in the 1890s—as if, raised in the physicalism of the 19th century as he was, he had told himself that something with such constant and massive effects in each succeeding generation must in the last analysis have, or at least have had, a basis in the material external world.

In the drive model, Freud had from the beginning endowed the unconscious fantasies with a somatic substrate in the form of the erotogenic zones of the body and the associated stages of libidinal development, and had added a genetic foundation to them with the concept of hereditary disposition. In other words, he assigned the body—that transitional sphere between inside and outside, between subjectivity and objectivity—a central place within the drive model. At the end of his twelfth metapsychological paper he supplements the somatic and hereditary foundations of his drive model with a reflection in terms of evolutionary biology on the phylogenetic disposition that underlies ontogenetic disposition.

He asks himself how these inescapably active, stereotypical forms of programming entered into the substrate of the body in the first place. He believes he can discern in them traces of catastrophic environmental events and violent social acts that *actually* took place in the external world in the mists of prehistory and which overwhelmed our ancestors—traces that are fixed somatically and transmitted by heredity, unmodified from generation to generation. In his phylogenetic fantasy, Freud indeed imagines these environmental events and social acts as *traumatic*: radical climate change, acute threats to life from hunger and cold, then expulsion and castration by the primal father, and finally the murder of the primal father.

Here, then, Freud is manifestly attempting to combine his drive model with elements of the trauma model. It is important to note that he transfers the traumatic influence into phylogenesis, thus separating it from present-day sufferers from psychoneurosis by a buffer of hundreds of millennia. In contrast to the former seduction theory, the experiences presumed to have been had by primal man are no longer primarily sexual transgressions. The notion of trauma already has a wider connotation. However, what matters for our present purposes is that in the twelfth metapsychological paper the drive model no longer appears as disjunctively opposed to the trauma model. In a word, the formulation is no longer trauma *or* drive, but drive *and* trauma.

II

With his phylogenetic fantasy Freud had indeed returned to a fundamental problem of his earlier research, when he developed the paradigm of psychoanalysis in his dialogue with Wilhelm Fliess. To recapitulate, my thesis is that in the second part of his twelfth metapsychological paper he embarked on a theoretical effort to incorporate the traumatic factors of pathogenesis into the fabric of the drive model. It is no coincidence that this occurred precisely in 1915, when Freud was witness to the extreme traumatization, both individual and collective, wreaked by the First World War.

We have become accustomed to discern two successively developed basic aetiological models in the Fliess documents and in Freud's publications of this period: the trauma model and the drive model. The former corresponds in its most specific version to the so-called seduction theory and the latter to the genuinely psychoanalytic aetiological theory. Let me now draw together some historical lines which are thoroughly familiar to you. In his clinical work with patients in the mid-1890s, Freud often heard accounts of experiences of sexual seduction in childhood. This led him to modify the aetiological theory he had developed together with Josef Breuer, which had also taken traumatic experiences into consideration, albeit with more emphasis on those occurring in youth and adulthood. From then on he attributed ever-increasing importance, in the causation of the psychoneuroses, to *sexual* experiences sustained *in childhood*. According to his then perfectly conventional view, children who have not yet attained sexual maturity are incapable of specifically sexual stimulation, sensations, and ideas, and are to that extent 'innocent'. A child who is made the victim of a sexual scene by an adult or an older child is unable to cope with the experience psychically, and takes fright. If at puberty—that is, during the course of sexual maturation—the child has another experience of a kind that arouses by association the memory of the first experience and confers the weight of sexual significance on it, the mechanism of repression is set in train, and this occurs *after the event*, after a period of latency. In other words, the flooding with stimuli, which is this time brought about endopsychically by the memory, necessarily triggers the defence. Considered in these terms, the memory aroused *after* sexual maturation has an incomparably more powerful impact; it has 'a greater unbinding effect' (Masson, 1985a: 163; translation corrected) and is therefore more *traumatic* than the prepubertal event itself. Admittedly, as long as the defence can be maintained, the situation substantially continues to resemble that of health. It is only the failure of the defence in any later conflict that gives rise to the formation of actual psychoneurotic symptoms.

So even in this comparatively early version of his aetiological theory Freud does not imagine the pathogenic effect as having arisen spontaneously by way of a simple mechanism of stimulus and response. Instead, he is postulating a *diphasic* pathogenesis, centring not only on sexual seduction but also on repression. From this point of view, the trauma model, in the guise of the seduction theory, already hypothesizes a complex causal relationship in the form of an intricate network of external *and* internal—that is, social, psychic, and somatic—conditions that are reworked in accordance with the rhythm of the process of *Nachträglichkeit*, of deferred action.

Yet Freud soon came to understand 'that there are no indications of reality in the unconscious, so that one cannot distinguish between truth and fiction that has been cathected with affect' (ibid., p. 264). When further exploration compelled the realization that his patients' reports of sexual seductions in childhood corresponded only in part to actual events, however, he did not disappointedly dismiss their fantasized communications as lies, but instead took these recurring fantasy configurations as the occasion for a further metamorphosis of his aetiological theory.

Against the background of a broadened conception of sexuality, Freud now recognized the sexual life of children, the various phases of libidinal development, in accordance with the erotogenic zones of the body assigned to them, and the structure of the Oedipus complex. Since psychoneurosis betrays more of the regularities of unconscious mental life and the early stages of ontogenesis, which had previously been subject to massive defence, than the normal adult constitution, he used it so to speak as the gateway to a new *general* psychology—that is, one that embraced *both* normal *and* pathological mental phenomena: namely, psychoanalysis. What made, and to this day probably still makes, the drive model appear so scandalous is that it applies to *everyone*—drawing attention to the fact of our imperishable infantile wishes, the ineluctability of our drive-based nature as enshrined in our bodies, and the psychic structure that is at risk in all of us, because it indelibly carries within itself, by virtue of its early development which is so liable to disturbances, the seeds of neurosis, psychosis, and perversion.

As is clear from a reading of the Fliess letters, none of this suited Freud's perfectly conventional bourgeois taste. Spontaneously, he would no doubt rather have remained faithful to the cliché of an inner childhood paradise, of an untroubled and harmonious parent–child relationship and, above all, of a sharp line of distinction between mental health and psychopathology. He may well have been constantly tempted to revert to the trauma model. To counter this temptation he as it were erected an intellectual bulwark by from then on elevating the admittedly major difference between the two aetiological conceptions to the status of an antagonism. This was already true in 1897, when, upon the discovery of the pathogenic effect of fantasies, a mainstay of his drive model, he wrote to Fliess of the 'collapse of everything valuable' (ibid., p. 266). In 1906 he stated: 'After I had made this correction, "infantile sexual traumas" were in a sense replaced by the "infantilism of sexuality"' (Freud, 1906a: 275); he did not write 'complemented'. And it remained so later, in his official accounts of the history of psychoanalysis, when he condemned the seduction theory as purely and simply an 'error' (Freud, 1925d: 33). Yet in reality the models are not antagonistic. In fact, we have before us two successive and mutually *complementary* versions of Freud's aetiological theory, one of which, the trauma model, accentuates the manifest external-world aspects, while the other, the drive model, shifts the focus to the invisible factors of the internal world.

III

Even after his rejection of the phylogenetic fantasy, Freud persisted throughout his life with his efforts to integrate the trauma and drive models in his writings. A cursory mention of only four instances is possible here. In the discussion of the traumatic neuroses, based on the example of the war neuroses, given in the *Introductory Lectures on Psycho-Analysis* (Freud, 1916–1917a), composed not long afterwards and still during the First World War, he admittedly still adopts a non-psychoanalytic approach. However, he stresses that traumatic experiences may play a part in the pathogenesis of the psychoneuroses too, in the sense of a 'complemental series' (ibid., p. 362 and p. 370), noting explicitly 'that there is no need to abandon the traumatic line of approach as being erroneous' (ibid., p. 276). So it is that in the diagram illustrating his aetiological formula in Lecture 23, Freud includes the traumatic aspect as a causative element at several points. As in the phylogenetic fantasy, hereditary disposition is for instance once again the factor whereby he considers traumatic experiences of our ancestors to be active transgenerationally in ourselves. So when patients report seductions, threats of castration and the like sustained in childhood, and all of these demonstrably fail to correspond to the facts, in his view these are not arbitrary lies but compelling *primal fantasies*—primal fantasies 'as a phylogenetic endowment' (ibid., p. 371).

The theme of primal fantasies also pervades the case history of the 'Wolf Man', likewise written down during the First World War, in which a real infantile seduction is central to the pathogenesis. As Freud emphasized: 'the old trauma theory [...] had suddenly come to the front once more' (Freud, 1918b: 95). He here refers to the primal fantasies as 'phylogenetically inherited schemata, which, like the categories of philosophy, are concerned with the business of "placing" the impressions derived from actual experience' (ibid., p. 119).

Freud made another attempt to link the trauma and drive models, albeit admittedly excluding the phylogenetic dimension, in 1920 in *Beyond the Pleasure Principle* (Freud, 1920g), the work in which he at the same time introduced the concept of the death drive. Still under the influence of the war neuroses, he sought to comprehend the typical rhythm of the working out and psychic binding of traumatic experiences through the notion of the *compulsion to repeat*. He writes that the need for such repetitive working out arises on account of the prior traumatic 'breach in the shield against stimuli' (ibid., p. 31). Whereas the flooding with stimuli may be due to *external* events, it can also be triggered by 'excitations *from within*' (ibid., p. 34; my emphasis)—that is, in particular, by the drives. In this case, then, the drive is in effect *itself* the trauma. At any rate, Freud here goes so far as to assert that the failure of psychic binding of such an *endogenous* flooding with stimuli gives rise to a disturbance 'analogous' (ibid., p. 35) to a traumatic neurosis of *exogenous* origin. Not long before, he had already noted, as a 'unifying hypothesis' of this kind, that 'after all, we have a perfect right to describe repression, which lies at the basis of every neurosis, as a reaction to a trauma—as an elementary traumatic neurosis' (Freud, 1919d: 210). In relation to the concept of the *compulsion to repeat* elaborated in *Beyond the Pleasure Principle*, it can at any rate be said—like that of *primal fantasies*, mentioned earlier—to be a kind of linking concept between the trauma and drive models.

However, it was only in old age, with *Moses and Monotheism* (Freud, 1939a), that last variation on the themes first addressed in *Totem and Taboo*, that Freud may be said to have truly re-assumed the 'phylogenetic fantasy'. This work, begun in Vienna under the influence of Hitler's seizure of power and excesses of anti-Semitism, and completed in exile in London with a premonition of the Second World War and of collective extreme traumatization on an unprecedented scale, shows us a Freud who manifestly feels under pressure to reflect one last time on trauma and its effects. Once more he establishes an analogy between the genesis of religion and the aetiology of the neuroses. He inquires anew into the *real* traumatic events in the external world—the 'historical truth' (ibid., p. 58)—that might ultimately be held responsible for the intensity of conviction and the obsessional character of religious faith and of pathogenic fantasies alike. And yet again he tells his tale of those violent prehistoric acts—the murder, castration, or expulsion of the sons, the patricide and devouring of the father, and so on—which are handed down by heredity, as *archaic heritage*, in the form of primal fantasies independent of individual life experience. With impressive obduracy, Freud here for the last time stands up for his neo-Lamarckian convictions against the conceptions of contemporary biology, with which he was perfectly conversant. It should, however, be mentioned that he does touch upon one other possible transgenerational mode of transmission—namely, the archaic, ubiquitous symbolism in language (ibid., p. 98f.).

On the level of ontogenesis, which features repeatedly in the Moses book, Freud counts as traumas not only sexual and aggressive transgressions but also, for the first time, 'early injuries to the ego (narcissistic mortifications)' (ibid., p. 74). The concept of trauma is thus once again expanded, with the addition of possible wounds inflicted on the subject's narcissism during the processes of primary structure formation, having concomitant effects in the form of permanent pathological alterations of the ego. So it was only in this final phase of his work that Freud attained the insight that 'the ego can be split' (Freud, 1933a: 58) and that with the genesis of a split-off, inaccessible psychical party, 'one might say, a State within a State, [...] the path to a psychosis lies open' (Freud, 1939a: 76). In the context of his late reflections on trauma and drive, then, Freud at the end of his life pushed forward the investigations of the defence mechanism of splitting that blazed a trail for the future of our discipline (Freud, 1940a).

IV

As we know, Freud hesitated for a long time before he published the three essays that make up his book on Moses. This was not only for political reasons, but also no doubt because he was here for the last time pursuing his endeavour to combine the trauma and drive models. In the 'Wolf Man' case history, the publication of which he also deferred, he unequivocally notes the following, in the context of the relative aetiological significance to be assigned to infantile fantasies on the one hand and to real traumatic childhood experiences on the other: 'I admit that this is the most delicate question in the whole domain of psycho-analysis. [...] no doubt has troubled me more; no other uncertainty has been more decisive in holding me back from publishing [...]' (Freud, 1918b: 103n). Freud manifestly held fast throughout his life to the attitude formed during the Fliess period—namely, the fear that the comparatively inoffensive trauma model, with its direct appeal to common sense, might jeopardize the then radically new, disagreeable, 'more difficult and more improbable' (ibid., p. 103n) drive model. When Otto Rank published his theory of the trauma of birth in 1924, Freud was alarmed lest 'our ingenious etiological construction be superseded by the crude birth trauma' (letter to Ferenczi of 26 March 1924; Falzeder and Brabant, 2000: 135; translation corrected). The tragic alienation from Sándor Ferenczi at the beginning of the 1930s, too, was ultimately attributable to the latter's highly original work on the *traumatic* experiences of very young children in relation to their primary objects—actually a kind of psychophysical aetiological trauma theory based on the first description and conceptual outline of what we nowadays call narcissistic personality disorders and borderline pathology.

As described above, Freud was assailed by conflict even in his own attempts to make progress in reconciling the two chains of causation, held back as he was by ambivalence. Put as starkly as possible, his concern could be summarized as follows: by drawing attention, in the aetiology of the neuroses, to the *external traumatic* factors, which are substantially apprehended via the visual sense—the perceptual modality whereby reality is most tellingly conveyed to us—one is wittingly or unwittingly opening up an escape hatch from the repulsive, threatening, and invisible *unconscious internal* world that so hurtfully dominates our feeling and thinking. Such a path might tend to lead away from psychoanalysis altogether. Given the helplessness and vulnerability of the human infant and child, Freud himself never lost sight of the external causal factors in the genesis of neurosis. However, in his published works he mentioned them explicitly as rarely as possible. For him, the traumatic element was always so to speak taken for granted and allowed for in the background together with other considerations.

For decades this attitude has been handed down from one generation of psychoanalysts to the next, presumably on a more unconscious than conscious level. Hence the fallacious impression that psychoanalysts refuse to perceive and take seriously the weight of the external world and the harmful effect of real traumas. Without making a fuss about it, since Freud's day they have in fact by no means concerned themselves solely with pathogenic fantasies, dreams, and drive vicissitudes, but have also at all times taken account of the direct and indirect consequences of traumatization due to flooding with stimuli from outside. This is so when they investigate the potential effects of the loss of one or both parents, physical and/or mental disability in siblings, illness in the subject himself or herself, surgical operations or hospitalizations, and so forth, during the course of childhood development, or, say, the possible consequences of war, torture, social, and cultural deracination, serious accidents, natural catastrophes, and so on, in adulthood. Although we are repeatedly warned not to overstretch the concept of trauma, it is nevertheless the case that exploration of the influence of pathological internal states and cumulatively harmful forms of behaviour by the primary objects on babies and young children belongs in this context. Finally, the study—even if commenced only after a prolonged phase of latency—of the effects of the Shoah on survivors and their offspring, as well as on the persecutors' children and grandchildren, has documented the preparedness of psychoanalysts to engage with the consequences of extreme traumatizations due to a real crime of unique proportions.

Was, and is, there any justification for Freud's concern that we might be tempted to exit from psychoanalysis as it were at the trauma end? In the 1980s and 1990s at any rate, the answer might well have been yes. At this time a storm was whipped up by the abstruse theories of Jeffrey Masson (1984) to the effect that, out of cowardice and opportunism, Freud had suppressed the true seduction theory in favour of untrue psychoanalysis. The clamorous debate about sexual abuse flared up at about the same time. These two media events abruptly highlighted the intensity of the need, felt by specialists and the general public alike, to cast off the complexity and travail inherent in genuine psychoanalytic thought by one-sidedly focusing on trauma.

V

Undisconcerted by, and independently of, this commotion, which has now died down, the psychoanalytic community has since continued the work commenced by Freud on bringing the trauma and drive models together. One comparatively spectacular sign of these efforts is the debate on the rediscovery and re-evaluation of the late work of Sándor Ferenczi—a debate that, despite the extreme polarization of its early stages, has now after all more or less ended in a substantial degree of integration. In this way a theoretical effort became manifest and ultimately impossible to overlook—an effort which, as retraced in my paper, Freud had begun quietly and in outline only, and which, no doubt partly with Ferenczi's advance resonating in his mind, he had pursued with greater intensity in his late work. Each in their own specific way, great psychoanalytic minds of subsequent generations such as Balint, Winnicott, Bion and, now, André Green, to name but a few, have continued this effort.

So the question Freud sought in vain to answer in the phylogenetic fantasy with its quasi-mythological transmission construct has since spawned new, less speculative hypotheses on transgenerational transmission. The metapsychological issue of aetiology, on which Freud's highly abstract reflections on trauma once centred, remains a focus of interest. However, it is mainly concrete *clinical* work, especially with extremely traumatized patients, that has yielded an impressively abundant phenomenology of the process and consequences of traumatization, as reflected in the latest psychoanalytic literature on the subject. In particular, it has been possible to give an even more specific description of the typical forms of defence deployed by trauma victims in the service of their psychophysical survival during and after exposure to traumatization.

In the theoretical, conceptual elaboration of the results of their research, the authors take account, as in the past, of the classical economic point of view, which is indispensable precisely in the context of trauma. But they benefit, too, from the psychoanalytic theory of object relations, now further elaborated. In this connection, however, it is easy to overlook the fact that the seeds of this relational expansion of the allegedly wholly solipsistic classical concepts were already sown in Freud's texts—in particular, 'Mourning and Melancholia' (see Ogden, 2002). The authors also exploit the progress made in the psychoanalytic understanding of the fundamental importance of the capacity for symbolization. We now understand better that—and why—massive traumatization due to flooding with external stimuli, together with the ego-paralyzing automatic anxiety that is thereby internally triggered, can actually lead to the lasting demolition of psychic structure. The annihilation of internalized good object representations—note that the issue is the loss not only of objects but of object representations—coupled with the loss of the capacity for symbolization that imparts meaning, has the consequence that the traumatic event in all its crudity persists only in the victim's body, and is thus pseudo-represented somatically. Besides massive bodily sensations, the predominant subjective experience is of disorientation along the chronological continuum of past-present-future—that is, in essence, personal timelessness—as well as total hopelessness and loneliness, extreme distrust, and the unimaginability of empathic concern.

The authors are manifestly agreed that where the capacity for symbolization has been destroyed, even the most rudimentary working out of the traumatic experience cannot get under way without psychotherapeutic help. It seems imperative for a good, empathic object in the shape of the analyst to make itself available in *reality*. The analyst must be capable of overcoming the disbelief, disavowal, and spontaneous refusal of empathy that are always and inevitably aroused by confrontation with the consequences of extreme traumatization. He or she must be prepared to take upon himself or herself the catastrophic burden of the trauma, and must attempt to symbolize what *actually* happened, to order it in the dimension of time (that is, to re-establish temporality) and also to reconstruct it historically—and all this must be done affirmatively rather than through interpretation. In the *real*, hope-creating experience of relating to the therapist, it may be possible for the patient, in small steps on the boundary between the somatic and the psychic, as it were, to reacquire a good internal object and the mental capacity for the formation of representations—that is, for binding extreme quantities of excitation. In other words, the issue in such treatments is at first nothing less than recovery of the structural prerequisites for the working out of the cataclysmic effects of the trauma. This working out, for its part, proceeds by way of a narration to be created jointly by patient and analyst, which must be intimately connected with the actual traumatic reality in the form of a historical reconstruction.

One is struck by the extent to which the attention of today's psychoanalytic trauma researchers is focused on the therapeutic process, on the treatment technique and, even more specifically, on the *real* relationship between patient and therapist. Some connotations of the concept of the real relationship are, of course, also included in the modern concepts of 'therapeutic holding' or 'therapeutic containing'. At this point I should like to forge a further link to the Freudian tradition. There is in my view a correspondence between the theoretical pair of concepts 'trauma model/drive model' on the one hand and the clinical pair of concepts 'real relationship/transference relationship' on the other. The trauma model and the real relationship appeal directly to common sense, whereas the drive model and the transference relationship represent the more difficult, more improbable, truly novel, and genuinely psychoanalytic conception. I said earlier that Freud always took the traumatic element for granted, comparatively seldom discussing it *explicitly* in his works, and the same is no less true of the aspects of the *real* analyst-patient relationship. In his writings on technique he predominantly stressed the transference relationship, presumably for the same reasons that induced him to give priority to the drive model in the aetiology of the neuroses.

We know from the numerous surviving reports of his analysands that he in fact assigned a great deal of space for the real relationship to unfold and certainly attributed considerable therapeutic significance to it. Late in life he complained that in the matter of clinical technique he had often been misunderstood because in his writings he had mainly emphasized the perils that were liable to hinder the development of the analytic process; for this reason his recommendations had been predominantly negative, directed towards what was if at all possible to be *avoided* (see, for example, a letter to Ferenczi of 4 January 1928; Falzeder and Brabant, 2000: 332). Extracts from notes made by Max Eitingon on the first meeting of the Vienna Psychoanalytic Society he attended in 1907 have recently been published. He records that Freud said in his intimate circle: 'The secret of our activity is that healing is healing through love.' According to Eitingon, Freud often repeated this statement orally. It may, however, be assumed that in a written text, and certainly in one intended for publication, he would be more likely to have used the term 'aim-inhibited love'. Yet Eitingon added in his notes that especially in the case of particularly difficult patients—perhaps including traumatized ones?—Freud also considered that by 'supreme *personal* effort' it might still be possible to reach such patients, 'but this would be at the cost of one's skin'. This was expressed even more tellingly as follows: 'More can be achieved in the treatment, but then one would have to cut strips out of one's own skin' (see Freud and Eitingon, 2004h: 938). This radical image is so to speak the unofficial, interpersonal anti-metaphor to his official, highly distanced likening of the analyst to a surgeon or a mirror. Having 'to cut strips out of one's own skin' at any rate graphically conveys the enormous strain imposed by therapeutic work with severely traumatized patients, where the *real* relationship between analyst and patient appears to be the very foundation upon which the therapy may in favourable cases after all succeed.

In conclusion, what I—and no doubt also Marianne Leuzinger-Bohleber—wanted to demonstrate by this presentation to our Panel is as follows. As psychoanalysts we possess a rich intellectual tradition that deserves to be remembered, and is and remains susceptible to extension in every direction. If something new is discovered, it can be integrated, and at the same time untenable earlier conceptions can of course be relinquished. However, this tradition, which, now as in the past, is inspiring not least by the questions it raises, need not be devalued as it sometimes is today. We are fortunate in having Sverre Varvin as a member of our Panel. On the basis of the conceptual tradition I have summed up in the phrase 'drive *and* trauma', and by virtue precisely of his openness to the concepts of other disciplines, such as, say, semiotics, as well as of his extensive clinical experience with severely traumatized patients, he has made innovative and in many respects also integrative contributions (including Varvin, 2000, 2002, 2003) to present-day genuinely psychoanalytic trauma research.

Bibliography

Falzeder, E. and Brabant, E. (eds) (1996). *The Correspondence of Sigmund Freud and Sándor Ferenczi*, vol. 2, 1914–1919. Cambridge, Mass. and London: Harvard University Press.

Falzeder, E. and Brabant, E. (eds) (2000). *The Correspondence of Sigmund Freud and Sándor Ferenczi*, vol. 3, 1920–1933. Cambrdige, Mass. and London: Harvard University Press.

Freud, S. (1906a). 'My View on the Part Played by Sexuality in the Aetiology of the Neuroses'. *S.E.*, 7: 271–79.

Freud, S. (1912–1913a). *Totem and Taboo. S.E.*, 13: 1–161.

Freud, S. (1915e). 'The Unconscious'. *S.E.*, 14: 166–204.
Freud, S. (1916–1917a). *Introductory Lectures on Psycho-Analysis. S.E.*, 15–16.
Freud, S. (1916–1917g). 'Mourning and Melancholia'. *S.E.*, 14: 222–35.
Freud, S. (1918b). 'From the History of an Infantile Neurosis'. *S.E.*, 17: 7–122.
Freud, S. (1919d). 'Introduction to Psychoanalysis and the War Neuroses'. *S.E.*, 17: 207–10.
Freud, S. (1920g). *Beyond the Pleasure Principle. S.E.*, 18: 7–64.
Freud, S. (1925d). *An Autobiographical Study. S.E.*, 20: 7–70.
Freud, S. (1933a). *New Introductory Lectures on Psycho-Analysis. S.E.*, 22: 5–182.
Freud, S. (1939a). *Moses and Monotheism. S.E.*, 23: 1–137.
Freud, S. (1940a). 'Splitting of the Ego in the Process of Defence'. *S.E.*, 23: 275–78.
Freud, S. (1985a[1915]). *Übersicht der Übertragungsneurosen: Ein bisher unbekanntes Manuskript*. Ediert und mit einem Essay versehen von I. Grubich-Simitis. Frankfurt am Main: S. Fischer. (English edition: Freud, S. *A Phylogentic Fantasy: Overview of the Transference Neuroses*. Edited and with an essay by I. Grubrich-Simitis. Cambridge, Mass. and London: Harvard University Press, 1987.)
Freud, S. and Eitingon, M. (2004h). *Briefwechsel 1906–1939*, vol. 2, ed. Schröter, M. Tübingen: edition diskord.
Grubrich-Simitis, I. (1981). 'Extreme Traumatization as Cumulative Trauma: Psychoanalytic Investigations of the Effects of Concentration Camp Experiences on Survivors and Their Children'. *The Psychoanalytic Study of the Child*, 36: 415–50.
Grubrich-Simitis, I. (1984). 'From Concretism to Metaphor: Thoughts on Some Theoretical and Technical Aspects of the Psychoanalytic Work with Children of Holocaust Survivors'. *The Psychoanalytic Study of the Child*, 39. 301–19.
Grubrich-Simitis, I. (1988). 'Trauma or drive—drive and Trauma: A Reading of Sigmund Freud's Phylogenetic Fantasy of 1915'. *The Psychoanalytic Study of the Child*, 43: 3–32. The German text appeared in *Psyche*, 41: 992–1023, 1987. Translated from the German by Philip Slotkin.
Grubrich-Simitis, I. (2003). 'Trauma ou pulsion—pulsion et trauma: Leçons à partir de la "fantasie phylogénétique" écrite par Sigmund Freud, en 1915'. In: Green, A., Grubrich-Simitis, I., Laplanche, J. and Schimek, J.G. *Sur la théorie de la séduction*. (Libres cahiers pour la psychanalyse, Etudes.) Paris: Editions In Press, 19–54.
Masson, J.M. (1984). *The Assault on Truth: Freud's Suppression of the Seduction Theory*. New York: Farrar, Straus and Giroux.

Masson, J.M. (ed.) (1985a). *The Complete Letters of Sigmund Freud to Wilhelm Fliess, 1887–1904*. Cambridge, Mass. and London: Harvard University Press.

Ogden, T. (2002). 'A New Reading of the Origins of Object-Relations Theory'. *The International Journal of Psychoanalysis*, 83: 767–82.

Varvin, S. (2000). 'Die gegenwärtige Vergangenheit: Extreme Tramatisierung und Psychotherapie'. *Psyche*, 54: 895–930.

Varvin, S. (2002). 'Body, Mind and the Other: Mentalising Extreme Experiences'. In: Varvin, S. and Stajner Popovic, T. (eds) *Upheaval: Psychoanalytic Perspectives on Trauma*. Belgrade: International Aid Network. pp. 153–191.

Varvin, S. (2003). 'Extreme Traumatisation: Strategies of Mental Survival'. *International Forum of Psychoanalysis*, 12: 5–16.

CHAPTER NINE

Pluralism in theory and in research—and what now?[1] A plea for connectionism

Anna Ursula Dreher

Abstract

For a long time now there has been an analytic discussion about the pluralism of theories; the author proposes that there is a second pluralism we must pay attention to, namely the one in the analytic research field. Introductory remarks on the development of conceptual research serve as *reference* to highlight the two pluralisms—relating to the Green-Wallerstein-debate about the *common ground* in psychoanalysis; and relating to considerations about the scientific status of psychoanalysis and about some current understandings of analytic research.

Psychoanalysis as a science 'between nature and culture' (in Green's and Wallerstein's words) would have to take both nature *and* culture into account, not only in its theoretical concepts but also in research and methodology. In doing so it would be desirable not only to lament those two pluralisms, but to understand both positively as resources in the search for the best problem solutions.

The author criticizes the idea of an unchangeable *common ground* in psychoanalysis. She points to Freud's work as *historical* ground, understanding Freud's image of man [*Menschenbild*] and his interest in knowledge [*Erkenntnisinteresse*] as a possible common backdrop for a constructive analytic discourse—against which a common ground would have to be worked out anew again and again. The prerequisites for such systematic 'controversial discussions' and for a connectionist view are discussed, which is seen as a workable alternative to fundamentalism or to a resigning acceptance of an arbitrary pluralism.

For many analysts who mainly work in clinical practice and who have an interest in research questions, our analytic research literature is meanwhile probably not so easy to survey. This is because there is not only the methodological interplay between conceptual and empirical *aspects* of any type of research, but because there are also many different subject *areas* of psychoanalytic research: psychotherapy research with process and outcome analyses, developmental research, and historical research or, for instance, conceptual research. There are many interesting studies on the most varied topics using different research paradigms. One can also find very different proposals to organize this psychoanalytic research field, a lot of classifications and divisions. So I can only attempt to shed some light on this vast field. I would like to do this from a basic perspective, namely, an epistemological one. Reflections of this kind are necessary from time to time, but are unfortunately also somewhat dry. André Green (2005: 629) has this in mind when he says: '*Reflection on the fundamental postulates of divergent theories is not the most beloved exercise of psychoanalysts*'. It is surely not 'the most beloved' exercise—but we know that, regrettably, the universe 'Beyond the Pleasure Principle' cannot be ignored ... definitely not for long.

I would like to present my reflections using the example of conceptual research, and begin with a few remarks on the development of this research area, in the course of which I will also refer to my own way to conduct conceptual research. This introduction will result in a brief development of some ideas on science and research in psychoanalysis in order to discuss—against the background of the pluralism in our analytic theories and of the debate about the *common ground*—a second pluralism in the field of psychoanalytic research; and will end with a plea for a 'connectionist' view.

Some thoughts on the development of conceptual research

My first contact with conceptual research was in the 1980s at the Sigmund-Freud-Institute in Frankfurt, Germany, through a research project initiated together with Joseph Sandler—discussing methods to explore the usage of concepts. At the time, the mere label 'conceptual research' provoked a certain scepticism amongst analytic researchers. One could study the Unconscious, the process and outcome of analyses, child development, and even specific illnesses—but concepts? How could that be done? Not only was our research subject considered strange by many, it also did not fit into the *Zeitgeist:* since the 1970s, neopositivistic empiricism has begun to gain ground in the analytic research field, not accidentally accompanied by an increasing *medicocentrism* (cf. Jacoby, 1983; Parin and Parin-Matthèy, 1986), which often regards psychoanalysis merely as a form of psychotherapy practised by physicians and psychologists, and which, for instance, sees few problems in adapting our nosology to the system of the International Statistical Classification of Diseases and Related Health Problems (ICD). It was not surprising then, that our project's 'conceptual research' at the time often met with an understanding that equated analytic research generally with analytic psychotherapy research. Quantitative-empirical psychotherapy researchers wanted to explore measurable aspects of inner and outer reality by using objective and reliable methods, but they did not make the use of analytic concepts their explicit topic of study. Clinicians also do research, they explore themselves, their patients, and the analytic situation, for instance, how unconscious processes work in the interplay of transference and counter-transference—but clinicians also usually do not systematically make the use of analytic concepts the topic of their research. Our Frankfurt research group, however, considered that a methodically well founded examination of the variety that exists in the use of analytic concepts, its change over time, and the imprecise and, at times, contradictory, use, would be a worthwhile undertaking.

What do we mean by 'conceptual research'?

The phrase 'conceptual research' has meanwhile become familiar to many, but has also suffered something of the same fate which we know from analytic concepts: different authors use it with different meanings. The phrase actually is a contraction; *originally* it did not designate the conceptual aspects of any research, but rather:

- the systematic investigation of different uses of concepts in different analytic cultures;
- the investigation of the historical change of the meaning of a concept over time; and
- the attempt to formulate proposals for a reasonable, clinically rich, and meaningful use (for a systematic introduction cf. Dreher, 2005).

'Conceptual research' is normally connected with the name of Joseph Sandler who introduced it into the analytic literature. The unfolding and constant differentiation of our concepts was one focus of the kind of conceptual studies which Sandler had proposed and had then carried out himself with different colleagues. This began with his work in the so-called 'concept group' at the Hampstead Index (Anna-Freud Centre London), continued with the Frankfurt research group, and included the work he had done together with Anne-Marie Sandler on *past and present unconscious*, and the work on internal object relations (Sandler and Sandler, 1999). The validity and usefulness of analytic concepts must show themselves in clinical practice. Sandler was convinced that the analytic situation was not only the place for this justification, but also the place where concepts arise, or where their meanings can change. These changes, in the beginning, tend to occur silently and implicitly. The Frankfurt research group (Sandler *et al.*, 1987) had thought up a set of methods to make the boundary between the analysts' *implicit* and *explicit* concept use more permeable—between explorative, carefully tentative attempts in the analytic situation and the 'official' communications about how concepts are understood. Only through publication can new ideas be made explicit, and only through discussion can these proposals be criticized (see Canestri, 2006).

A central intention of Sandler's research work on concepts was to elicit these processes of conceptualization as they occur during clinical work, and as a direct result, to make suggestions for improved concept usage. This work in turn, especially the joint work in Frankfurt on the changes in the use of the concept 'psychic trauma', later became the practical example and the starting point for me to introduce epistemological and methodological reflections about the role and status of such a conceptual research programme (Dreher, 2000). We normally use our analytic concepts quasi-automatically; they are our categories when we describe, organize, and communicate our thoughts and experiences in language. We are certain of this usage, usually without being aware of problems, as long as we do not leave our respective analytic culture. It requires some effort to take a distanced and reflective attitude when our own concept use is being put to the test. A very human problem, obviously, and one to which Lewis Carroll once hinted: 'When *I* use a word,' Lewis Carroll has Humpty Dumpty say in a rather scornful tone to Alice, 'it means just what I choose it to mean—neither more nor less.' 'The question is,' replies Alice, 'whether yon *can* make words mean so many different things.' 'The question is,' retorts Humpty Dumpty, 'which is to be master—that's all' (quoted after Carroll 1960/70: 269 [orig. 1872]). Indeed, when someone is criticized for his or her concept usage, this may provoke different affects. Some react with 'a rather scornful tone', and often the question is asked: Who has the monopoly of interpretation over concepts? Who is the 'master' in the house? Of course there are not only 'personal', but also other factors which make the study of concepts complicated. These are factors such as the consequences of psychoanalysis being embedded into different cultures, into different medical and thus economic systems of different countries, and so forth; epistemologically speaking: the consequences of the embedding of our concepts into different language games.

About the change of concepts

Concepts do change; this they have in common with scientific theories and world views. Freud (1915: 117) confronted the changes of his concepts with equanimity: 'The advance of knowledge … does not tolerate any rigidity … in definitions. … even basic concepts that have been established in the form of definitions are constantly being altered in their content'. In the history of psychoanalysis, many theories, models, and concepts have come under pressure to change, even 'basic concepts'. But: not everything old is bad, and not everything new is good. Green (2005: 631) refers to the relevance of the 'old' classic literature, when he, somewhat wistfully, complains, that Freud is today 'no longer an author worth reading'. Green is right; of course, Freud should be read, not for reasons of idolatry, but because, up to this day, Freud's intentions and also parts of our psychoanalytic history are preserved in our concepts—this is especially so for our clinical concepts. As a result, this makes an important demand on our research: to find a prudent balance between preservation and change in the 'advance of knowledge'.

Thomas Kuhn (1962) has compellingly shown how change processes occur in scientific theories; they do not only proceed in a linear, continuous way, but often by crisis-like leaps. He has also shown that scientific progress happens not only through the steady accumulation of new research findings in times of normal science. Progress can also be initiated through paradigm change, for example through new methods, through changes in the scientific world view, or in mentalities. Prominent examples for such processes of change in the life sciences are the movement towards cognitive science, towards evolutionary biology, or nowadays, to the neurosciences. Changes in concepts occur rather similarly. Right now we can notice how concepts from the cognitive memory research such as 'declarative and procedural memory' gradually flow into our analytic concepts about memory and the unconscious. Let me highlight one important finding from Kuhn's studies: changes in scientific theories—and I think this is also true for changes in the meaning of concepts—are not only based on scientific arguments. A number of other non-negligible, but well-known parameters, are, for instance, struggles for institutional power, for prestige and dominance, or simply for research money grants. Another known parameter is a kind of territorial thinking, the insistence on such conceptual understandings as they have been codified by idealized authorities. All of these influences affecting the meaning of our concepts are at times opaque and certainly difficult to grasp; nonetheless, they constitute the background for different concept usages.

Problems of the variety in concept use—and an attempted solution

Differences in the understanding of even central concepts do not always receive the same evaluation from the analytic community: to some, this is a lamentable Babel of languages, to others, it is not. Some recognize a creative evolutionary potential in this manifoldness, others see a danger for the consistency of our theory. There are good reasons behind both points of view. Nevertheless, the, to my mind, justified complaints about the *semantic vagueness* of our concepts and about their inconsistent usage have predominated for quite some time. These complaints make us irrefutably aware of a—from a scientific point of view—severe problem regarding the meaning of our concepts. The question remains: how can we actually guarantee that we are all referring to the same clinical phenomena and that we all mean the same thing when we use the same concept?

The idea that conceptual research could offer a constructive contribution to solving this problem and thus might yield gains for clinical work *and* scientific endeavours, has become accepted by many in contemporary psychoanalysis. The Hampstead Index and later the Frankfurt research group had initially used Sandler's phrase 'conceptual research' only as a working title. But in the last decade the label has in fact established itself. In this sense 'conceptual research' is indeed a historically grown phrase, but, of course not a protected, patented one, and nowadays it is also itself being used with different meanings: its usage spans quite a range from conceptual reflection to systematic conceptual research. Therefore, it appears to make sense, to take another, closer look at the history of the origin of conceptual research. What is specific about it? The phrase 'conceptual research' in fact refers to a special kind of *empirical phenomena*, namely the use of concepts. It describes activities related to the *systematic investigation* of analytic concepts in their clinical and extra-clinical usage. It is thereby assumed that a concept does not stand alone in the world, but rather is situated in connection with other concepts in a conceptual field, and that it is not used solipsistically by individual analysts, but rather by different members of a specific scientific community. Therefore, empirical questions must be answered first and foremost: in addition to the question of how one understands and uses a concept, it must be clarified how others understand and use it. Consequently, the procedure of our Frankfurt research study included, along with the always important conceptual *reflections*, a series of further methodical steps, and was oriented at the following beliefs:

- Conceptual research—like other complex research activities today—requires teamwork by researchers who are connected through a common research interest; at best they come from differing perspectives and disciplines.
- Besides selecting concepts of interest, it is necessary to consider the 'sample' of users, namely: which concept users are relevant for

answering the research questions, which analysts, which experts, and whom from neighbouring disciplines?

- The collection and evaluation of data are based on a research-design which has to specify precisely the kind of data to be gained through the application of what type of methods, from which individuals, and over what timeframe. The Frankfurt research group, which here serves only as programmatic prototype, implemented for the investigation of the trauma concept—in addition to a systematic literature analysis—semi-structured interviews with a number of trauma experts. Then, the method of group discussion was used for evaluating the data. Of course, other qualitative or quantitative, philological or hermeneutic methods, can also be used.

Conceptual research as a standardized procedure does not exist, just as psychotherapy research as such or the experiment as such do not exist. Conceptual research, therefore, is not a concrete method, but rather a *research programme*.

As to its procedure, it is:

- empirical, by investigating and describing the meaning space and actual usage of a concept in the context of interest;
- historico-reconstructive, by tracing the development of a concept through essential points of change; and
- evaluative, by critically discussing the collected data and by working out meaning aspects of a concept which, from an analytic perspective, are indispensable, and perhaps by also making suggestions for better concept use.

It is understood that those aspects can only be grasped with different methods, and in so far conceptual research is always *multimethodical*. It is therefore, in my view, a central misunderstanding in the current discussions on the methodological status of conceptual research if it is equated with qualitative research, or if it is demarcated from quantitative-empirical research. It may have become clear by now that conceptual research—as it was conceptualized—may make use not only of qualitative, but also of quantitative, methods. Methods are a means to an end, and the all-important question is whether or not they serve this end. Other research approaches may define themselves by the methods they deem admissible; *conceptual research defines itself by its subject matter, the use of concepts, and by its aim, the clarification of the meaning of concepts.*

Possible elements of a conceptual research programme

Thus, the first phase of a research programme may be concerned with methods that examine the logical consistency of concepts; another phase may be about the objective and reliable measuring of a concept's usage with the help of standardized instruments. Nevertheless—as the work on concepts has to do essentially with the use of language and with meaning aspects—it is obvious that the analysis of our analytic literature, the interpretation of expert interviews, or the critical discussion in a research team, are central aspects; that is, the application of hermeneutic methods, with which we analysts are indeed very familiar. In the course of such a research process, a concept is being tested again and again from new vantage points. In this, the respective individual pre-knowledge within the research team, and also the joint knowledge, systematically acquired in the course of the work, serve as a background. This procedure has the purpose of gradually elaborating the relevant meaning field of a concept. Such 'working through' is at its best that 'progressive spiral' which was described in the context of the Hampstead Index. Structured reflection and discussion within a research team are part and parcel of how an analytic research process proceeds. However, it is not quite so obvious that the interpretative and discursive moments are systematically applied and considered to be decisively important. But without any such communication about the rules of concept usage and without the search for a consensus on them, the aim of conceptual research, which is to clarify the meanings of concepts, would be difficult to attain. There have been, in the history of psychoanalysis, a number of attempts to clarify concepts in discourse, like the concept study groups of mainly US-American analytic institutes, or the Panel-discussions on individual concepts, associated with the idea of overcoming contradictory or outdated meanings of our concepts and of making our concepts *fit* for new developments. And while consensus is the aim, at times we only succeed in highlighting the dissent more sharply.

Empirical phenomena do not describe and name themselves. The *person,* the concept *user,* is always in the game, and thus the dependency of the concept's meaning from whoever is using the concept, from his or her being embedded in historically grown and socially shared language games. By focusing on the discourse and on the concept users (clinicians or researchers) it becomes clear that the relationship between a concept and the pertaining empirical phenomena, that is, between language and the world, cannot be regarded as only a two-digit relation. Rather, this relationship must be seen as triangular, in accordance with semiotic and pragmatic tradition: there is the concept, there are the phenomena to which the concept refers, and there is the person who uses the concept in line with his or her understanding. Thus, the meanings of concepts are embedded in and interact with different human life forms. Adequate consideration of this will make one sensitive to the fact that concept use is *contingent* (dependent also on the *Zeitgeist* and on mentalities), which, by the way, is not that uninteresting an aspect in our international psychoanalysis, given that we use our analytic concepts across different continents and cultures. Therefore, conceptual studies can—in order to take into account such cultural bindedness—additionally take on Freud's cultural theory perspective, which, along with clinical and metapsychological theory, is the third classic pillar in the history of psychoanalytic theory.

So much for the intentions of conceptual research. Whichever way these intentions may be put into practice in the future, it can be noted that the sensitivity towards the described problem area has grown. To do research on concepts and their usage tends to be understood as quality assurance. As many of our concepts are also being employed outside of the analytic situation, it is all the more important to preserve the essential *analytic* meaning aspects of our concepts.

But what does the analytic research field look like in which conceptual research had to find its position?

Some thoughts on psychoanalysis, research, and science

What is understood by research in psychoanalysis?

Not only can our analytic concepts have different meanings for different users, but so can our methodological concepts. As we know, there is no uniform understanding of 'research' in psychoanalysis today. At times it is understood as a loose metaphor, at other times as a methodologically sophisticated programme, and in any case there exist a host of activities under its label. If we refer this only to analytic *psychotherapy* research, then, for instance, at one end of this vast field there is an understanding of research based exclusively on Freud's work, and at the other end we have an understanding of research which orients itself on the ideas formulated by neopositivistic empiricism, or on cognitivism, or lately, on the neurosciences. This opens up a particularly interesting methodological field of tension between, on the one hand, the ideographic view oriented on the individual single case, and, on the other, the nomothetic view oriented on the taking of samples and on universal laws—two positions in the analytic research field which are usually relatively irreconcilable.

For some, psychoanalysis—according to classical analytical conviction—represents by its practice alone a special kind of research: we analysts *research* unconscious processes of our patients, and at best, also our own; and we reflect on our cases and publish these reflections in often fascinating case studies. Generations of analysts have shared this self-image, which is expressed in Freud's (1927: 256) 'conjunction between cure and research'. To call each analyst also a researcher, as this dictum demands, makes for a sometimes flattering self-image, but in a modern understanding of science, it can be seen as a rather problematic use of the term 'research'. Not quite unjustly, this understanding of research is called somewhat naïve today, as it is based upon Freud's 19th-century understanding of science. The understanding of research and the criteria which scientific research would have to meet have of course changed since Freud's times. Thus, critics usually point out a series of deficits in this so-called conjunction-research: along with the danger of merely selective or distorted—in Grünbaum's (1988) words: 'epistemically contaminated'—reporting from the analytic situation, one of the problems indicated is that such research is often only a one-person-endeavour, that it produces not easily replicable and criticizable results, and that its findings cannot always be reconstructed due to insufficient information. The idea that a researcher, on his or her own, generates hypotheses, gathers and interprets the data, and thus structures the whole research process alone, is of course not easy to bring into agreement with the convictions arising out of research understandings oriented on the standards of intersubjectivity.

On the other hand, those modern understandings of research which are empiricism-orientated appear naïve and deficient to a convinced conjunction-researcher. For one, because the research process is often far removed from the analytic situation, too far away from direct subjective experience; and then because unconscious processes, which can only be inferred via hermeneutic methods, are to be quantitatively grasped and measured; and because often the analyst him- or herself does not occupy a privileged role in the research process.

The more one goes beyond pure psychotherapy research and opens up the complete research field in psychoanalysis, then there is the conviction, and increasingly so, that psychoanalysis cannot shut itself off from modern ideas of research as they have developed in the 20th century in natural, human, and the social sciences. It has become more and more acknowledged that not only the genuine analytic path of research, but also that research practice generated by, for example, empiricism and cognitivism, but also and above all by the hermeneutic sciences, could be of interest for us. The relevance of the analytic practice in the various research areas, however, remains unquestionable for most of us: the analytic situation with its emphasis on subjectivity, interaction, shared experience, and unconscious processes remains the core, the important empirical basis, and also indispensable place of justification. This particularity undoubtedly sets the *constraints* for the import of other research technologies into psychoanalysis.

To conclude this little excursion: there is a broad, multi-layered understanding of research within psychoanalysis (cf. also Leuzinger-Bohleber *et al.*, 2003a), and whenever research is discussed, the respective understanding of research—that is to say the epistemological perspective—is always present. It would therefore be desirable if the discussants were to acknowledge this and would more frequently explicate their own understanding of research. And this in turn is no doubt connected with the question of what they in fact consider 'scientific'. For, whoever speaks about research always refers—at least implicitly—to the sciences, as today it is the sciences which essentially codify how research functions. If we analysts are not seeking splendid isolation (which we possibly cannot afford as long as analytic therapy as a *scientifically* recognized procedure is paid for by national health insurers), we will at least have to engage with the current discussions about criteria for research. *Critically* engage—for of course psychoanalysis can assert its own way of thinking and its own view of the world (*Weltbild*) and can itself proffer suggestions, based on its own very specific model of the mind. To look over the fence can be beneficial—and at times both sides may learn from each other (an approach of this kind in psychotherapy research is certainly the multi-perspective. catamnestic study of the German Psychoanalytic Association, Leuzinger-Bohleber *et al.*, 2003b).

Is psychoanalysis regarded as a science?

It seems appropriate to elucidate briefly the relationship between psychoanalysis and the sciences—a varied history, occasionally interspersed with moments of acknowledgement, but more often with moments of devaluation. Psychoanalysis is and definitely has been treated with little affection by the established sciences. Often, it has not even been conceded 'scientific' status. Questions of status, however, as everyone knows, are not trivial questions, as they determine public standing and admission to government (medical and social) institutions, or will determine university affiliation and research grants.

From our analytic position, the relationship with the established sciences is also an ambivalent one. Some of us even question whether psychoanalysis should seek any kind of proximity with other sciences; whether it is not a science in its own right, autonomous in all essential features—with its own subject matter: the Unconscious, and then with its own specific research methods for understanding and interpreting this Unconscious. And there are still those among us who advise to generally keep a distance between us and other sciences. André Green (2005: 632), for instance, concisely postulated some time ago, in the debate with Robert Wallerstein about the *common ground* in psychoanalysis: 'Psychoanalysis in my view is neither a science nor a branch of hermeneutics. It is a practice based on *clinical thinking* that leads to theoretical hypotheses.' This statement, that psychoanalysis is a practice leading to theory, refers to Freud's characterization of psychoanalysis as a method, a cure, and a theory. This is to say, that our work does not only deal with science or with the application of theoretical insights, but also with personal knowledge and experience, with practical skills, with learned abilities, perhaps even artistic ones, with intuition, self-reflection, and also with ethical convictions.

In any case, 'practice leads to theory'—and precisely that has always been claimed by psychoanalysis, namely that it is a practice *and* a theory, for instance a clinical or a developmental theory, and it has also claimed to have a model of the mind. But there is a problem here: regarding the understanding of what theories, models, or 'theoretical hypotheses' (Green) are, psychoanalysis certainly does not have an exclusive monopoly on definition. What hypotheses and theories are, which structures and which functions they have, how they are tested, how they change, how new theories arise, why some disappear—all of this is also discussed in the sciences, especially in epistemology.

All of this is itself subjected to change: the question of what is considered scientific, and thus what is correspondingly considered good research, the question of which theories, which methods are deemed the best, all of this is contingent. Each so-called *turn* in the last century has generated new belief systems in this respect, the *behaviouristic turn* as well as the *linguistic turn*, the *cognitive turn*, as well as the current *neuro turn*. And each *turn* has produced modifications in the view on phenomena that were considered relevant, and also in the evaluation of those research methods judged admissible. And of course these modifications in the scientific world views have always had an impact on psychoanalysis, too, and have coloured our understanding of science and research. Thus, in the course of its history, psychoanalysis has approached changing scientific positions and has attempted to adapt their respective methodological convictions for its own needs. We know the discussions that say that psychoanalysis—if it is a science at all—is most likely a hermeneutic one, a science of understanding and interpretation. Or, that psychoanalysis—if it is a science—is most likely a neo-positivistic one, a science of explanation and prediction. Still others see psychoanalysis as being close to the cognitive sciences and their memory theories. Currently for some the biological or the neuro-sciences have become the leading science.

There is definitely a colourful discussion in psychoanalysis on the subjects of science and research! The conviction, which relation psychoanalysis has with the sciences, determines to a considerable extent what kind of research is regarded as most suitable, as important, right, and useful. But which science and which logic of research offer at which time the best paradigm for psychoanalysis? This question is answered differently by different voices. Thus we not only find the described variety in theory, but *also* variety within the analytic *research field*. And this is a problem, of course. At first glance, there is nothing wrong with having different convictions; the question is only how respective protagonists deal with this. Will they listen to each other, will they try to understand the other's position, or will they only be interested in their own position? All of this will have consequences for a possible dialogue.

Conceptual research in the force field of two pluralisms

In psychoanalysis, we have over the course of time become familiar with discussions about the pluralism of our theories, perhaps even the pluralism in clinical practice. And by now the very term 'pluralism' may set off a reaction of discomfort in some, as at times it appears only to gloss over the fact that the different analytic communities do not have so much to say to each other any more. On occasion, convictions other than one's own are devalued, and on other occasions the well-known attitude of 'anything goes' is taken.

Yet 'pluralism' does not need to have only negative connotations, but can also be understood as referring to a constructive diversity from which a competing, fair search for the best problem solutions can result. And in this sense I would see each research approach, like here conceptual research, in the force field of this diversity of convictions, of which, so my thesis, there are two kinds:

1. There is the very familiar pluralism of psychoanalytic theories and schools, which I would like to call here—to keep things simple—*theory-pluralism*. Thus, for example, conceptual research at all times moves within the labyrinth of divergent theories, of the huge historically grown variety of analytic traditions, classified by geographic or cultural aspects, or often by the names of those authorities to which one feels particularly obligated qua analytic socialization.
2. But each research approach also finds itself confronted with another kind of pluralism; namely, the multitude of convictions as to which scientific maxims psychoanalytic research should adhere to. These beliefs are usually connected with a preference

for a methodological position, or with a leading science which psychoanalysis should follow epistemologically. I will call this *second* pluralism—again keeping things simple—*research-pluralism*.

It would be useful, therefore, when discussing a research activity, to consider its relationship to these *two* pluralisms. Of course, this does not make things easier, as a consideration within the framework of the one pluralism is already difficult enough. Green (2005: 629) describes a regrettable consequence of theory-pluralism: 'the Kleinians read only the Kleinians, just as the Lacanians cite only the Lacanians'. And we can observe similar tendencies in the field of research-pluralism. Empiricists tend to quote empiricists, just as conjunction researchers often only make reference to conjunction researchers. Everyone likes to be by themselves. Closed quoting circles may increase the rankings in the respective scientific community, but do not necessarily facilitate the earlier described 'search for the best solution'—a pity when one is convinced of the necessity of constructive discourse, but obviously unavoidable; and perhaps only to be understood better if we used our own analytic tools.

With the example of conceptual research here I can only describe the questions and problems that arise in the field of tension that these two pluralisms create. I do not have definite answers. It would be a good start indeed, and very useful, if those awful devaluations were to stop: to call someone with a different analytic theoretical tradition non-analytic, or to from the outset label anyone who has another understanding of research as unscientific. But there has been one question that leads in a good direction: in the debate about the *common ground* in psychoanalysis, Wallerstein (2005b: 636) directed a rhetorical question to Green: 'Who decides when it is *truly* psychoanalytic thought?' I would like to paraphrase this question with regard to the research-pluralism and ask: 'Who decides when it is truly scientific research in psychoanalysis?'

Theory-pluralism and research-pluralism—debates about the common ground

Two pluralisms—perhaps one can better answer the question of what *truly* is *research* in psychoanalysis, and what the status of individual research programmes is, if one took a closer look at the difficulties, presented by the research-pluralism, against the background of the more familiar discussion about the theory-pluralism. A prominent, more recent example, of this discussion is the earlier mentioned controversy between Green and Wallerstein about the *common ground.*

The Green–Wallerstein debate

Both protagonists enter this debate with clear statements. Wallerstein (2005a: 623) is optimistic; he is convinced of a *common ground* which characterizes all analysts as adherents of a shared psychoanalytic discipline. Green (2005: 627), on the other hand, is sceptical: 'Freud's monopoly has ended'; he considers the *common ground*-idea merely *'a political act'* which, to his mind, is an unsuitable attempt to overcome 'geographical and ideological boundaries' in an international analytic community. Both notice insufficient communication within psychoanalysis, and Wallerstein gives as an important reason for this a language barrier between Anglo-Saxon and French authors. As to pointing out language barriers, he is certainly correct. For some time, English has been the most relevant language in psychoanalysis. And whoever wants to be heard internationally from a Spanish, Italian, French, German, or other language background must publish in English and come to terms with the respective language barrier. But is what Wallerstein refers to here really only a language barrier, that is to say, only a problem of language competency and translation? Even within a language community things are not so uncomplicated and we must already grapple with more than the usual language barriers. This aspect has been beautifully illustrated by the British Rock poet Sting in his song 'I'm an alien, I'm a legal alien, I'm an Englishman in New York.'

As Green notes, not only are we dealing with language barriers, but also, at all times, with *geographical and ideological boundaries,* and thus, as it were, with cultural barriers—historically grown differences, based on different mentalities and on differently developed understandings of psychoanalysis and also of science. Green (2005: 631), perhaps a little disappointed, complains about one possible consequence of these barriers when he describes the reception of French authors in Anglo-Saxon discussions: 'French authors were considered ... as smooth talkers of no interest'. I assume that Green alludes, amongst other things, to the beliefs of some empiristically oriented researchers for whom what counts is only 'hard' quantitative data, and everything else is nothing but 'soft' talk.

In answer to the question of what *true* research is, I would like to pick out two aspects in this debate which appear fundamental to me.

The first has to do with the already mentioned question of status: Is psychoanalysis a *science* at all? For Green, as we have heard, psychoanalysis is neither a science nor a branch of hermeneutics. Wallerstein (2005b: 635) has a different belief; for him psychoanalysis is an independent discipline, 'rooted in the exploration of workings of unconscious mental processes, but with interfaces with ... philosophy and linguistics at the one end of the spectrum, to cognitive psychology and modern neuroscience at the other end'. In this I agree with Wallerstein. For, renouncing the claim of being scientific is not only incompatible with our history, but would also hold the danger that psychoanalysis withdraws from all scientific discourses, and therefore from an essential part of our social reality—and, at worst, fragments into a loose assembly of fundamentalist, sect-like, associations. And, as already pointed out, our participation in government health systems would also be at stake ...

The second aspect has to do with another status question. Because Green in this debate argues so decidedly against psychoanalysis as a science, one cannot simply ask: What kind of science psychoanalysis is after all? But one has to ask: Where does one locate psychoanalysis *epistemologically*? For Green (2005: 632), psychoanalysis forms the bridge between nature and culture. Wallerstein sees this similarly, that psychoanalysis draws nourishment from both natural and cultural sources. But remarkably enough he then proceeds to exclude the cultural sources from his scientific consideration. For him, *science* can only study *one* aspect—nature and natural sources (Wallerstein, 2005b: 637). Sciences, in the English-speaking world, are generally understood as *natural* sciences (such as biology, chemistry, and physics), the others (such as sociology, psychology, and philosophy) are *humanities* or *arts* 'that do not rely on the scientific method' (The American Heritage Dictionary, 2001: 48). Wallerstein's view then does of course have consequences for the kind of research methods he considers appropriate.

Psychoanalysis between 'nature and culture'—what are the consequences?

It does make a big difference, whether—moving in the fields of epistemology and research—one sees oneself grounded only in the *'natural world'*, then one would argue more from a natural scientist's point of view and therefore prefer their pertaining research methods (for example, experiments) and research aims (for example, causal *explanations*); or whether one wants to take up the, what Green calls, 'bridging function' between nature and culture. I would agree with Green's view—with the reservation, however, that I see psychoanalysis as a science. But then one cannot limit oneself to the language games and research maxims of the natural sciences alone. One would have to critically evaluate how one could do justice to both sides, thus one would also have to include the language games and research methods of the social and cultural sciences, with the aim to *understand* and to reconstruct meaning. In its choice of methods, conceptual research, by the way, oscillates between both classes of methods, which are not, after all, disjunctive.

Paying attention to this culture-side of the bridge means focusing in a specific way on the human being as an individual, and thus also on analyst and patient as interacting subjects, each with their own subjectivity. It means keeping in mind that their experiences are woven into biographical, cultural, and historical contexts. In all this, our analytic language, that is to say, our theoretical language, including its concepts, has been, since Freud, a suitable medium for describing and reflecting the double interwoveness of the individual in nature *and* culture. By the way: when concepts and conceptual fields are investigated by conceptual research, then this double functionality of analytic concepts—namely to grasp the biological nature of the individual, and, at the same time, his or her biographically grown individuality and subjectivity—is always one of the themes.

The summary of this short epistemological excursion: there is reason enough to see psychoanalysis as a scientifically based endeavour—then one would be more in line with Wallerstein than with Green. And there are also enough reasons to take psychoanalysis seriously in its bridging function between nature and culture, which in turn is more in line with Green, and less with Wallerstein. What does such a belief ('science between nature and culture') mean for the question of *true* research? Who decides questions like these? Some would like an authority to decide, but this will not help those who do not believe in that authority. How could one come closer to a reasonable answer? A further short detour may be useful to explore this.

Common ground and specific (pre-)understanding: An example

By now, I think it has become clear that a decisive role in taking a position on what is 'true' research is played by the personal belief systems which we have all developed. Of course, Wallerstein, Green, and all of us who participate in these debates on status and *common ground* come from totally different scientific cultures, from *specific grounds*, so-to-speak. What it can mean to be socialized into a specific understanding of science, and thus eventually into a specific understanding of psychoanalysis already during one's studies and further education, I would like to illustrate with an example: my own scientific socialization. I choose this in scientific contexts' somewhat unusual form of a 'case vignette' (which definitely cannot be left out of any analytic paper), because I want to point out some of those pre-assumptions which often remain implicit and which characterize my (any) understanding of research and my (any) *specific ground*. The attempt to explicate one's own scientific world view may better elucidate how useful it can be in discussions about a *common ground*, also in psychoanalysis, to clarify one's own perspective as far as possible—for oneself, but also for others. This might facilitate the recognition that, regarding scientific beliefs, a (continuously developing) specific *ground* always comes into play.

In most countries, the path to becoming an analyst follows a two-phase educational process. Many have academic degrees mostly in medicine, or psychology. As a psychologist, like many from my generation, I was influenced by the debates in the social sciences that took place in Germany in the 1970s, following the fundamental debates of the late 1960s. This may imply that up to now I value such research traditions which, in their images of man, see the individual as a cultural and historical being, not merely as a biological system. In my Central-European understanding, science, or

Wissenschaft, is (as I have discussed above) not only natural science. In Germany and in other countries of continental Europe, many disciplines are assigned equal status as sciences: natural sciences and equally the human, social, or cultural, or linguistic sciences—with their respective differing *scientific* methods. Freud, by the way, in his idea of a psychoanalytic university, wanted to see gathered the whole canon of sciences, all the sciences of his time concerned with the human being.

And so, in the times of my studies in psychology, I grew—like others too—into a rather broad, in no way one-sided, understanding of science. Beside this, empiricism in academic psychology was not yet so dominant; qualitative and interpretative methods for the exploration of the psyche were deemed as equally admissible as the quantitative-empirical methods. One did not have to experiment, or test statistical hypotheses, or build computer models, in order to be recognized as a scientist. From the start, it was conveyed to me that there are two basic entities in psychology: *facts*, which are mainly graspable with the methods of the natural sciences, and *meanings*, which are mainly graspable with the methods of linguistics and cultural sciences. This is why I am convinced, to this day, that in psychoanalysis and in psychoanalytic research we have to take into account the *interplay* of both, facts and meanings. And for me, human beings are individuals who process meanings and generate meanings, and are actually not merely information-processing systems. I further learnt, through the *ordinary language turn* (which does away with the strict separation between scientific and everyday language) that language and its rules and structures, and its diverse use in science and practice can be the subject of independent scientific investigation—a useful approach indeed for a talking cure like psychoanalysis (and self-evident in conceptual research).

All in all, this conveyance of a multi-layered understanding of science has made me somewhat sceptical from then on towards authors who unfailingly believe that science only works in the way that they practise it, and in particular only with their methods. In some important aspects, I was thereafter epistemologically socialized by the Frankfurt school of philosophy with its central tenets orientated at the American pragmatism. 'In important aspects' means, for instance, their departure from a correspondence theory of truth and their preference for a *consensus theory* of truth. What is temporarily true is that which a scientific community can agree on in an exchange of rational arguments, which of course includes empirical findings. And what is true is that which a scientific community deems useful and workable for the solution of the respective problems. There is not 'the one unchangeable', the 'eternal' truth. In science, there is always only the arduous road towards a 'best problem solution' in the context of a historical situation. Last but not least, I have also learnt the following through Popper and Kuhn: our own beliefs, even more so our own theories and hypotheses, may always need correction or may prove to be wrong. What is considered a secure base, secured knowledge, or state of the art, needs constant updating. Above all one must try to again and again communicate and look for consensus. Science may go wrong; nowadays it is only religion that still promises absolute certainty. In a science we are not only looking for evidence to support our hypotheses—surely an important aspect. In a science we must also acknowledge the criticism of others; and we must definitely accept the relativity of the beliefs of our own scientific reference group. How science and research interact with social, political, and often, economic conditions was of course also emphasized in the thinking of the Frankfurt school. Even scientists are just children of their time.

In my *psychoanalytic* training in the 1980s, the pluralistic labels that are so familiar today did not initially play such a big role. This was most certainly due to the specific situation in Germany. For, of course, psychoanalysis and its institutions were suffering from the effects of National Socialism, which up to this day are a central theme in German psychoanalysis. Mainly in the English-speaking analytic world decisive theoretical developments in theory and research had taken place after the Second World War. Not only we analysts in training tried first of all to reconnect with Freud's ideas, and then only gradually with these new approaches. As a consequence, we read essentially Freud at that time, and then only gradually added in other kinds of analytic literature: in time the ego-psychologists and the object relation theorists; we did not think Kohut was so terrible; on the horizon, Kleinian approaches were emerging more and more; Lacan guided our attention to the importance of language … I only slowly got to know the subtle differences and the sometimes intimate animosities among the diverse competing analytic and scientific schools—which became more clear to me mainly during the systematic reading for the revision of the book *The Patient and the Analyst* (Sandler *et al.*, 1992). Green (2005: 627) probably rightly referred to some 'bloody duels', to anger and bitterness in those debates about the 'correct', the 'true' *common ground* in psychoanalysis.

What plays a lesser important role today—compared to the times of my analytic training—is certainly the broad and public dialogue of psychoanalysis with other sciences such as philosophy, ethnology, and also the literary sciences. We met with a lively interest which was in our theory but also in our interpretative method of understanding unconscious aspects of the mind. One thing is indeed strange: on the one hand, interpretation (*Deutung*) is one of our main tools in psychoanalysis. And also in the *evaluation* of empirical data, the interpretation of the results is an acknowledged and creative activity of a scientist. On the other hand, however, when today someone says in a research context that he or she is applying interpretative or hermeneutic methods to *generate* data, this is often considered unscientific, because supposedly such methods do not meet the criteria of objectivity. In my academic socialization, interpretative methods were always part of the admissible canon of methods, as a 'rational reconstruction of meaning', which of course must take into account the interplay of facts and meaning mentioned earlier.

Against the background of this specific scientific socialization, conceptual research later seemed of interest to me for three reasons:

- it attempts to integrate new knowledge, whether it comes from psychoanalysis or neighbouring disciplines;
- it remains grounded through its reference to the analytic situation and analytic practice—and has no reservations against the use of interpretative methods; and
- team work plays a decisive role in its projects, be that in the search for consensus, or for precision regarding dissent.

A research programme which had as its subject the investigation of change in the use of our concepts, and in doing so attempted to largely preserve the analytic substance of our concepts, and at the same time sought to integrate the view of different concept users, and always kept an eye on the validity and usefulness of our concepts for clinical practice—that was really something. Conceptual research—understood in this sense—might contribute to sharpening the analytic profile of our concepts, and therefore eventually our theories, too. Thus the task would be, in the current dialogue with memory researchers, for example, to clarify the conceptual field surrounding our analytic concept 'unconscious', and one would have to work out the specific analytic connotation of 'dynamic unconscious'—so that 'unconscious' is not equated with 'implicit', as often happens.

Enough about my case. A 'case vignette', by nature, can only highlight a few aspects at a time. Its purpose was only to illustrate from which *specific ground* and with which scientific pre-knowledge one can enter the psychoanalytic research field. It should thus underline my argument that—with reference to both pluralisms—epistemological and methodological questions can hardly be dealt with in discourse successfully, if one does not pay attention to the specific and different scientific backgrounds of the discussants.

A plea for connectionism

Theory-pluralism and research-pluralism—and what now? The answer to the question 'Who decides when it is truly psychoanalytic thought or research?' remains open. Whoever expresses convictions in the fields of psychoanalysis and epistemology does this neither from an extraterrestrial position, nor from a position of absolute truth, superior to others. Besides choosing resignedly the path of the often lamented postmodern arbitrariness, there are strictly speaking only two other ways to escape this dilemma. One can claim that one's own belief represents the truth, and then one would have a good answer to the question of 'Who decides?'—at least for oneself. Or, one seeks a way of approaching and communicating with those that have a different view. Then things become definitely more complicated. Not only are there different voices, beyond that they often appear to be working rather unconnectedly, at times more in rivalry than cooperation. (By the way, many years ago, there was also an ignoring coexistence—namely between researchers and clinicians—that motivated Sandler to make a suggestion for the structure of the annual IPA *Research Conference* in London: analytic researchers were to report on their work; clinically working analysts were to discuss this work from their perspective, with a view to its clinical relevance. The other sequence would of course have been conceivable, too: a clinician presents a case, and an analytic researcher discusses this case from his or her research perspective. And this could possibly even be a researcher from another discipline, whereby such interdisciplinary exchange of knowledge would not have to be a one-way-street.)

The functioning of ideas, which are directed towards a critical dialogue with reference to each other, is generally dependent on important requirements: on mutual interest and mutual acknowledgement of the *specific* scientific beliefs, on renouncing a claim of exclusiveness, and on reflecting the contingency of one's own position. To fulfil those requirements seems to be the more difficult part of the endeavour. The intended 'domination free discourse' may be seen as utopian, and perhaps it is. On the other hand, we know the power of dreams … And indeed, what we currently experience is very much a growing critical discourse in the international debate about our occasionally almost incompatible understandings of psychoanalysis. Why not think of a similar critical discourse in our research field? To listen to others and to respect them does not preclude one from pursuing one's own interests, does it?

Maybe the idea of a *common ground* has now generally become wishful thinking, really only an illusion (as Green calls it), especially the thought that this *common ground* existed in a 'general theory' (which Wallerstein has in mind) and that through such a unifying theory the various international analytic cultures could be integrated. But, if one cannot renounce the idea of a *common ground*, even if one wants to conjure it up again and again merely for political reasons, why not simply refer to the origins of our science and take recourse to Freud's work? For it is here that the large majority of analysts seems to agree: *historically* speaking Freud's theory is definitely our *common ground*. And why not keep our eyes on this *ground*, the beginnings of our science, as reference basis? Interestingly enough, people outside psychoanalysis have few problems seeing the unifying force of our analytic roots.

Freud, in his classic understanding of science and in his concern about the recognition and prestige of the young science, saw the basis of psychoanalysis in the agreement to central tenets. 'The assumption that there are unconscious mental processes, the recognition of the theory of resistance and repression, the appreciation of the importance of sexuality and of the Oedipus complex—these constitute the principal subject-matter of psychoanalysis and the foundations of its theory. No one who cannot accept them all should count himself a psychoanalyst' (Freud, 1923a: 247). That is how simple it once was. At the same time Freud was scientist enough—in all his efforts to keep the analytic community in line—to emphasize that his statements were all subject to historic change as expressed, for instance, in his belief that the advance of knowledge does not tolerate any rigid definitions, up to his radical assumption that one day biology 'will blow away the whole of our artificial structure of hypotheses' (Freud, 1920: S. 60).

If one were to stop seeing a *common ground* as a set of *unchangeable* theoretical beliefs or axioms—as the smallest common denominator of all analysts, so-to-speak—then, a totally different view might open up. Particularly Freud's image of man, his epistemological interest, his analytic-exploring, critical-understanding, and reflecting look at the human psyche—at nature *and* culture—all this could be the model for us analysts up to today when wrestling with a continually changing *common ground*. Neither concepts, nor theories, nor epistemological beliefs, are static quantities, and I actually think that no *common ground* should have the status of an eternally unchangeable creed; it, too, must be discussed and elaborated again and again. And of course in dialogue, however arduous this may be at times. As analysts we could easily understand how much the complexity of such a discourse about our analytic thinking and practice invites the avoidance of such arduous work, and we could analyse which function the illusion and the wish for uniformity have in all this.

Guided by a common view of man and by a common interest in knowledge controversial discussions about a common ground in both fields—the field of analytic theory and the field of epistemological approaches to the human mind—could lead to a more dynamic understanding of a common ground. The term 'controversial discussion' is intentionally chosen here in analogy to the British *controversial discussions*. These were discussions which, at the time, did not lead to a unified theory, but helped to precisely describe the dissent and to this day have led to a (relatively) tolerant cooperation. Such a path would surely be more modest than the working out of a general all-encompassing theory. But I think it is also more realistic and perhaps can even be libidinously cathected: the hope of a unifying theory would have to be replaced by the hope of a constructive discourse for a *common ground*.

In any case, I think we have to acknowledge *both* our existing pluralisms worldwide and not 'celebrate' them (as Wallerstein [2005b] critically notes). Why not understand them as a sign of vitality? In science diversity must, pluralism must, however, have contours; it must be clearly defined so that its positive aspects can come to fruition. And an attempt must always be made to show convergences within the variety. Constructive controversial discussions would make this possible, splitting would not, nor would indifference. Therefore, the maxim must be: *from a pluralism of indifference to connectionism.* This term, too, has been intentionally chosen, in analogy to its use in the neurosciences. There, connectionist models of the human brain can clearly show how it is possible that, despite the multitude of instances and functions, a holistic operation can be achieved. A systematic networking with reference to each other and a systematic accompanying epistemological reflection are indispensable for favourable conditions of quality assurance in science and research.

If this path of controversy and connectionism is chosen, then someday it might also be much easier to answer the question 'Who decides, when it is truly psychoanalytic thought and research?' with a 'We all decide—and from time to time our decision might look slightly different!'

Note

1. This text—translated in cooperation with Eva Ristl—is based on ideas developed in a paper for the IPA Research Conference in London in 2006: 'In Celebration of the 105th Anniversary of Sigmund Freud's Birth: The Current State of Psychoanalytic Research' (Section: epistemology, conceptual research and psychoanalysis). A former version was published in German in *Forum der Psychoanalyse* 2007 (23: 288–307): *'Pluralismus in Theorie und Forschung—was nun?'*

Bibliography

Canestri, J. (2006). *Psychoanalysis: From Practice to Theory.* Whurr Publishers Ltd.

Carroll, L.C. ([1872]1960, 1970). *Through the Looking Glass.* Penguin Books.

Dreher, A.U. (2000). *Foundations for Conceptual Research in Psychoanalysis.* Madison CT: International Universities Press.

Dreher, A.U. (2005). 'Conceptual research'. In: Person, E.S., Cooper, A.M. and Gabbard, G.O. (eds) *Textbook of Psychoanalysis.* Arlington, VA: American Psychiatric Publishing, Inc..

Freud, S. (1915). Instincts and their vicissitudes. In: SE 14. The Hogart Press and The Institute of Psa, London.

Freud, S. (1920). Beyond the pleasure principle. In: SE 18. The Hogart Press and The Institute of Psa, London.

Freud, S. (1923a). Two encyclopaedia articles (A) Psychoanalysis, (B) The libido theory. In: SE 18. The Hogart Press and The Institute of Psa, London.

Freud, S. (1927). Postscript to *The Question of Lay Analysis.* In: SE 20. The Hogart Press and The Institute of Psa, London.

Green, A. (2005) 'The illusion of common ground and mythical pluralism'. *IJP*, 86: 627–32.

Grünbaum, A. (1988). 'Précis of The Foundations of Psychoanalysis: A Philosophical Critique'. In: Clark, P. and Wright, C. (eds). *Mind, Psychoanalysis and Science.* Oxford: Oxford University Press. pp. 3–31.

Jacoby, R. (1983). *The Repression of Psychoanalysis: Otto Fenichel and the Political Freudians.* New York: Basic Books.

Kuhn, T.S. (1962). *The Structure of Scientific Revolutions.* Chicago: IL, University of Chicago Press.

Leuzinger-Bohleber, M., Dreher, A.U. and Canestri, J. (eds) (2003a). *Pluralism and Unity? Methods of Research in Psychoanalysis.* London: International Psychoanalysis Library.

Leuzinger-Bohleber, M., Stuhr, U., Rüger, B. and Beutel, M. (2003b). 'How to study the quality of psychoanalytic treatments and their long-term effects on patient's well-being: a representative, multiperspective follow-up study'. *Int J Psychoanal.*, 84: 263–290.

Parin, P. and Parin-Matthèy, G. (1986). Medicozentrismus. In: Subjekt im Widerspruch. Syndikat. Frankfurt am Main: 61-80.

Sandler, J., Dreher, A.U., Drews, S., *et al.* (1987). Psychisches Trauma: Ein Konzept im Theorie-Praxis-Zusammenhang. Materialien aus dem Sigmund-Freud-Institut Frankfurt am Main: 5.

Sandler, J., Dare, C. and Holder, A. (1992). *The Patient and the Analyst: The Basis of the Psychoanalytic Process.* 2nd edn. Revised and expanded by Sandler, J. and Dreher, A. U. London: Karnac.

Sandler, J. (1998). *Sandler A.M.: Internal Objects Revisited.* London: Karnac.

The American Heritage Dictionary (2001). 4th edn. NY: Random House.

Wallerstein, R.S. (2005a). 'Will psychoanalytic pluralism be an enduring state of our discipline?' *IJP*, 86: 623–626.

Wallerstein, R.S. (2005b). 'Dialogue or illusion? How do we go from here? Response to André Green'. *IJP*, 86: 633–638.

CHAPTER TEN

New orleans congress panel: What does conceptual research have to offer?

Jorge L. Ahumada and Roberto Doria-Medina

To the question, 'What does conceptual research have to offer?' the short answer is: everything. Shorn of it, psychoanalysis dissolves as a discipline. However, it speaks of its intricacies that we write this paper as a dialogue, to keep to our distinct stances.

J.L.A.: Freud was immersed in a lifelong conceptual struggle with what emerged from his clinical findings. Empirical work—gathering the relevant evidences—and conceptual work go hand in hand, this being valid for each and every observational discipline. Thus, the Galapagos Islands as a natural experiment lent Darwin the evidential path to his theory of the evolution of species, providing him the exemplars needed for accessing what went on, and to do so from multiple perspectives. When they expound on what the scientific method purportedly is, philosophers of science studiously skip such prime exemplars of knowledge buildup coming from the observational sciences.

R.D-M.: The distinction between conceptual and empirical research is indeed schematic and an oversimplification. So we should also ask: 'What does empirical research have to offer?' and then, vitally: 'To whom?'

Among philosophers of science and on the philosophy of science several perspectives have to be considered. Are we talking about methodologists who speak after discoveries have been done and then intend to tell what good science is? Do we take into account epistemologists and their epistemologies? How do we differentiate the epistemic from the logical aspects of inquiry? How do we deal with historic and sociological considerations on the actual practice of research?

The crucial issue of evidence includes modes of evidence (Gil, 1993, 1998, 2000), domains of evidence for various disciplines, the relations between evidence, truth and proof, and so forth. *The central theme for us psychoanalysts being psychoanalytic research.*

J.L.A.: Scientific concepts, and notably our psychoanalytic ones, are *'open concepts'* (Pap, 1958: 312ff.; emphasis in original), modified and redefined in their different contexts of use. As Reichenbach (1947: 22) put it, empirical 'definitions in use' must define and redefine their elements in terms of concrete observational ones. Far from Cartesian univocities and deducticisms, objectivity is context-dependent also in the exact sciences. To say that objectivity means to be observer-independent leads nowhere: how would we get to knowledge in case we were not human observers is plain nonsense. While all knowledge is in this sense irreducibly subjective, objectivity results in ample fields of science from informal verification. Only in the 'ideal' or 'formal' sciences which have no empirical reference, and in the 'exact' sciences which mimic them in their formal hypothetico-deducticist structure dealing with the inert and unthinking by way of *reduction,* verification uses formal theories. This was well-known to Pascal but a Popper or a Grünbaum carefully omit it.

R.D-M.: Science is much easier when it is more formalized because formalization transforms irreducible conceptual difficulties in transitory technical difficulties that can be overcome by means of dedicated apprenticeship (Levy-Leblond, 1996). In that sense the strength and the weakness of the so-called exact sciences lies in that they let us avoid thinking continually and they develop through mechanization. Mathematics, the foremost example of formalized science, is a purely algorithmic and syntactic activity in which signs do not have any determined meaning; its source is simply convention, it develops through deductive instruments building new demonstrations and inventing new axiomatic systems which eventually might produce potential instruments to obtain knowledge from the real (Klimovsky, 2000). Algorithms and axiomatic systems are way afar of the nature of psychoanalysis. *Psychoanalytic practice is a practice of research, ultracomplex research I would dare say, initiated by a genius who was one of the most skilled and trained scientists of his time and who had the ability to deal creatively with the vanguard of scientific knowledge of his age. Our psychoanalytic findings are always contrasted from the consulting room to our culture and with other sciences, they circulate and reverberate in different composites of knowledge and according to different parcellings of reality, not free of the tensions generated by the oldest philosophical controversies that today can be reproduced in terms of nominalism versus constructivism in the current war of sciences* (see Hacking, 1999).

I propose a fourfold categorization of research and psychoanalysis. In each fold there is no empirical/conceptual distinction, each one includes different modalities of research pertinent to psychoanalysis. *The first comprises clinical, extraclinical, and experimental research. The second includes systematic (with gradients of formalization) and descriptive research: both, systematic and descriptive, can deal with single case studies or collective gathering of samples. The third delineates the possibilities of research from the inside of psychoanalysis, from the outside, during psychoanalysis and after. The fourth includes research about psychoanalysis, research from psychoanalysis on, and research in, psychoanalysis.* Research programmes carve the realm of psychoanalysis differently (see, for instance, Brakel 2000; Sandell *et al.*, 2000; *J. Amer. Psychoanal. Ass.* Special volume on Varieties of Research, 2002).

J.L.A.: *It must be stressed that empirical certainty is a myth.* Thus Charles Peirce, who was both a mathematical genius and a field worker in geodetics, held over a century ago that the idea of empirical certainty was irresistibly comical. Similarly, in what Landsberg (2000: 706) calls Einstein's uncertainty principle, he had sustained in 1924 that 'insofar as the propositions of geometry apply to reality, they are not certain; insofar as they are certain, they do not apply to reality'.

Peirce avows that we have only two types of thinking, mechanical (formal) and anthropomorphic, which divides the so-called exact sciences and the observational sciences. The Established Truth of the Pythagorean-Cartesian-Popperian tradition is that a mathematically posited formal theory is a must for objectivity, for verification, and for science to be such: this functions, says Toulmin (1990: 149), as long as one restricts the field of study to the inert, inanimate, and unthinking. Strict predictibility depends on reducing processes to 'well-behaved', that is, mechanical-like, variables.

In the observational sciences the complexities and often the contradictoriness of their objects of study allows scant reliance on formalization. Here attempts at 'theory' often usurp the place of enquiry: then an *ordo exponendi,* a didactical order of exposition, substitutes for the *ordo inveniendi,* the discernment of the incoming events.

R.D-M.: How are we to determine the moment of truth between subject and observer, the analyst being both at the same time?: this problem is not an exclusive prerogative of psychoanalysis (see Devereux, 1967). Psychoanalysis has also domain specificity, in the sense that concepts are not all the same and the structure of knowledge differs according to the areas of content that require particular capabilities and expertise that are developed by the actual use of persistent cognitive subsystems (see Hirschfeld and Gelman, 1994). Psychoanalytic exploration is a formidable endeavour of discovery and its chronicles can be pondered by all those interested in the findings of new lands and who might be ready for participating in the adventure. Every NASA expedition provides huge amounts of data for scientific scrutiny, empirical and conceptual, of course. In any case the practical aspects of getting into outer space provoke conceptual treatment of what is going on and defy established concepts about cosmological matters with collateral gains for all sciences. Although technology is grossly present in the illustration it serves to underline that methodologists are not necessarily good astronauts and nor do they necessarily contribute in developing the new fields of astrophysics. It is not through questionnaires, hundreds of questions before, during, and after the expedition, questions that include ethnicity and flying experience from playing with kites and being a passenger in commercial airlines to piloting Jumbo jets or STEALTH bombers, that the cosmos will unveil the incommensurate multiplicity of reality (in this reference see Vaughan *et al.*, 2000). We are in need of smart methods rather than rigorous ones so that robust correlations (Wimsatt, 1994) are obtained and relevant clues are separated from rubbish data. As Freud (1912: 114; italics Freud's) noted 'exact reports of analytic case studies are of less value than might be expected. Strictly speaking, they only possess the *ostensible* exactness of … 'modern' psychiatry … [Those] unwilling to take analysis and the analyst seriously, will pay no attention to accurate verbatim records of the treatment either. This is not the way, it seems, to remedy the lack of convincing evidence to be found in psychoanalytic reports'. Psychoanalytic research is neither a tour for sophisticated tourists in need of an expert guide, nor a surveyor's task with the appropriate surveyor's level, as it is not a speculative exercise in current theories. The psychoanalytic encounter is a complex expedition that involves a plurality of cognitive resources, intricate emotional logistics, and multiple levels of communication. In Freud's (1913: 123) words: 'The extraordinary diversity of the psychical constellations concerned, the plasticity of all mental processes and the wealth of determining factors oppose any mechanization of the technique'.

J.L.A.: As I understand it, our clinical situation puts to work a *logica utens*, which signs Freud's conception of method and theory building as explained in 'The Resistances to Psychoanalysis' (1925a: 214–16) and in 'An Outline of Psycho-analysis' (1940: 161). The New Introductory Conferences in 1933 further detail that '*Progress in scientific work is just as it is in an analysis.* We bring expectations with us into the work, but they must be forcibly held back. By observation, now at one point and now at another, we come upon something new; but to begin with the pieces do not fit together. We put forward conjectures, we construct hypothesis, which we withdraw if they are not confirmed, we need much patience and readiness for any eventuality, we renounce early convictions so as not to be led by them into overlooking unexpected factors, and in the end our whole expenditure of effort is rewarded, we get an insight into a whole section of mental events, we have completed our task and now we are free for the next one' (p. 174; emphasis added). The *Autobiographical Study* expounds that scientific concepts are open ones: 'Zoology and botany did not start from correct and adequate definitions of an animal and a plant … Physics itself, indeed, would not have made any advance if it had to wait until its concepts of matter, force, gravitation, and so on, had reached the desirable degree of clarity and precision. The basic ideas or most general concepts in any of the disciplines of science are always left indeterminate at first and are only explained to begin with by reference to the realm of phenomena from which they are derived; it is only by means of a progressive analysis of the material of observation that they can be made clear and can find a significant and consistent meaning … a science based on observation has no alternative but to work out its findings piecemeal and to solve its problems step by step' (1925b: 58).

For Peircean fallibilism which takes experience as its start, indication (pointing, ostension, deixis) is as indispensable as it is irreducible (Sebeok, 1995: 224). Inquiry and treatment coincide, says Freud, in the unfolding of the clinical material. The psychical sciences, Peirce noted, present arduous problems of inference the resolution of which—he sustains, as Freud later did—must come out indexically or ostensively from observations in particular instances. Our concepts, holds Thomas Kuhn (1974), do not cluster in discrete sets with appreciable distances between them: set in Venn diagrams they cluster as overlapping classes with no precise limits. Small wonder then that for our different 'schools' terms such as ‚narcissism' have widely different contents.

Going now into the polemic on what the terms 'research' and 'empiry' apply to, we can all agree on that the kernel of our concepts, fuzzy as they are, has come from psychoanalytic clinical work. So when it is stated that attempts to restrictively redefine what research has set in motion 'anxieties about status, territory, exclusion' (Target, 2002: 714), the issue is whether such anxieties are legitimate or not. When the term 'empirical' risks being sectorially appropriated, which despoils the hard-won empiricity of psychoanalytic clinical work, such anxieties are to my mind fully justified. Samely for the injunction 'that we do not repeat the mistake of inventing our own research methodology which is neither accepted nor understood by neighbouring disciplines' (Target, 2002: 715). Sorry to say it, we clinical analysts have been long devising and improving our own research methodology, the psychoanalytic method, and it would be preposterous to ask that we surrender it in favour of what neighbouring disciplines might manage to grasp. The request that we graciously relinquish the empiricity of our clinical method to an assumedly superior variables-defined 'empiry' mimicking reductive ideas of science I find divisive and bound to raise legitimate opposition.

Whatever space is gained by what I prefer to call 'programmed research' or 'nomological research' must come from an appraisal of its results, not from bids at epistemic superiority. And, while valuable work must be done in conceptual research, we should take heed of Freud's (1918: 48) warning that 'No sooner has one begun to depart from the material on which one ought to be relying, than one runs the risk of becoming intoxicated with one's own assertions and, in the end, of supporting opinions which any observation would have contradicted', this being why, he holds, as a rule purely theoretical controversy is unfruitful.

In order to gain a fruitful place, conceptual research must not tie itself to the chariot of programmed research. Whatever their virtues, experimental approaches on the basis of reduction to variables are bound to introduce a bias, as Gregory Bateson (1973) has shown for the case of Pavlovian psychology. *Induction is an inference to the best available explanation*, this being why instead of speaking of a hypothetico-deductive method we might better speak of a *hypothetico-inferential method*. Importantly, up to what point the complexities and contradictoriness of the analytic process can be usefully reduced to variables remains to be seen.

Our conceptual research should not aspire to function as a theoretical superscience imposing itself on the context of open discussion which is the hallmark of our discipline. To put it in Orwellian terms, about the very last thing we need is a Ministry of Truth intoxicating itself, and all of us, with its own assertions.

R.D-M.: We need to be much aware of the perils of worshiping Idealized Science, at the same time that we acknowledge that there is bad science, necessary anyway for many researchers to make a living. Psychoanalysis is just part of the whole scientific endeavour. Those who believe that there are more mature methods than the psychoanalytic method can do better in related fields and contribute from there. Psychoanalysis may benefit from many areas of research, from new developments in non-classical logic, for example, in particular paraconsistent logic (Asenjo, 1986; Da Costa and Lewin, 1995; Priest, 2001; Palau, 2002), from the transdisciplinary efforts of the sciences of discourse and the history of ideas (Van Dijk, 1997; Tasic, 2001), from the multiple debates in the philosophy of mind, from the pertinent contributions of the neurosciences, and from the multiple methodologies in the field of historical studies (Burke, 1991, 1997), or the contrasting viewpoints of anthropology (Kuper, 1999), just to name a few. As a passing remark lets consider the rudimentary quality of the protocols of most medical research in recent years, so far away from the complex nature of things and the candent topics of scientific debate. In fact the reorganization of knowledge goes far back from its production (Lévy-Leblond, 1996).

In the field of validation conceptual research is a must. If a pragmatic theory of meaning is considered (Habermas, 1999), the key concept is not truth but the generalized concept of validity, used epistemically in the sense of 'rational acceptability'. Similarly when considering the history of a concept or the structure of a concept we should acknowledge that the understanding of a linguistic expression means knowing how that expression can be used to get some understanding with someone about something in the world. What role we are going to attribute to mentalism, and how we are going to relate towards pragmatism or pragmaticism (Appel, 1967, 1987) are questions of enormous import when deciding on matters of validation. Are epistemological considerations outmoded? The problem of justification acquires very different perspectives if realism is adopted or rather contextualism is opted for, if there is a deflationist consideration about truth or an epistemic approach that expands justification towards truth as the limit of it (Habermas, 1999). Empirical research cannot stand for ignorance of conceptual difficulties or in place of indispensable conceptual clarifications.

J.L.A.: Inference on our clinical facts is highly complex—an issue Charles Peirce was well aware of, as was Freud. This, and that counterinduction has a privileged place in accessing those facts (Ahumada, 1994, 1997), map the inbuilt limits of programmed research. Which helps grasp that, as adroitly held by Shedler (2002), speaking from such research, its reductions cannot attain the sharpness of the objectivations gained in the detailed lived revision of examples in the analytic process. To put it mildly, the issues that the multi-levelled and paradoxical nature of the access to insight confront us with are not compliant enough for the methods of programmed research. Its efforts might likely be better focused on issues more suited to its methods.

Given that the objectivity gained in the clinical process goes further than whatever objectivity our concepts may attain, our conceptual research must fall back once and again, as Freud urged, on clinical observation. Our 'open concepts' are at the opposite pole from formal ones, so our conceptualizations must be enquired on both clinically and historically, and they cannot be put to work by themselves.

R.D-M.: Clinical, historical, and theoretical lines of enquiry intertwine in an tangled conceptual matrix. Just picking the historical approach implies dealing with numerous epistemological and methodological problems pertaining to the varieties of historical investigation (see Burke, 1991, 1997).

Demonstrations by proof and by evidence must be set apart. Evidence dispenses of proof (Gil, 1993). Evidence has no need of recurring to dispositives of external assessment: it is patent by itself and for everybody. Although the relation between evidence and intuition is in debate since scholastic times with the antagonism posed by Scotus and Occam, two modes of intuition of evidence are to be distinguished (Gil, 1998): evidence that imposes itself more perceptually, and evidence of a logical import, more signalled by language. These two modes have to be related to the epistemic factors of conviction and certitude (Gil, 2000), whose unconscious determinants have not been fully explored.

J.L.A.: What about the sweet, fashionable enticements of scientific reductionism? Freud (1930) masterly held that modern man seeks to become a prosthetic god. Technologies are built on mechanical and reductionistic understandings, and our serfdom to the pleasure principle yearns for theories and technologies permitting us to skip the efforts and pains of psychic evolution. Under the aegis of the Techno-Pleasure Principle, Brain replaces Mind: replacement of the paradigm of 'psyche' is by that of 'brain' in the currently ruling techno-sciences goes right across what we psychoanalysts have been striving for in the last century. The substitution of Mind by Brain as part of an all-around, prosthetic Techno-Mimesis runs against what André Green (1993: 1,032) voiced, that 'psychoanalysis [is] the effort to stay lucid'. The insights for emotional growth are hardy, they must be personally gained, and they can't be mass-produced.

R.D-M.: Scientific reductionism includes the simplistic, although multi-axial, taxonomies advocated by the crudest researchers who in the name of a neo-Kraeppelinian approach pretend to categorize patients by means of lists of disorders supposedly free of conceptual bias. Disorders that are nominated without psychopathological considerations and without a meaningful semiology, gathered under the ideological umbrella of pharmacology and the brain, as if the mythology of the brain had not passed away in the XIX century, and with the pretense that science deals only with the quantitative or numerical treatment of variables of observation. The necessary imprecision of psychoanalytic nosography, as Baranger (1992) put it, is part of the richness of psychoanalysis.

What does psychoanalytic research have to offer? More psychoanalysis for all types of researches. More serious controversies for psychoanalysts (Bernardi, 2002). More psychoanalysis on psychoanalytic method, psychoanalytic writings, and psychoanalytic theories (Gubrich-Simitis, 2000; Doria-Medina, 1991, 1997; Doria-Medina and Kijak, 1990). We should apply and extend psychoanalysis to our own psychoanalytic production as we can extend our psychoanalytic method to other fields.

Bernardi (2002) very aptly noted that there is an absence of systematic confrontation between psychoanalytic approaches, and the obstacles to the progress in argumentation, the reduction of the field of discussion, require epistemologic analysis plus psychoanalytic understanding of the unconscious factors that hamper true dialogue and fruitful debate. As he stated: the purely philosophical debate has to be separated from the consequences for psychoanalytic practice of particular philosophical ideas, critical reflexion on theoretical concepts has to be coupled with clinical and extraclinical research, and self-analysis or re-analysis have to ascertain the personal limitations to get involved in open interchange under common laws for the mutual benefit that arises from confrontation due to reformulation of the premises that govern established knowledge.

It is time to follow Perelman (1977) and develop our own particular applications of the new rhetoric to psychoanalytic argumentation. Once we procure evidences, we have to discuss them if they are debatable and it is necessary to establish a specialized methodology of argumentation, psychoanalysis being a discipline of a distinct genre.

As Bion (1976) puts it, we analysts see things that the rest of the world cannot see and there is a world in which it is impossible to see what an analyst sees. Our research is the way we strive to bring psychoanalysis beyond the psychoanalytical world if the existence of such a world is plausible enough.

Bibliography

Ahumada, J.L. (1994). 'What is a clinical fact? Clinical psychoanalysis as inductive method'. In: *The Logics of the Mind. A Clinical View.* London: Karnac. pp. 15–36.

Ahumada, J.L. (1997). 'Counterinduction in psychoanalytic practice. Epistemic and technical aspects'. In: Ahumada J.L. *et al.* (eds) *The Perverse Transference and other Matters: Essays in Honor of R. Horacio Etchegoyen.* Northvale NJ: Aronson, pp. 181–202.

Appel, K.-O. (1967). 'Charles S. Peirce: From pragmatism to pragmaticism'. New Jersey: Humanities Press.

Appel, K.-O. (1987). *Teoría de la verdad y ética del discurso.* Barcelona: Paidós.

Asenjo, F.G. (1986). 'La verdad, la antinomicidad y los procesos mentales'. *Revista latinoamericana de filosofía, Vol VIII, N° 1.*

Baranger, W. (1992). 'De la necesaria imprecisión en la nosografía psicoanalítica'. *Rev de Psicoanál., N° especial 1*: 83–97.

Bateson, G. (1973). *Steps to an Ecology of Mind.* Herts., Paladin.

Bernardi, R. (2002). 'The need for true controversies in psychoanalysis'. *Int. J. Psychoanal.*, 83: 851–73.

Bion, W. R. (2000[1976]). 'Evidence'. In Bion, F. (ed.) *Clinical Seminars and Other Works.* London: Karnac. pp. 312–20.

Brakel, L.A.W. (2000). 'The primary process and the unconscious: experimental evidence supporting two psychoanalytic presuppositions'. *Int. J. Psychoanal.*, 81: 553–69.

Burke, P. (1991). *New Perspectives on Historical Writing.* London: Polity Press.

Burke, P. (1997). *Varieties of Cultural History.* Madrid: Alianza.

Da Costa, N. and Lewin, R. (1995). 'Lógica Paraconsistente'. *Enciclopedia Ibero Americana de Filosofía.Vol VII.* Barcelona: Trotta. pp. 185–204.

Devereux, G. (1967). *From Anxiety to Method in the Behavioural Sciences.* Moutton.

Doria-Medina, R. (1991). 'On Freud and monotheism'. *Int. Rev. Psychoanal.*, 18: 489–500.

Doria-Medina, R. (1997). 'Notes on Psychoanalysis, Freudian Studies and Psychic Reality'. In: Ahumada J.L. *et al.* (eds) *The Perverse Transference and Other Matters.* Northvale NJ: Aronson. pp. 422–432.

Doria-Medina, R. and Kijak, M. (1990). 'Investigación psicoanalítica sobre "El Moisés de Miguel Angel"'. *Rev. de Psicoanálisis*, 47: 478–85.
Freud, S. (1912). 'Recommendations to physicians practising psycho-analysis'. *S.E.* 12.
Freud, S. (1913). 'On beginning the tratment'. *S.E.* 12.
Freud, S. (1918). 'From the history of an infantile neurosis'. *S.E.* 17.
Freud, S. (1925a). 'The resistances to psycho-analysis'. *S.E.* 20.
Freud, S. (1925b) 'An autobiographical study'. *S.E.* 20.
Freud, S. (1930). 'Civilization and its discontents'. *S.E.* 21.
Freud, S. (1933). 'New introductory conferences on psycho-analysis'. *S.E.* 22.
Freud, S. (1940). 'An outline of psycho-analysis'. *S.E.* 23.
Gil, F. (1993). *Traité de L'évidence.* Grenoble, J. Millon.
Gil, F. (1998). *Modos da Evidencia.* Lisboa: Imprensa Nacional.
Gil, F. (2000). *La Conviction.* Paris: Flammarion.
Green, A. (1993). 'Culture(s) et civilization(s), malaise ou maladie?' *Revue française de psychoanalyse*, 57: 1,029–56.
Gubrich-Simitis, I. (2000). 'Metamorphoses of "The Interpretation of Dreams": Freud's conflicted relations with his book of the century'. *Int. J. Psychoanal.*, 81: 1,155–83.
Habermas, J. (1999). *Verdad y justificación*, Madrid: Trotta.
Hacking, I. (1999). *The Social Construction of What?* Boston MA: Harvard Univ. Press.
Hirschfeld, L.A. and Gelman, S.A. (1994). *Mapping the Mind: Domain Specificity in Cognition and Culture.* Cambridge Univ. Press.
J. Am. Psychoanal. Ass. (2002). Varieties of Research, Special Volume.
Klimovsky, G. (2000). *Las ciencias formales y el método axiomático.* Buenos Aires, A-Z.
Kuhn, T. (1974). 'Second thoughts on paradigms'. In: *The Essential Tension: Selected Studies in Scientific Tradition and Change.* Chicago: Univ. of Chicago Press. pp. 293–319.
Kuper, A. (1999). *Culture: The Anthropologists' Account.* Boston MA: Harvard Univ. Press.
Landsberg, P.T. (2000). 'An uncertainty principle for geometry'. *Nature*, 404: 705–6.
Lévy-Leblond, J.-M. (1996). *Aux contraires: Le exercise de la pensée et la pratique de la science.* Paris: Gallimard.
Palau, G. (2002). *Introducción Filosófica a las Lógicas no Clásicas.* Barcelona: Gedisa.
Pap, A. (1958). *Semantics and Necessary Truth.* New Haven: Yale Univ. Press.

Perelman, C. (1977). *L'Empire Rhétorique: Rhétorique et Argumentation.* Paris: Vrin.

Priest, G. (2001). *An Introduction to Non-Classical Logic.* Cambridge U. Press.

Reichenbach, H. (1947). *Elements of Symbolic Logic.* New York: Macmillan.

Sandell, R. *et al.* (2000). 'Varieties of long-term outcome among patients in psychoanalysis and long-term psychoanalytic psychotherapy: a recent review of findings in the Stockholm outcome of psychoanalysis and psychotherapy project (STOPPP)'. *Int. J. Psychoanal.,* 81: 921–42.

Sebeok, T.A. (1995). 'Indexicality'. In: Ketner, K.L. (ed.) *Peirce and Contemporary Thought.* NY: Fordham Univ. Press. pp. 222–42.

Shedler, J. (2002). 'A new language for psychoanalytic diagnosis'. *J. Amer. Psychoanal. Ass.* 50: 429–56.

Target, M. (2002). 'Book review of Foundations of Conceptual Research in Psycho-analysis by Anna Ursula Dreher'. *Int. J. Psychoanal.,* 83: 712–16.

Tasic, V. (2001). *Mathematics in the Roots of Postmodern Thought.* Oxford: Oxford Univ. Press.

Toulmin, S. (1990). *Cosmopolis: The Hidden Agenda of Modernity.* Chicago: Univ. of Chicago Press.

Van Dijk, T.A. (1997). *Discourse as structure and process. Discourse studies: A Multidisciplinary Introduction, Vols 1–2.* London: Sage.

Vaughan, S. C. *et al.* (2000). 'Can we do psychoanalytic outcome research? A feasibility study'. *Int. J. Psychoanal.,* 84: 513–27.

Wimsatt, W. (1994). 'The ontology of complex systems: levels of organization, perspectives and causal thickets'. In: M. Matthen and R.X. Ware (eds) *Biology and Society: Reflections on Methodology, Canadian Journal of Philosophy, Suppl. to Vol. 20.*

INDEX

Academic achievements 13
Adaptability 100
Adult
personality 89
schizophrenic patients 167
Affect-motor sphere 148
Aggressive behaviour 13
Aggressive-destructive impulses 196–197, 200, 202
Ahumada, Jorge L. 35, 153, 175, 267
American academy of child and adolescent psychiatry 12
American pragmatism 259
American Psychiatric Association 108
Analysis terminable and interminable 34, 114–115
Anna-Freudian terminology 87
Antagonism 227
Anterior hypothalamus (MPOA) 61
Anti-Semitism 229
Approach/withdrawal 100
Asperger, Hans 154
Attachment 53–71
and the arms-race 60–61
categories 15
clinical illustration 67–70
clinical implications 65–67
developmental risks and their sequelae 77–84
hyperactivity 62
neurobiology of 61–65
theory and trauma 58–59
understanding of 60–65
Attachment, trauma, and psychoanalysis
psychoanalysis meets neuroscience 87–92

Attention Deficit Disorder (ADD) 8, 154
Attention Deficit Hyperactivity Disorder (ADHD) 3, 9, 14, 33
anamnestic information on parents and their history 126–129
and culture 29–30
and extraordinarily talented children 30
and trauma 28
as precursor to ADHD 107
biological roots of 6
biomedical models of 143–145
cases 126
central psychological deficits 9
children 11–18, 26, 36, 150
children in social situations 5
children treatment 132–135
clinical picture of 150
cognitive-behavioral/medical treatments of 16
complexities of 39
controversional theoretical positions with treatments 11–17
current status of overdiagnosis of 98–105
development of 146
diagnosis and severe behavioural problems 25
diagnosis 6, 21, 27, 105, 107, 120, 139, 145, 150
dramatic increase in treating 7
dysfunctions in 4
early development and its disturbances 51
from empirical and clinical perspectives 143–151
frontal lobe contribution to 19
genesis of 14, 185
in Frankfurt Prevention study (FP) 191
in psychoanalysis with child and adult 185–203
in psychoanalytic psychotherapy 189
in psychoanalytic terminology 145
inappropriate diagnosis of 106
initial meeting with 129–132
Michael's 23
molecular genetics network 119
motion and meaning 123–140
mourning or depression 31–33
multidimensional model of 83
multimodal treatment of 6, 12
neural differences in 18
neuro-imaging studies 9
neurological syndrome 16
Parenting Practices of Mothers of Children 80
phenotype 119
primitive defence mechanisms 125
psychiatric diagnosis of 145
psychoanalytic concepts on the aetiology of 17
psychoanalytic inquiry of 123–140
psychoanalytic understanding of 5
psychoanalytic view 105
relationship of temperament 105
remarks on questions of technique 135–136
resilience of children with 25
Robert's symptoms 26
stringent definition 107
symptomatic 145
symptoms 26, 29, 187
symptoms of Rahel 32

syndrome 5, 22
transvestite symptoms 27
understanding children with 16–17
Autism, evolution of the concept 153–157
Autistic
child 168
contiguous defences 151
disturbances of affective contact 154
mimetic dynamics 165–171
spectrum disorders (ASD) 175–176
Autistic Barriers in Neurotic Patients 156
Autobiographical memory 83
Autotomy 168
Auto-sensuality 170

Bartels's and Zeki's fMRI-findings 89
BASICS profile of behavioural adjustment 103, 110
Battles on the Setting and First Settlements 132
Behavioural adjustment, BASICS profile of 103
Behaviouristic turn 252
Berna, Jaques 197
Beyond the Pleasure Principle 229
Bion, Wilfrid 57, 155
concept of 'containment' 125
proto-emotive 170
proto-mental 170
special reference to theory of thinking 153–171
theory of thinking to account for autistic-mimetic dynamics 165–171
clinical case 176–179
Sophia's
clinical narrative 157–162
conceptual comments 162–165
conceptual discussion 179–182
'going on being' 177
mimetic autism 153–171
personal space 165
Biopsychosocial model 12
Bipolar disorder
current status of overdiagnosis of 98–105
Bowlby, John 58
attachment theory 213
Brain-imaging data 18
Brain mechanism 8
self-awareness 59–60
Brain organic problem, in children 22–25
Branik, Emil 36
Breast-feeding 127
Busch de Ahumada, Luisa C. 151, 153, 175

Canestri, Jorge 3, 34, 113
Cantwell, Dennis 9
Carey, William B. 34, 97, 113, 118, 120
Causation 6
Central-European understanding 258
Cerebral dysfunctions 12
Changed childhood 11
Child
idiosyncratic psychological 21
psychiatrists 84
psychiatry and psychotherapy 143
psychoanalysis 192
psychoanalysts 84

psychosis 154
temperament on parents 102
Childhood mimetic autism 168
Children's temperament, coping with 97–111
Child-stimuli parameter 78
Cognitive
behavioural 12
turn 252
Cognitivism 250
Comorbid
mental health condition 107, 120
symptoms 13
Concept group 242
change of 243–244
problems of variety in 244
Conceptual research programme 247–248
Conduct disorder 9
Connectionism 239–265
plea for 262–265
Corrective emotional experience 105
Counter-transference 91
Clinical research in psychoanalysis 35
Conception of Wholes and Parts in Early Infantile Autism 154
Counter-transference reactions 36
Crisis-of-two-ness 164

Darwin left evolutionary theory 210
DBH gene 119
Diagnostic and Statistical Manual (DSM-IV-TR APA 2000) 105, 119, 154
diagnosis 106
implicitly adheres 119
problems with diagnostic system 108–109
Diphasic pathogenesis 226
Disruptive Disorders in Childhood 9
Distractibility 100
Domination free discourse 263
Dopamine transporter gene (DAT1-allel) 81
Dopamine-deficit hypothesis 144
Dopamine-ß-hydroxylase 119
Doria-Medina, Roberto 267
Dreher, Anna Ursula 38, 239
Drive and trauma 219–236
DSM-II 8
Dual Arousal Systems Model 63

Ego
capacity 147
functions 147
integration 170
psychology 92, 186
Ego-paralyzing automatic anxiety 234
Eitingon, Max 235
Elements of Psychoanalysis 57
Embodied Cognitive Science 35, 37
Emotional distrurbances 13
Emotional trauma 105
Empirical attachment theory 15
Endogenous factor 115
Entangled mothers 190
Environmentalism 35
EPF (European Psychoanalytical Federation) 214
Epidemiological characterization 9
Evidence-based medicine,
Externalizing mechanisms 139

Face-to-face relationship 136
Fairbairn, R.D. 186
FAUSTLOS 5
Feldman, Ruth 78

Ferenczi, Sándor 233
Ferro, Antonino 166
First World War 225
Fischer, Annette Streek 35
Fixation 115
fMRI (functional Magnetic Resonance Imaging) 119
Fonagy, Peter 53, 189
  discussion of his paper 77–92
  mentalization and psychosocial developmental model 81
Frankfurt Prevention Study (*FPS*) 4, 21–22, 32
French psychoanalysts 92
Freud, Anna 87, 211
  conception of method and theory 271
  hypothesis of narcissism 213
  second theory of aggression 211–212
  theories of aggression 211
Freudian concept of
  complementary series 34, 114
Freudian equation 118
Freud's greatest contribution 56
Freud, Sigmund 221
  conception of sexuality 227
Frontal lobe functions 19
Functional Magnetic Resonance Imaging (FMRI) 23
Fundamental emotional systems 136

Gaddini, Renata 156
Gene-environment-interactions 81
German Psychoanalytic Association 251
Goeppel, Gerlinde 26
Göttinger Form repreoduktions-Test 23
Green, André 157, 240, 251
Greenson, Miss C. Ralph 91
Green–Wallerstein debate 255–257
Grubrich-Simitis, Ilse 38, 219

Hanly, Charles 185, 209
Hauser, Stuart 25
HAWIK (Hamburg Wechsler Intelligence Test) 23
Hippocampal damage 67
Hitler's seizure of power and excesses of anti-Semitism 229
Hyperactive
  child syndrome 8
  reaction of childhood 8
Hyperkinetic
  impulse disorder 8
  symptoms 13
Hypothetico-deductive method 273

Ice Age 223
Imaginative mental activity 55
Independent arousal systems 63
Index, Hampstead 242, 245
Industrial century 10
Infantile seduction 228
Infantile sexual traumas 228
Infantilism of sexuality 228
Information-processing systems 259
Institute for Psychoanalytic Treatments of Children and Adolescents 5
Intensity 100
International Psychoanalytic Association 87
International Psychological Associations's Conceptual Research Committee 220
International Statistical Classification of Diseases and Related Health Problems (ICD) 241
Intrinsic cerebral malfunction 105

Introductory Lectures on Psycho-Analysis 228
IPA Congress 3

Jacobson, Edith 64
Johi's serious social problems 29
Joseph Sandler Research Conference 6, 37
Journal of the American Academy of Child and Adolescent Psychiatry 9
Joyce, Angela 175

Kächele, Horst 35
Kandel, Eric 77
Kantian space and time 212
Kleinian conceptual
  bearings 155
  framework 154–156
Klein, Melanie 154
  distinction 188
  path-breaking research 156
  self-consistent 216
Klein, Sydney 156
Kohutian theory 212
Kölner Mutimodale Therapiestudie 13
Kramer Intelligence Test 31
Kuhn, Thomas 244, 272

Lamarckian mode of transmission 223
Lehmkuhl, Gerd 77
Leuzinger-Bohleber, Marianne 3, 22, 35, 120, 185, 220–221, 236
Linguistic and social cognitive capacities 94
Linguistic turn 252
Long-lasting chronic stress 147

Mahler, Margaret 156
  autism and symbiosis 154
MAOA gene 117
Marty, Pierre 92
Massive traumatization 233
Masson, Jeffrey 232
Maternal sensitivity 15
Mayes, Linda 87
MCD (Minimal Cerebral Dysfunction) 192
McDevitt, Sean 102
McGill University 8
Medina, Doria 38
Mental health and psychopathology 227
Mentalization 55, 60, 64, 66, 93
  ability of 148
  attachment and the arms-race 60–61
  capacity for 191
  concept of 91
  decouples 70
  developmental risks and their sequelae 77–84
  imaginative leap of 69
  successful process 80
Mesocorticolimbic dopaminergic reward circuit 94
Metzler, Donald 155
Michael´s probability score 23
Michael's oedipal developmental phase 24
Michael's retarded sensory motor development 23
Mimetic autism 163
Mimetic mirroring 169
Mimetic/symbiotic component 163
Mind–body problem 5
Minimal brain damage 8
Minimal brain dysfunction 8, 24
Mitrani, Judith 157
Modern psychiatry 271
MonoAmine Oxidase A 117
Mood 100
Mother–baby dyad 88

Mother–child interaction 77, 79
Mother–infant psychoanalytic
 treatment 90
Motor skills 124
Multi-factorial models of
 illness 115

Narcissistic
 depressive disorder 146
 disorder 146
 mortifications 230
 neuroses 223
National socialism 260
Nature/nurture polarity 115
Nature/nurture relationship 115
Nature Neuroscience 37
Negative mother–child
 interactions 9
Neo-Lamarckian
 convictions 230
 lines 224
Neopositivistic empiricism 249
Neuro turn 252
Neurodevelopmental disorder 105
Neuropsychiatric disorders 3
Neuroscientific-attachment theory
 58–60
New Introductory
 Conferences 271
New Orleans Congress panel
 267–277
New York Longitudinal
 Study 99, 113
New York Psychoanalytic
 Institute 220
Newton's theory 210
Non-genetic physical factors 118
Non-psychoanalytic scientists 36

Oedipal developmental phase 24
Oedipus complex 212, 227, 263
Oppositional Defiant Disorder 9
Ordinary language turn 259
Organic brain 21
 pathology 23
Organicism 35

Panksepp 20
Paranoid-schizoid 57
 position 188
Parent–child interaction,
 micro-analysis of 78
Parent–infant bond 77
Parent-infant-interactions 77
The Patient and the Analyst 261
Pavlov, Ivan 99
Peaceful and concentrated
 togetherness 136
Peircean fallibilism 272
Persistence/attention span 100
Peterson, Bradley 37
PET (Positron Emission
 Tomography) 119
Phylogenetic fantasy 222, 225,
 228–229
Pluralism
 in theory and research 239–265
 of psychoanalytic
 theories 253
 simple research 254
 simple theory 253
Positive masculine model 139
Postencephalitic behaviour
 disorder 8
Post-Freudian
 psychoanalytic culture 118
 theorizing 211
Post-Kleinian object 88
Post-natal maturation process 125
Post-traumatic subjective 56
Poustka, Fritz 36
Pre-natal maturation process 126
Pre-schizo-paranoid 171
Primary seduction 88

Projective identification 64
  Melanie Klein's conception of 64
The Protective Shell in Children and Adults 156
Pseudo mental subnormality 193
Pseudo scientific classification 8
Psychiatric disorder 10
Psychic
  binding 229
  equivalence, non-mentalizing mode of 70
  reality 57
  suffering 166
  trauma 242
  truths 188
Psychism 170
Psychoanalysis 3, 34, 36, 53–71, 93, 143, 211, 231, 239, 249, 251, 273
  between nature and culture 257
  clinical implications 65–67
  complete research field in 250
  contemporary 17, 245
  epistemology of 217
  meeting of neuroscience 53–71, 87
  object with such patients 65–66
  present-day 220
  research in 254
  role of memory work in 70
  thoughts on 248–251
  understandings of 255
Psychoanalytic
  aetiological theory 225
  community 232
  conceptualization 16
  development phenomenology 55
  formulations 89
  knowledge 210, 214
  pluralism, contemporary 210
  schools 16
  self-psychology 188
  therapy 23, 28
The Psychoanalytic Quarterly 209
Psychoanalytic research
  early development and ADHD 3–40
  hopes, views, controversial discussion 207
  in logic, meaning, and truth 209–218
Psychoanalytic theory 4
  unified mainstream 209
  unity and verifiability in 209–218
Psychodynamic causation 82
Psychological integrity 59
Psychoneurotic symptoms 226
Psychopathology
  CNS-based 34, 113
  development of 78
  current status of overdiagnosis of 98–105
  on on-going development 179
Psychopharmacological treatments 12–13
Psycho-physiological—abstraction 170
Psycho-social
  environment 118
  factors 9
  stress factors 79
  synchronization 83
Psychotherapeutic assistance 126
Psychotherapeutic help 234
Psychotropic drugs 113
Ptolemaic belief 216

Quantitative-empirical psychotherapy researchers 241
Quasi-mythological transmission 233

Reactive behaviour problems
100, 106
Research-pluralism 254–255, 262
Retarded sensory motor
development 23
Rhythmicity 100
Rio de Janeiro Congress 119
Ritalin® 4, 98, 113, 126
Role of Genotype in the Cycle of
Violence in Maltreated
Children 117
Rough-and-tumble games 20, 27

Salomonsson, Björn 36, 87
Sandler, Anne-Marie 56, 91
Sandler, Joseph 241
Scales, Conner 21
Schizo-paranoid 171
Schizophrenia, symptomatic triad
diagnostic for 153
Second world war 260
Secure attachment behaviour 15
Seduction theory 225
Segal, Hanna 57
Self-awareness 59–60, 63
Self-fragmentation 94
Self-harming behaviour 82
Self-object differentiation 156
Self-regulating functions 78
Semantic vagueness 244
Sensitive moment-by-moment
adaptation 78
Sensoriality 170
Sensory threshold 100
Sexual
stimulation 226
transgressions 225
Sigmund-Freud-Institute 16, 36, 240
Sleed, Michelle 87
Slow-to-warm-up children 101
Social anxiety disorder 120
Social brain, evolution 59
Social referencing 188
Social/sexual activity 61
Sophia's
clinical narrative 157–162
conceptual comments 162–165
mimetic autism 153–171
personal space 165
Specific psychiatric disorders 9
Staufenberg, Adelheid 35
Staufenberg, Heidi 123
Stauffenberg, Frau 146
Stern, Daniel 189
Strange Situation 15
Streeck-Fischer, Annette 143
Super ego 132
Swain, James 77
Symbiotic psychoses 162

Target, Mary 3, 189
mentalization and psychosocial
developmental model 81
Temperament
assessment 102
coping with children's 113–121
current status of knowledge
and research 104
definition 98–99
differences in children 98
early development and its
disturbances 113–121
environment misfit 106
goodness or poorness of fit 101
history 99
management 104
neurological explanation 105
NYLS dimensions of 100
of child 102
origins and stability 101–102
pathologized 107
practical importance 102–104
problems with DSM diagnostic
system 108–109

psychological
interpretations 105
relationship to ADHD and
other psychopathology
105–106
relationship to other
psychopathology 108
role of 105–106
traits and clusters 100
variation 108
Theory-pluralism 254–255, 262
Therapeutic holding or therapeutic
containing 235
Thomas, Alexander 99
Totem and Taboo 223, 229
Transference interpretations 91
Trauma 53–71
clinical illustration 67–70
clinical implications 65–67
developmental risks and their
sequelae 77–84
hyperactivity 62
model 226, 235
neurobiology of 61–65
recovering memories 66–67
understanding of 60–65
Trauma model/drive model 235
*Trauma triggers the attachment
system* 58
Tustinian conceptual frame,
autism-derived 153

University Clinic for Child and
Adolescent Psychiatry 28

Varvin, Sverre 236
Vasopressin sensitive circuit 61
Vienna Psychoanalytic Society 235

Waldung, Christina 26
Wallerstein, Robert 251
unsustainable argument 210
Winnicott, Donald 64
theory of 'holding 179
Wissenschaft 35
Womblike communal situation 161

Zepf, Siegfried 92

For Product Safety Concerns and Information please contact our EU representative GPSR@taylorandfrancis.com Taylor & Francis Verlag GmbH, Kaufingerstraße 24, 80331 München, Germany

Batch number: 10726011

Printed by Printforce, the Netherlands